Our Modern Services

Our Modern Services

Anglican Church of Kenya

© Anglican Church of Kenya and Uzima Publishing House 2002, 2003, 2008

First published by Uzima Publishing House,
P.O. Box 48127-00100, Nairobi, Kenya
uzima@wananchi.com
www.uzimapublishinghouse.org

ISBN 9966-855-73-4

This edition published with permission for the North American and South
American Market by the General Secretary Ekklesia Society,
P.O. Box 118526 Carrollton TX 75011-8526 US.

Table of Contents

Preface

The completion of this book gives me great relief, because it is a wonderful fulfilment of one of my dreams and visions when I was the chairman of the Provincial Liturgical Committee, and when I was enthroned the 3rd Archbishop of the Anglican Church of Kenya in 1997, I considered liturgical renewal a major priority in my ministry as Archbishop. This book is a gift to the Anglican Church of Kenya in the 3rd millennium of the Christian era, and the 21st Century. It was my great desire to see the Church develop a new alternate prayerbook that would be both relevant and contemporary because the Book of Common Prayer, great and useful as it has been, has nevertheless been culturally outlived. This new alternate book, Our Modern Services whose work was pioneered by the publication of the Modern Service of Holy Communion in 1989 and the Modern Services in 1991 takes into great account the needs of today's Anglican Christians in Kenya. It has so many new and interesting liturgies.

However it must be remembered that it is not necessarily a new prayerbook that will make worship lively; more so, it is the creativity of those who will be using it in leading the worship or conducting the various services. Our clergy and lay leaders must learn to be creative and innovative and make our worship time as enriching as possible. I want to sincerely thank all who have made the production of this new prayerbook possible: Venerable Sam Mawiyoo the chairman of the prayerbook committee; the vice chairman the Rt Rev Dr Gideon Githiga and all the committee members.

I also wish to greatly thank the Provincial Liturgical coordinator Rev Joyce Karuri Kirigia who has marshalled all her talents in ensuring that this book becomes a reality. The work which Joyce has done has already become internationally recognised as she is a member of the International Anglican Liturgical Consultation and its steering committee. We commend and deeply appreciate the work she has done.

I also greatly thank our overseas friends and partners: Bishop Colin Buchanan of England, Paul Gibson of Canada who is also the liturgical consultant for the Anglican Consultative Council (ACC), and the Rev Dr Graham Kings formerly Principal of St Andrew's College of Theology Kabare, Kenya, and now vicar of Islington Parish in England. These three took time to read the draft prayerbook and made very useful editorial and professional comments. I Sincerely thank all and sundry who have contributed in one way or another to make this book a reality.

My thanks to all of you bishops for sharing in this vision and for the encouragement you have accorded Joyce and her committee. I know you will continue in this spirit and encourage Christians in your dioceses to buy this book and make full use of it. We are aware that we shall not be able to get to the grassroot congregations effectively until we have translated this book into vernacular languages. This is going to be the next phase of this project and plans are already underway for translation work to begin.

When we appointed the liturgical coordinator in late 1999, we had no money but we had faith that if God is on our side, nothing can be against us. Although we could not get money from sources that we had initially identified, God opened other doors. I sincerely thank the following: Church Missionary Society (England) who set us moving with their initial generous donation and did not stop there but continued sending more funding; the Archbishop of Canterbury Fund for a very generous gift; and likewise the United Thank Offering (USA). We are very grateful for their financial support.

The outgoing Archbishop of Canterbury George Carey requested that this book be made available to all the Anglican Provinces in Africa as an encouragement to their own liturgical renewal efforts. Southern Africa and Kenya are far ahead of the rest in terms of liturgical renewal. This book which was my dream and my vision as chairman of the liturgical committee and as 3rd Archbishop of the Anglican Church of Kenya is a retirement gift to you all. Am glad the book has been published just before my retirement in September 2002. May God bless you as you celebrate and worship God in your congregations, etc. Indeed I can now sing *Nunc Dimittis* and say, "let your servant retire in peace for my eyes have seen the onset of liturgical and musical transformation of worship in the Anglican Church of Kenya which I have served as Bishop for 22 years, and 5 years as Archbishop until my retirement at midnight on 16th September 2002." May God the Father, God the Son and God the Holy Spirit be glorified through the worship of his people. Amen.

The Most Rev Dr David Mukuba Gitari
Archbishop of Kenya and Bishop of Nairobi
January 1997 to 16th September 2002.

General Notes to the Prayerbook

Preparedness of the Leaders
This book comes as a guide to worship in all the Anglican Church of Kenya churches. It is suggested that the worshipper does not use this book rigidly but rather the Spirit of God must be allowed to permeate every word and every line of every service. This calls for the spiritual preparedness and alertness on the part of the leaders so that the services make meaning and meet the people's real inner needs.

Singing
It has been observed that a lot of times the congregations seem to prefer choruses to hymns until the beauty of hymns is overshadowed. It is a general acceptance that where a hymn is suggested, a chorus may also be allowed but balance must be maintained. Every congregation should have a choir and choir leaders who lead the congregation effectively in song.

Greetings
It is important that during every gathering of God's people, a time for greetings is accorded to the worshippers. Worship must not necessarily be people-leader oriented; it should also be people to people and this aspect can be enhanced by allowing people to know who is sitting beside them and for them to chat out some greetings. This moment is provided for in some services like Holy Communion; the sharing of peace, but it should also be introduced in other services even without having to set any liturgical rules.

Exhortation on Giving
It is encouraged that giving for the Lord's work be taken seriously and that Christians be exhorted to desire to give and to do so with cheerfulness and thankfulness to God for all his goodness. Therefore always before offertory, the leader should read some scripture and expound on it briefly before inviting people to give. During giving, appropriate hymns should be sung.

Congregational Participation
The members of the congregation should be encouraged to own a prayerbook especially where the same is not provided in the pews. Worship comes alive when the congregation is moving together with the leader. Wherever bold occurs, it is a response by the respective party.

Burial of the Departed

There are three burial services. It shall be appropriate for the family to be involved in the decision as to which of the three services suits the departed. Otherwise it is considered expedient that we bury our dead with dignity.

Gender

It is not always easy to maintain gender balance in the application of pronouns due to the influence of the masculine domination in the English language and its gender specifics. Where necessary we have tried to be gender inclusive by italicising the masculine pronouns. Any oversight regarding this is regretted. Otherwise we have also at times applied the him/her, he/she style, but with limitation otherwise this can cause the text flow to be quite clumsy.

Ordinations

It is the recommendation of the committee that no two ordination services may take place together, for instance Ordination of Deacons and Ordination of Priests.

The Dignity of the Diaconate

It is further recommended by the International Anglican Liturgical Consultation (IALC), that the Diaconate does not necessarily have to be a stepping stone to priesthood. It can and should be treated as a dignified order in its own right.

Services Held in the Context of Holy Communion

The entry points into the Holy Communion are rather varied for the different services depending on the liturgical merits of each.

Reference to: Priest, Minister, Pastor, Celebrant, Leader

The first three may refer to the same office. We have not strictly referred to the ordained person as a priest owing to the contemporary interchangeable three applications which usually mean the same. Where the reference is to Celebrant or leader, the opening notes and rubrics should explain who is eligible.

Amen

Whenever it occurs, it is for all; hence it is (supposed to be) in bold.

Bible Versions
I attempted to maintain one Bible version (New International Version) but it wasn't easy and so I gave up. This is because some of the texts for services already done earlier on seem to have very varying versions. We might conclude that as long as the quotation is from the Bible it probably may not matter too much which version it is. But largely, the version applied is the NIV.

Notes and Rubrics
For nearly every service there is a bulleted list of guide notes explaining the purpose of the service and the mode in which it is to be conducted. These notes should be read carefully before the onset of the service. Likewise, the leader should study the rubrics well before the service begins for purposes of familiarization in order to be able to lead the service with confidence and competence.

Missing: The Psalter, and the Lectionary
Due to cost implications the Psalter has deliberately been left out in this edition. It is suggested that this need be met in the use of the Bible preferrably the New International Version. About the Lectionary, time factor was the culprit especially because we had to have this book printed before the retirement of Archbishop David M. Gitari. For the time being, we will have to make do with what is available from Uzima Press (that is, *Taratibu ya Masomo,* and the *Church Pocket Book and Diary*).

The Church Calendar Seasons

Advent
The First Sunday of Advent
The Second Sunday of Advent
The Third Sunday of Advent
From 17 December (O Sapientia) begin the eight days of prayer before Christmas Day
The Fourth Sunday of Advent
Christmas Eve

Christmas
Christmas-25 December
The First Sunday of Christmas
The Second Sunday of Christmas
The days after Christmas Day until the Epiphany traditionally form a unity of days of special thanksgiving.

Epiphany
The Epiphany –6 January
The Baptism of Christ- The Sunday of Epiphany
The Second Sunday of Epiphany
The Third Sunday of Epiphany
The Fourth Sunday of Epiphany
The Presentation of Christ in the Temple (Candlemas)-2 February

Ordinary Time
This begins on the day following the presentation
The Fifth Sunday before Lent
The Fourth Sunday before Lent
The Third Sunday before Lent
The Second Sunday before Lent
The Sunday next before Lent

Lent
Ash Wednesday
The First Sunday of Lent
The Second Sunday of Lent
The Third Sunday of Lent
The Fourth Sunday of Lent- *Mothering Sunday*

The Fifth Sunday of Lent *(Passiontide begins)*
Palm Sunday
Monday of Holy Week
Tuesday of Holy Week
Wednesday of Holy Week
Maundy Thursday
Good Friday
Easter Eve

Easter
Easter Day
Monday of Easter Week
Tuesday of Easter Week
Wednesday of Easter Week
Thursday of Easter Week
Friday of Easter Week
Saturday of Easter Week
The Second Sunday of Easter
The Third Sunday of Easter
The Fourth Sunday of Easter
The Fifth Sunday of Easter
The Sixth Sunday of Easter
Ascension Day
From Friday after Ascension Day
begin the nine days of prayer before Pentecost
The Seventh Sunday of Easter – Sunday after Ascension Day
Pentecost (Whit Sunday)

Ordinary Time
This is resumed on the Monday following the day of Pentecost
Trinity Sunday
The Thursday after Trinity Sunday may be observed as
The Day of Thanksgiving for the Institution of Holy Communion
    (Corpus Christi)
The First Sunday after Pentecost
The Second Sunday after Pentecost
The Third Sunday after Pentecost
The Fourth Sunday after Pentecost
The Fifth Sunday after Pentecost
The Sixth Sunday after Pentecost

The Seventh Sunday after Pentecost
The Eighth Sunday after Pentecost
The Ninth Sunday after Pentecost
The Tenth Sunday after Pentecost
The Eleventh Sunday after Pentecost
The Twelfth Sunday after Pentecost
The Thirteenth Sunday after Pentecost
The Fourteenth Sunday after Pentecost
The Fifteenth Sunday after Pentecost
The Sixteenth Sunday after Pentecost
The Seventeenth Sunday after Pentecost
The Eighteenth Sunday after Pentecost
The Nineteenth Sunday after Pentecost
The Twentieth Sunday after Pentecost
The Twenty-First Sunday after Pentecost
The Twenty-Second Sunday after Pentecost
Dedication Festival – *The First Sunday in October or The Last*
Sunday after Pentecost, if date unknown
All Saints' Day – 1 November
The Sunday between 30 October and 5 November may be kept as
All Saints' Sunday or as:
The Fourth Sunday before Advent
The Third Sunday before Advent
The Second Sunday before Advent
Christ the King – The Sunday next before Advent

Festivals and Holy Days

The naming and circumcision of Jesus *(1 January)*

The week of Christian Prayer and Unity *(18 to 25 January)*

The conversion of Paul *(25 January)*

Joseph of Nazareth *(19 March)*

Annunciation of our Lord *(25 March)*

Mark the Evangelist *(25 April)*

Philip and James, Apostles *(1 May)*

Matthias the Apostle *(14 May)*

The visit of Blessed Virgin Mary to Elizabeth *(31 May)*

Barnabas the Apostle *(11 June)*

The birth of John the Baptist *(24 June)*

Peter and Paul, Apostles *(29 June)*

Thomas the Apostle *(3 July)*

Mary Magdalene *(22 July)*

James the Apostle *(25 July)*

The Transfiguration of our Lord *(6 August)*

The Blessed Virgin Mary *(15 August)*

Bartholomew the Apostle *(24 August)*

Holy Cross Day *(14 September)*

Matthew, Apostle and Evangelist *(21 September)*

Michael and all Angels *(29 September)*

Luke the Evangelist *(18 October)*

Simon and Jude, Apostles *(28 October)*

Christ the King *(Sunday next before Advent)*

Andrew the Apostle *(30 November)*

Stephen, Deacon, First Martyr *(26 December)*

John, Apostle and Evangelist *(27 December)*

The Holy Innocents *(28 December)*

A pioneering example of African liturgical renewal and a gift for the whole Anglican Communion. This new prayerbook is rooted in Biblical, African and Anglican traditions, open to contextual insights, vivid in its metaphors and delightfully surprising in its range of services. The Archbishop and the Editor of the Anglican Church of Kenya Liturgical Commission are to be warmly congratulated on this historic publication.

Canon Dr. Graham Kings, Vicar of St. Mary Islington, London and a member of the Church of England Lirtugical Commission.

Morning Worship

NOTES

- The psalms of the day are sung or read antiphonally.

- Songs/canticles may be sung or said antiphonally.

- An alternative declaration of pardon as well as an alternative form of benediction are provided for use by a lay minister in the absence of a minister.

- Offertory: In this as well as other services, it is encouraged that the leader first exhorts the Christians to give generously for the Lord's work, by reading and explaining texts related to giving and stewardship.

SENTENCES
One or more may be said after the introduction.
If a wicked man turns away from the wickedness he has committed and does what is just and right, he will save his life. *(Ezekiel 18:27)*

Rend your heart and not your garments. Return to the Lord your God, for he is gracious and compassionate, slow to anger and abounding in love, and he relents from sending calamity.
(Joel 2:13)

Delight yourself in the Lord and he will give you the desires of your heart. *(Psalm 37:4)*

For with you is the fountain of life; in your light we see light.
(Psalm 36:9)

My soul yearns, even faints, for the courts of the Lord;
My heart and my flesh cry out for the Living God. *(Psalm 84:2)*

God you are my God, early will I seek you:
O God, you are my God, earnestly I seek you;
my soul thirsts for you, my body longs for you. *(Psalm 63:1)*

Whom have I in heaven but you?
And earth has nothing I desire besides you. *(Psalm 73:25)*

Wash and make yourselves clean.
Take your evil deeds out of my sight! Stop doing wrong and learn to do right! *(Isaiah 1:16-17a)*

"Come, let us go up to the mountain of the Lord, ... he will teach us his ways, so that we may walk in his paths." *(Isaiah 2:3)*

Before they call I will answer; while they are still speaking I will hear. *(Isaiah 65:24)*

This is the one I esteem:
he who is humble and contrite in
spirit and trembles at my word. *(Isaiah 66:2)*

And what does the Lord require of you?
To act justly and to love mercy and to walk humbly with your God. *(Micah 6:8)*

Do not think that I have come to abolish the law or the prophets; I have not come to abolish them but to fulfil them. *(Matthew 5:17)*

Blessed are you who are poor, for yours is the Kingdom of God.
Blessed are you who hunger, for you will be satisfied.
Blessed are you who weep now, for you will laugh.
Blessed are you when people hate you, ... because great is your reward in heaven. *(Luke 6:20-22)*

Fear not, little flock, for it is your Father's good pleasure to give you the kingdom. *(Luke 12:32)*

I tell you there will be more rejoicing in heaven over one sinner who repents, than over ninety-nine righteous persons who do not need to repent. *(Luke 15:7)*

"I will set out and go back to my father and say to him: 'Father, I have sinned against heaven and against you. I am no longer worthy to be called your son.' " *(Luke 15:18)*

ORDER OF SERVICE

1   *At the entry of the procession the people stand. A hymn is sang after which the people remain standing and the leader welcomes them with the following words:*

Leader   The Lord be with you.

People   **And also with you.**

Leader   We have come together, the people of God, drawn by his Spirit, longing for his word, to praise the holy name of the Lord, to share his glorious news of grace, to pray for our needs and the pain of the world, to rejoice in his love and be sent in his peace.

Leader	We are heirs of the Father;
People	**joint heirs with the son,**
Leader	renewed in the Spirit,
People	**together we are one.**

2   *SENTENCES*
A few may be said, see previous pages.

Leader	If we say we have no sin we deceive ourselves and the truth is not in us. If we confess our sins, in repentance and trust, God is faithful and just, and will forgive us our sins. So let us confess them to our Father.

People kneel.

3   *All*   **Eternal Father, God of our ancestors, before your power all things tremble but through your son, we approach your throne. We have done wrong and neglected to do right; our sins weigh heavily on our hearts: Lord have mercy, count them not against us. Grant us the joy of forgiveness and lighten our hearts with the glory of Christ, who died and rose again for us. Amen.**

4   *Minister*   The God and Father of our Lord Jesus Christ rejoices at repentance and declares his acceptance. The dead are alive, the lost are found. His goodness and mercy will follow you all the days of your life, and you will live in the house of the Lord for ever. **Amen.**

5   *When a minister is not present the lay leader uses the following prayer.*
   Leader   Lord of mercy, grant us your pardon and peace; that cleansed from our sins and with peace in our hearts, we may be free to serve you; through Jesus Christ our Lord. **Amen.**

6 *Leader*	Blessed are those who live in your house:
People	**They will always be singing your praise.**
Leader	Praise the Lord.
People	**The name of the Lord be praised.**

People stand.

Leader	Glory to the Father in whom all things began,
All	**Glory to the Son who became the Son of Man,**
	Glory to the Spirit who inspires and renews.
	The Lord our God for ever! Alleluia!

7 *Between Christmas and Epiphany Sunday, and between Easter Day and Pentecost Sunday, the following version of the gloria may be said instead of the above.*

| *Leader* | The glorious Son of God on high |
| *People* | **is born for us through Mary's womb:** |

| *Leader* | The homeless Prince of Peace on earth |
| *People* | **is crushed and lies in Joseph's tomb:** |

| *Leader* | The reigning Lord of Life and death |
| *People* | **breaks the bonds of time and doom.** |

8 JUBILATE SONG, VENITE, OR THE SONG OF HABAKKUK

JUBILATE SONG (SONG OF JOY) PSALM 100:3

1   **I will enter his gates with thanksgiving in my heart:**
    I will enter his courts with praise.

2   **I will say this is the day that the Lord has made:**
    I will rejoice for he has made me glad.

3   **He has made me glad, he has made me glad:**
    I will rejoice for he has made me glad.

4   **He has made me glad, he has made me glad:**
    I will rejoice for he has made me glad.

VENITE (SONG OF TRIUMPH) PSALM 95

1   **O come, let us sing out to the Lord;**
    let us shout in triumph to the Rock of our salvation.

2   **Let us come before his face with thanksgiving:**
    and cry to him joyfully in psalms.

3   **For the Lord is a great God:**
    and a great King above all gods.

4   **In his hand are the depths of the earth:**
    and the peaks of the mountains are his also.

5   The sea is his and he made it:
    his hands moulded dry land.

6   Come let us worship and bow down:
    and kneel before the Lord our maker.

7   For he is the Lord our God:
    we are his people and the sheep of his pasture.

8   If only you would hear his voice today:
    for he comes to judge the earth.

9   He shall judge the world with righteousness:
    and the peoples with his truth.

Glory to the Father, Son, and the Holy Spirit;
as it was in the beginning, is now and ever shall be.
Amen.

SONG OF HABAKKUK (Habbakuk 3:17-18 adapted)

1   Though the mango tree does not blossom,
        nor the fruit be on the vines,

2   the crop of the coconut fails,
        and the fields yield no food,

3   Though the flock be cut off from the fold,
        and there be no herd in the stall,

4   yet I will rejoice in the Lord,
        I will be joyful in the God of my salvation.

Glory to the Father, Son and the Holy Spirit;
as it was in the beginning, is now and ever shall be.
Amen.

9   *PSALM APPOINTED, may be sang or said antiphonally and
    should end with:*

Glory to the Father, Son and the Holy Spirit;
as it was in the beginning, is now and ever shall be.
Amen.

10   *FIRST READING* from the Old Testament

At the end of the reading the reader says:

This is the word of the Lord.
All **Thanks be to God.**

11 SONG OF THE MESSIAH, SONG OF ZECHARIAH
OR THE SONG OF PAUL

*SONG OF THE MESSIAH (Genesis 12:3, Deuteronomy 18:15f,
2 Samuel 7:12f, Isaiah 53:4, Daniel 7:13-22)*

1   **Jesus the Seed of Abraham blesses the nations:**

2   **Jesus the Prophet like Moses frees the oppressed:**

3   **Jesus the Lord of King David leads his people:**

4   **Jesus the Servant of the Lord suffers and saves:**

5   **Jesus the Son of Man destroyed and raised.**

**Glory to the Father, Son, and the Holy Spirit;
as it was in the beginning, is now and ever shall be.
Amen.**

SONG OF ZECHARIAH (Benedictus: Luke 1:68-79)

1   **Blessed be the Lord God of Israel:
     for he has come to his people and set them free.**

2   **He has raised up for us a mighty Saviour:
     born of the house of his servant David.**

3   **Through his holy prophets he promised of old:
     that he would save us from our enemies,
from the hands of all that hate us.**

4   **He promised to show mercy to our fathers:
     and to remember his holy covenant.**

5   **This was the oath he swore to our father Abraham:
     to set us free from the hands of our enemies,**

6   **Free to worship him without fear: holy and righteous
in his sight all the days of our life.**

7 You my child shall be called the prophet
   of the Most High: for you will go before
   the Lord to prepare his way,

8 to give his people knowledge of salvation
   by the forgiveness of all their sins.

9 In the tender compassion of our God:
   the dawn from on high shall break upon us,

10 to shine on those who dwell in darkness
   and the shadow of death:
   and to guide our feet into the way of peace.

   Glory to the Father, Son and the Holy Spirit;
   as it was in the beginning, is now and ever shall be.
   Amen.

SONG OF PAUL (Colossians 1:15-18)

1 You are the image of the invisible God,
   the first born over all creation.

2 By you, O Christ, were all things created,
   in heaven and on earth, visible and invisible,

3 Thrones and dominions, powers and principalities;
   all were created through you and for you.

4 You are before everything and
   in you all things hold together.

5 You are the head of your body, the Church,
   you are the beginning, the first born from the dead,
   that over everything you may be supreme.

   Glory to the Father, to the Son and to the Holy Spirit;
   as it was in the beginning, is now and ever shall be.
   Amen.

12 *SECOND READING from the New Testament.*

   At the end of the reading the reader says:

   This is the word of the Lord.
All **Thanks be to God.**

13 SONG OF JESUS, SONG OF THE CHURCH OR THE SONG OF REVELATION

SONG OF JESUS (Luke 6:27-28; Matthew: 25:35-36; Luke 7:22-23; Luke10:21)

1   Love your enemies:
      do good to those who hate you,

2   bless those who curse you:
      pray for those who ill-treat you.

3   For I was hungry and you gave me something to eat:
      I was thirsty and you gave me something to drink.

4   I was a stranger and you invited me in:
      I needed clothes and you clothed me.

5   I was sick and you looked after me:
      I was in prison and you came to visit me.

6   The blind receive sight:
      the lame walk, lepers are cured.

7   The deaf hear, the dead are raised:
      the good news is preached to the poor,
      and blessed are those not offended at me.

      Glory to the Father, the Lord of heaven and earth:
      Glory to the Son, to whom all things are given.
      Glory to the Spirit, in whom the Son rejoices,
      Now and for ever. Amen.

TE DEUM LAUDAMUS (SONG OF THE CHURCH)
(verses 14-18 may be omitted)

1   You are God and we praise you:
      you are the Lord and we acclaim you.

2   You are the eternal Father:
      all creation worships you.

3   To you all angels, all the powers of heaven:
      Cherubim and seraphim sing in endless praise,

4   Holy, holy, holy Lord, God of power and might:
      heaven and earth are full of your glory.

5   The glorious company of apostles praise you:
    the noble fellowship of prophets praise you
    the white-robed army of martyrs praise you.

6   Throughout the world the holy Church acclaims you:
    Father of majesty unbounded;

7   your true and only Son worthy of all worship:
    and the Holy Spirit advocate and guide.

8   You Christ are the King of glory:
    the eternal Son of the Father.

9   When you became man to set us free:
    you did not abhor the Virgin's womb.

10 You overcame the sting of death:
    and opened the kingdom of heaven to all believers.

11 You are seated at God's right hand in glory:
    we believe that you will come and be our judge.

12 Come then Lord and help your people;
    bought with the price of your own blood;

13 and bring us with your saints:
    to glory everlasting.

14 Save your people Lord and bless your inheritance:
    govern and uphold them now and always.

15 Day by day we bless you:
    we praise your name for ever.

16 Keep us today Lord from all sin:
    have mercy on us Lord, have mercy.

17 Lord show us your love and mercy:
    for we put our trust in you.

18 In you Lord is our hope:
    let us not be confounded at the last.

SONG OF REVELATION
(Revelation 19:6-8; 4:11; 5:9-10; 15:3-4, 5:13)

1   Alleluia! For the Lord our God the Almighty reigns:
    Let us rejoice and be glad and give him the glory.

2   Worthy is the Lord our God:
    for he created everything.

3   Worthy is the Lamb who was slain:
    for by his blood he ransomed us for God
    from every tribe and tongue, people and nation.

4   Great and wonderful are your deeds, Lord God the
    Almighty:
    just and true are your ways, O king of ages!

5   Who shall not fear and praise your name O Lord?
    For you alone are holy.

6   All nations shall come and worship in your presence:
    for your just deeds have been revealed.
    To him who sits on the throne and to the lamb be
    blessing and honour, glory and might,
    for ever and ever. Amen.

14 *Notices*

15 *Hymn*

16 *Sermon*

17 *APOSTLES' CREED*

    Leader   We stand together with Christians throughout the
                centuries, and throughout the world today, to affirm our
                faith in the words of the Apostles' Creed.

    All   I believe in God, the Father Almighty,
                creator of heaven and earth.
                  I believe in Jesus Christ,
                his only Son, our Lord,
                who was conceived by the Holy Spirit,
                born of the Virgin Mary,
                suffered under Pontius Pilate,
                was crucified, died and was buried;
                  he descended to the dead.

On the third day he rose again;
he ascended into heaven,
he is seated at the right hand of the Father,
and he will come to judge the living
and the dead.
I believe in the Holy Spirit,
the holy catholic Church,
the communion of saints,
the forgiveness of sins,
the resurrection of the body,
and the life everlasting. Amen.

18 *Leader*   The Lord be with you.
   People   **and also with you.**

   Leader   Let us pray.

19 *People kneel and say or sing:*

   All   **Ask and it shall be given unto you,**
        seek and you shall find,
        knock and the door shall be opened unto you.
        Allelu, alleluia.

20 *Leader*   As our Saviour taught us, we are bold to pray:

   All   **Our Father in heaven,**
        hallowed be your name,
        your kingdom come,
        your will be done,
        on earth as in heaven.
        Give us today our daily bread.
        Forgive us our sins,
        as we forgive those
        who sin against us.
        Lead us not into temptation
        but deliver us from evil.
        For the kingdom,
        the power and the
        glory are yours,
        now and for ever. Amen.

OR THIS VERSION OF THE LORD'S PRAYER IN SONG

All   **Our Father, who is in heaven,**
          hallowed be your name,
      your kingdom come your will be done,
          hallowed be your name,
          hallowed be your name.

      On earth as it is in heaven,
          hallowed be your name,
      give us this day our daily bread,
          hallowed be your name,
          hallowed be your name.

      Forgive us our trespasses,
          hallowed be your name,
      As we forgive those who trespass against us,
          hallowed be your name,
          hallowed be your name.

      Lead us not into temptation,
          hallowed be your name,
      but deliver us from all that is evil,
          hallowed be your name,
          hallowed be your name.

      For yours is the kingdom, the power and the glory,
          hallowed be your name,
      for ever and ever, for ever and ever,
          hallowed be your name,
          hallowed be your name.

21 *Leader*   Show us your mercy, O Lord;
    People   **and grant us your salvation.**

    Leader   O Lord, guide our President;
    People   **and give him your wisdom and justice.**

    Leader   May your ministers serve you faithfully;
    People   **and your royal people joyfully.**

    Leader   In the valley of the shadow of death;
    People   **protect us with your rod and staff.**

    Leader   Like trees planted by the waterside;
    People   **grant us the fruit of your Spirit.**

Leader	Send us out as the salt of the earth;
People	**and as the light of the world.**

Leader	May the earth be filled with your glory;
People	**as the waters cover the sea.**

22 *PRAYER FOR THE DAY*

23 *PRAYER FOR PEACE*

Either

Almighty and everlasting God,
Father of the Prince of peace,
in returning and rest we are saved,
in quietness and trust is our strength.
Grant us the blessing of making peace,
and the joy of seeking justice.
Take from our souls all strain and stress,
and let our ordered lives confess,
the beauty of your peace;
through Jesus Christ our Lord. **Amen.**

OR

O God, creator of peace and lover of unity,
through knowing you we have eternal life,
and in serving you we find perfect freedom.
Defend us in all attacks of our enemies,
so that trusting only in your defence,
we may be free from all fear;
through the power of Jesus Christ our Lord. **Amen.**

24 *PRAYER FOR GRACE*

EITHER

Almighty God,
You have been our Guard through the night,
keep us in your care through the day;
walking in the light, bearing witness to your way,
seeking first your kingdom and seeing you in everyone;
guide us in the footsteps of your Son,
and lead us on the path to your everlasting Day:
through Jesus Christ our Lord. **Amen.**

OR

Lord our heavenly Father,
Almighty and ever living God,
who has brought us safely to the beginning of this day.
Protect us today with your mighty power,
so that we do not fall into any sin, or meet any danger;
but all our deeds may be directed by you,
and that we may do every day what is good in your sight;
through Jesus Christ our Lord. **Amen.**

25 *Prayerful choruses (or hymns) may be sang.*
People may join in open prayers concerning contemporary, personal,
national and world needs and/or use the prayers here below, for the nation
and the Church. Other prayers are to be found in the last section of this
book and are to be used as may suit the need.

26 *PRAYER FOR THE NATION*

Almighty God,
you rule all nations and direct them according to your will.
We pray that you will guide our President
and all leaders of our country,
so that they may always use the authority
which you have given them
for the peace of the world,
the benefit, honour and development of our nation,
and the good of your holy Church;
through Jesus Christ our Lord. **Amen.**

27 *PRAYER FOR THE CHURCH*

Almighty and eternal God,
the only source of power.
Grant to our bishops, pastors and all
the people of our churches
your health-giving Spirit of grace;
and, in order that they may truly please you,
pour on them the continual dew of your blessing.
Grant this for the sake of our advocate and
mediator, Jesus Christ. **Amen.**

28 *A moment of silent intercession may be observed.*
The leader uses the following prayer:

Your silence is full, irresistible;
your presence is joy unspeakable.
People drifting into mind
we lift to you and pray they find
health in sickness,
life in deadness,
strength in weakness,
light in darkness.
Their loss you bear, mysteriously;
your peace you share, eternally.

29 *PRAYER OF SAINT CHRYSOSTOM*

Almighty God,
by your grace we have come together at this time
to bring our united prayers to you;
and you have promised by your Son Jesus Christ,
that where two or three are gathered in his name
he will be in the midst of them.

Fulfil now, O Lord,
our desires and petitions as may be best for us;
granting us in this world knowledge of your truth,
and in the world to come life everlasting;
through Jesus Christ our Lord. **Amen.**

30 *OFFERTORY*
The minister makes some biblical exhortation on giving for the Lord's work.
A hymn is then sang during which offering is taken.
After the offering the following form of response may be used:

31 *Leader*   All things come from you O Lord.
    People   **And of your own have we given.**

32 *BLESSING*

When a minister is not present, a lay leader shall finish the service with the
Grace, or the alternative form of ending in section 33.

Minister   May the God and Father of our Lord Jesus Christ fill
               you with all joy and peace in believing, that by the
               power of the Holy Spirit, you may abound in hope: And
               the blessing of God almighty, the Father, the Son and
               the Holy Spirit, be among you and remain with you
               always. **Amen.**

OR

The Lord bless you and keep you;
the Lord make his face shine upon you and
be gracious to you;
the Lord turn his face towards you and give you peace.
(Numbers 6:24-26).
And the blessing of God almighty, the Father, the Son,
and the Holy Spirit, be among you and remain with you
always. **Amen.**

OR

Now to him who is able to do immeasurably more than
all we ask or imagine, according to his power that is at
work within us, to him be glory in the church and in
Christ Jesus throughout all generations, for ever and
ever! *(Ephesians 3:20-21).*
And the blessing of God almighty, the Father, the Son,
and the Holy Spirit, be among you and remain with you
always. **Amen.**

OR

The peace of God, which passes all understanding, keep
your hearts and minds in the knowledge and love of
God, and of his Son, Jesus Christ our Lord *(Philippians
4:7).* And the blessing of God almighty, the Father, the
Son, and the Holy Spirit, be among you and remain
with you always. **Amen.**

OR

*This adapted traditional blessing which may vary according to the local
crops and livestock and which may be said outside the Church, with the
minister stretching out his hand towards the fields etc.*

May the Lord of the harvest bless your crops:
    your maize and beans,
    your rice and potatoes,
    your tea and coffee.

May the Lord of creation bless your animals:
    Your cattle and camels,
    your sheep and goats,
    your chickens and pigs.

May the Lord of all life bless your families:
  your husbands and wives,
  your sons and daughters,
  your brothers and sisters.

May the Lord of mercy have compassion on:
  all our sick ones in hospitals and at home,
  all who mourn your loved ones, and
  all orphans and widows.

And the blessing of God Almighty,
  the Father, the Son and the Holy Spirit,
  be among you and remain with you always.
  Amen.

Lay leader Let us join together in the words of the Grace:

All **The grace of our Lord Jesus Christ,
the love of God, and the fellowship of
the Holy Spirit, be with us now and for evermore.
Amen.**

OR

33 Now may our Lord Jesus Christ himself, and God our Father, who
loved us and gave eternal comfort and good hope through grace,
comfort our hearts and establish them in every good work and word.
**And may the grace of our Lord Jesus Christ,
the love of God, and the fellowship of the Holy Spirit be with us
now and for evermore. Amen.**

34 *RECESSIONAL HYMN.*

Evening Worship

1   *Hymn, after which the leader welcomes the people.*

    Leader   The Lord be with you.
    People   **And also with you.**

    Leader   We have come to the sun's hour of rest,
                the lights of evening round us shine,
                we praise the Father, Son and Holy Spirit divine.

                Glory to the Father in whom all things began,
    All   **Glory to the Son who became the Son of Man,**
                Glory to the Spirit who inspires and renews,
                The Lord our God for ever! Alleluia!

2   *SENTENCES*
One or more may be said. Those at the beginning of the Service of Morning Worship may also be used.

I will lie down and sleep in peace, for you alone,
    O Lord, make me dwell in safety. *(Psalm 4:8)*

He who dwells in the shelter of the Most High
    will rest in the shadow of the Almighty.
I will say of the Lord, "He is my refuge and my fortress,
    my God, in whom I trust". *(Psalm 91:1)*

I lift my eyes to the hills, where does my help come from?
    My help comes from the Lord, the maker of heaven and earth.
    (Psalm 121:1-2)

Stay with us, for it is nearly evening;
    the day is almost over. *(Luke 24:29)*

3   *Leader*   If we say we have no sin we deceive ourselves and the
             truth is not in us; if we confess our sins, in repentance
             and trust, God is faithful and just and will forgive us
             our sins. So let us confess them to our Father.
    All   **Eternal Father, God of our ancestors,**
             before your power all things tremble,
             but through your Son, we approach
             your throne.

**We have done wrong and neglected to
do right;
our sins of commission and omission weigh
heavily on our hearts;
Lord have mercy, count them not
against us.
Grant us the joy of forgiveness and
lighten our hearts with the glory of
Christ, who died and rose again for us,
Amen.**

4   *Minister*   The God and Father of our Lord Jesus
Christ rejoices at repentance and declares
his acceptance. The dead are alive, the lost
are found. His goodness and mercy will
follow you, all the days of your life and you will
live in the house of the Lord for ever. **Amen.**

When the minister is not present the lay leader uses the following prayer:

Lord of mercy, grant us your pardon and
peace; that cleansed from our sins and
with peace in our hearts, we may be free
to serve you; through Jesus Christ our
Lord. **Amen.**

Leader   Blessed are those who live in your house:
All   **They will always be singing your praise.**

Leader   Praise the Lord.
All   **The name of the Lord be praised.**

5   *PSALM 134 (in song)*

1   **Come bless the Lord all you servants of the Lord:
who stand by night in the house of the Lord.**
2   **Lift up your hands in the holy place,
come bless the Lord, come bless the Lord.**

6   *Psalm appointed, which ends with:*

**Glory to the Father, Son and the Holy Spirit;
As it was in the beginning, is now and ever shall be. Amen.**

People sit.

7   *First Reading from the Old Testament*
     At the end of the reading the reader may say:

    This is the word of the Lord.
All **Thanks be to God.**

8   HYMN OF MARY OR SONG OF MARY,
     OR SONG OF BLESSINGS.

HYMN OF MARY (Luke 1:46-55)
(Tune: *How sweet the name of Jesus sounds)*

My soul proclaims the Lord my God,
My spirit sings his praise:
He looks on me, he lifts me up,
And gladness fills my days.

All nations now will share my joy,
His gifts he has outpoured:
His little one he has made great,
I magnify the Lord.

His mercy is for evermore,
His name I praise again:
His strong right arm puts down the proud,
And raises lowly ones.

He fills the hungry with good things,
The rich he sends away:
The promise made to Abraham
is filled to endless days.

OR SONG OF MARY (Magnificat. Luke 1:46-55)

1   **My soul proclaims the greatness of the Lord:**
     my spirit rejoices in God my saviour;

2   **for he has looked with favour on his lowly servant:**
     from this day all generations will call me blessed;

3   **the Almighty has done great things for me:**
     and holy is his name.

4   **He has mercy on those who fear him**
     in every generation.

5   **He has shown the strength of his arm:**
     he has scattered the proud in their conceit.

6   He has cast down the mighty from their thrones:
     and has lifted up the lowly.

7   He has filled the hungry with good things:
     and the rich he has sent away empty.

8   He has come to the help of his servant Israel:
     for he has remembered his promise of mercy.

9   The promise he made to our fathers:
     to Abraham and his children for ever.

     Glory to the Father, Son and the Holy Spirit;
     as it was in the beginning, is now and ever shall be.
     Amen.

OR SONG OF BLESSINGS *(Matthew 5:3-10)*

1   Blessed are the poor in spirit,
     for theirs is the kingdom of heaven.

2   Blessed are those who mourn,
     for they shall be comforted.

3   Blessed are the meek,
     for they shall inherit the earth.

4   Blessed are those who hunger and thirst for
     righteousness, for they shall be satisfied.

5   Blessed are the merciful,
     for they shall obtain mercy.

6   Blessed are the poor in heart,
     for they shall see God.

7   Blessed are the peacemakers,
     for they shall be called sons of God.

8   Blessed are those who are persecuted for
     righteousness sake, for theirs is the kingdom of heaven.

     Glory to the Father, Son and the Holy Spirit;
     as it was in the beginning, is now and ever shall be.
     Amen.

People sit.

9   SECOND READING *from the New Testament.*
    At the end of the reading the reader may say:

      This is the word of the Lord.
All **Thanks be to God.**

10 *SONG OF SIMEON (Nunc Dimittis. Luke 2:29-32)*

  1 **Lord now let your servant go in peace:**
     your word has been fulfilled.

  2 **My own eyes have seen the salvation:**
     which you have prepared in the sight of every people;

  3 **A light to reveal you to the nations:**
     and the glory of your people Israel.

  Glory to the Father, Son and the Holy Spirit;
  as it was in the beginning, is now and ever shall be. Amen.

OR SONG OF THE KINGDOM (Matthew 6:25-33)

  1 **Do not be anxious about your life;**
     what you shall eat,
  what you shall drink,
  or what you shall wear.

  2 **Look at the birds of the air;**
     they neither sow nor reap nor gather into barns
  and yet your heavenly Father feeds them.

  3 **Consider the flowers of the field;**
     they neither toil nor spin,
  yet Solomon in all his glory
  was not clothed like one of these.

  4 **Seek first the kingdom of God**
     and his righteousness,
     and all these things shall be yours as well.

  Glory to the Father, Son and the Holy Spirit;
  as it was in the beginning, is now and ever shall be.
  Amen.

OR SONG OF CHRIST'S MISSION (Philippians 2:5-11)

  1 **You, O Christ, were in the form of God:**
     but did not cling to equality with God.

  2 **You emptied yourself taking the form of a servant:**
     and were born in the likeness of men.

3   Being found in human form you humbled yourself:
    and became obedient unto death, even death on a cross.

4   Therefore God has highly exalted you:
    and given you the name above every name,

5   that at the name of Jesus every knee should bow;
    in heaven and on earth and under the earth;

6   and every tongue confess that you are Lord:
    to the glory of God the Father.
    Glory to the Father, Son and the Holy Spirit;
    as it was in the beginning, is now and ever shall be. Amen.

11   *Notices*

12   *Hymn*

13   *Sermon*

14   *APOSTLES' CREED*

Leader   We stand with Christians throughout the
            centuries, and throughout the world today,
            to affirm our faith in the words of the Apostles' Creed:

All   **I believe in God, the Father Almighty,
            creator of heaven and earth.
              I believe in Jesus Christ,
            his only Son, our Lord,
            who was conceived by the Holy Spirit,
            born of the Virgin Mary,
            suffered under Pontius Pilate,
            was crucified, died and was buried;
              he descended to the dead.
            On the third day he rose again;
            he ascended into heaven,
            he is seated at the right hand of the Father,
            and he will come to judge the living
              and the dead.
            I believe in the Holy Spirit,
            the holy catholic Church,
            the communion of saints,
            the forgiveness of sins,
            the resurrection of the body,
            and the life everlasting. Amen.**

15 *Leader* The Lord be with you.
   People **and also with you.**

   Leader Let us pray.

16 *People kneel and say or sing:*

   All **Ask and it shall be given unto you,
         seek and you shall find,
         knock and the door shall be opened unto you.
         Allelu, alleluia.**

17 *THE LORD'S PRAYER*

   Leader As our Saviour taught us, so we pray:

   All **Our Father in heaven,
         hallowed be your name,
         your kingdom come,
            your will be done,
         on earth as in heaven.
         Give us today our daily bread.
         Forgive us our sins,
         as we forgive those
            who sin against us.
         Lead us not into temptation
         but deliver us from evil.
            For the kingdom,
         the power and the
         glory are yours,
         now and for ever. Amen.**

   OR THE LORD'S PRAYER IN SONG

   All **Our Father, who is in heaven,
            hallowed be your name,
         your kingdom come your will be done,
            hallowed be your name,
            hallowed be your name.**

         **On earth as it is in heaven,
            hallowed be your name,
         give us this day our daily bread,
            hallowed be your name,
            hallowed be your name.**

         **Forgive us our trespasses,
            hallowed be your name,**

As we forgive those who trespass against us,
hallowed be your name,
hallowed be your name.

Lead us not into temptation,
hallowed be your name,
but deliver us from all that is evil,
hallowed be your name,
hallowed be your name.

For yours is the kingdom, the power and the glory,
hallowed be your name,
for ever and ever, for ever and ever,
hallowed be your name,
hallowed be your name.

18 *Leader* Show us your mercy, O Lord;
People **and grant us your salvation.**

Leader O Lord, guide our President;
People **and give him your wisdom and justice.**

Leader May your ministers serve you faithfully;
People **and your royal people joyfully.**

Leader In the valley of the shadow of death;
People **protect us with your rod and staff.**

Leader Send us out as the salt of the earth;
People **and as the light of the world.**

Leader Like trees planted by the waterside;
People **grant us the fruit of your Spirit.**

Leader May the earth be filled with your glory;
People **as the waters cover the sea.**

19 *PRAYER FOR THE DAY*

20 *PRAYER FOR PEACE*
Either [All] **O God our Father,
you made us for yourself
and our hearts are restless
till we find our rest in you:
watch our sleeping, guard our waking,
that awake we may watch with Christ
and asleep we may rest in peace;
through your Son, the Prince of Peace. Amen.**

OR

O God,
the source of all good desires,
all right judgements, and all just works:
give to your servants that peace
which the world cannot give;
that our hearts may be set to obey
your commandments,
and that freed from the fear of our enemies,
we may pass our time in rest and quietness;
through Jesus Christ our Lord. **Amen.**

21   *PRAYER FOR PROTECTION*

Either   Lighten our darkness,
Lord, we pray;
and in your mercy defend us
from all perils and dangers of this night;
for the love of your only Son,
our Saviour Jesus Christ. **Amen.**

Or

Watch now, dear Lord with those who wake,
Or watch or weep tonight,
And give your angels charge over those who sleep.
Tend your sick ones O Lord; rest your weary ones,
Bless your dying ones,
Soothe your suffering ones, pity your afflicted ones,
Shield your joyous ones;
And all for your love's sake. **Amen.**

22   *Prayerful choruses (or a hymn) may be sang. People may join in open prayers concerning contemporary personal, national and world needs and/or use some of the prayers in the last section of this book.*

23   *OFFERTORY*
The minister makes some biblical exhortation on giving for the Lord's work. A hymn is then sang during which offering is taken. After the offering the following form of response may be used:

Leader   All things come from you O Lord.
People   **And of your own have we given you.**

24 *BLESSING OR FINAL PRAYER*
Other forms of blessing may be found in section 32 of Morning Worship.
When a minister is not present a lay leader shall finish the service with the
Grace.

Minister The Lord bless you and keep you,
The Lord make his face to shine upon you,
and be gracious to you.
The Lord look kindly on you and give you peace.
And the blessing of God almighty, the Father,
the Son and the Holy Spirit,
be among you and remain with you always. **Amen.**

25 *Lay leader* Let us join together in the words of the Grace:

All **The grace of our Lord Jesus Christ,
the love of God, and the fellowship of
the Holy Spirit, be with us now and for evermore.
Amen.**

OR

Now may our Lord Jesus Christ himself, and God our
Father, who loved us and gave eternal comfort and good
hope through grace, comfort our hearts and establish
them in every good work and word.
And may the grace of our Lord Jesus Christ, the love of
God, and the fellowship of the Holy Spirit be with us
now and for evermore. **Amen.**

26 *RECESSIONAL HYMN*

Late Evening Prayer
(Compline)

NOTES:

- This service is for use at late evening when people break to go to sleep.

- It may be used in church, in conferences, at home, or (for) any other appropriate place or purpose.

- It may be conducted by an ordained minister or a lay person.

- The Blessing is to be declared by the ordained minister who may also use other forms of blessing in the Morning Worship. The lay person may use the words of the Grace.

- At the end of the service, people are to disperse quietly.

ORDER OF SERVICE

1 *Hymn*

2 *Leader*   The Lord be with you;
           And also with you.

           Come to us this night Lord;
           Come to us with light.

           Speak to us this night Lord;
           Speak to us your truth.

           Dwell with us this night Lord;
           Dwell with us in love.

           You are our hiding place;
           You protect us from trouble
           and surround us with songs of deliverance.

3 *CONFESSION*
   This form of confession (or the one in either the Morning
   or Evening Worship) may be used. People sit or kneel.

   He who conceals his sins does not prosper;
   But whoever confesses and renounces them finds mercy.
   We confess our sins before you Lord;
   We confess them all.

Sins of commission and sins of omission;
We confess them all.

Cleanse us and forgive us O loving Saviour;
Cleanse and forgive us.

4   *People may prayerfully join in this verse from the hymn
     Rock of Ages or another appropriate verse/chorus.*

> **Nothing in my hands I bring,**
> **Simply to thy cross I cling,**
> **Naked come to thee for dress,**
> **Helpless look to thee for grace,**
> **Foul, I to the fountain fly,**
> **Wash me Saviour or I die**

A moment of silence may be observed.

5   *One of the following psalms is read (antiphonally). People stand.*

PSALM 4

1   **Answer me when I call to you, O my righteous God.
     Give me relief from my distress; be merciful to me and
     hear my prayer.**

2   **How long, O *people*, will you turn my glory into shame?
     How long will you love delusions and seek false gods?**

3   **Know that the Lord has set apart the godly for himself;
     the Lord will hear when I call to him.**

4   **In your anger do not sin;
     when you are on your beds search your hearts and be silent.**

5   **Offer right sacrifices and trust in the Lord.**

6   **Many are asking, "Who can show us any good?"
     Let the light of your face shine upon us, O Lord.**

7   **You have filled my heart with greater joy than
     when their grain and new wine abound.**

8   **I will lie down and sleep in peace, for you alone,
     O Lord, make me dwell in safety.**

PSALM 91:1-11

1   He who dwells in the shelter of the Most High
    will rest in the shadow of the Almighty.

2   I will say of the Lord, "He is my refuge and my fortress
    my God, in whom I trust."

3   Surely he will save you from the fowler's snare
    and from the deadly pestilence.

4   He will cover you with his feathers
    and under his wings you will find refuge;
    his faithfulness will be your shield and rampart.

5   You will not fear the terror of night,
    nor the arrow that flies by day,

6   nor the pestilence that stalks in the darkness,
    nor the plague that destroys at midday.
    A thousand may fall at your side,
    ten thousand at your right hand,
    but it will not come near you.

7   You will only observe with your eyes
    and see the punishment of the wicked.

8   If you make the Most High your dwelling,
    even the Lord, who is my refuge,

9   then no harm will befall you,
    no disaster will come near your tent.
    For he will command his angels concerning you
    to guard you in all your ways.

After the psalm:

Glory to the Father, Son and the Holy Spirit;
as it was in the beginning, is now and ever shall be.
Amen.

6   *Some of the following or other suitable Scriptures may be read,*
    preferably by different people.

He who watches over you will not slumber, indeed he who watches
over you will neither slumber nor sleep. The Lord watches over you.

The Lord is your shade at your right hand; the sun will not harm you by day nor the moon by night. The Lord will keep you from all harm, he will watch over your life.
(Psalm 121:3-7)

Unless the Lord watches over a city, the watchmen stand guard in vain. In vain you rise early, and stay up late, toiling for food to eat, for he grants sleep to those he loves.
(Psalm 127:1-2)

This is what the Lord Almighty, the God of Israel, says: "When I bring them back from captivity, the people in the land of Judah and its own towns will once again use these words: 'The Lord bless you O righteous dwelling, O sacred mountain.' People will live together in Judah and all its towns—farmers and those who move about with their flocks. I will refresh the weary and satisfy the faint." At this I awoke and looked around. My sleep had been pleasant to me.
(Jeremiah 31: 23-26)

Other scripture readings may also be taken from:
Proverbs 3:21-24; Ezekiel 34:24-31; Luke 22:41-46;
Matthew 26:36-46; Mark 13:28-37; (among others).

7   *Hymn*

8   *Homily (if desired)*

9   *PRAYERS OF INTERCESSION, starting with the Lord's prayer.*

Leader   *As our Saviour taught us, let us boldly pray:*

Our Father in heaven,
hallowed be your name,
your kingdom come,
your will be done,
on earth as in heaven.
Give us today our daily bread.
Forgive us our sins,
as we forgive those who sin against us.
Lead us not into temptation
but deliver us from evil.
For the kingdom, the power, and the
glory are yours,
now and for ever. Amen.

Extempore prayers may be offered at this juncture and then the
following prayers; that is,

Prayer for protection

Lighten our darkness,
Lord we pray;
And in your mercy defend us
From all perils and dangers of this night;
For the love of your only Son,
Our Saviour Jesus Christ. Amen.

OR

Lord keep us safe this night,
Secure from all our fears
May angels guard us while we sleep,
Till morning light appears. Amen.

The following verse may also be sang or said.
(Hymn number 701 in "Golden Bells").

Through the day Thy love has spared us
Now we lay us down to rest;
Through the silent watches guard us;
Let no foe our peace molest:
Jesus, Thou our Guardian be;
Sweet it is to trust in Thee. Amen.

10 *Prayer for the blessing of sleep*

Grant us Lord tonight your gift of sweet, uninterrupted sleep,
that free from the anxieties, stress and busy-ness of the day's
activities, our minds and bodies may be refreshed and
rejuvenated for tomorrow's work.
Grant that we shall enjoy tonight's sleep and thank you
in the morning as we stretch out ourselves in readiness for
the tasks ahead.
Through Jesus Christ our Lord we pray. **Amen.**

11 *Prayer of St. Augustine*

Almighty God,
To turn away from you is to fall,
To turn towards you is to rise,
And to stand in you is to live for ever.

Grant us in all our duties your help,
In all our problems your guidance,
In all our dangers your protection,
And in all our sorrows your peace;
Through Jesus Christ our Lord. **Amen.**

12 *BENEDICTION*

Minister   The Lord bless you and keep you,
            The Lord make his face to shine upon you and be
            gracious to you.
            The Lord look kindly on you and give you peace;
            And the blessing of God almighty, the Father, the
            Son and the Holy Spirit, be among you and
            remain with you always. **Amen.**

Lay leader Now may our Lord Jesus Christ himself, and God
            our Father, who loved us and gave eternal comfort
            and good hope through grace, comfort our hearts
            and establish them in every good work and word.
            And may the grace of our Lord Jesus Christ, ...

    OR

            May the grace of our Lord Jesus Christ,
            the love of God, and the fellowship of the
            Holy Spirit, be with us now, and for evermore.
            Amen.

13 *People disperse.*

Service of Baptism

NOTES

- The service is designed to be a complete service in itself, but when adults are being baptised the service should lead to Holy Communion.

- Baptism should normally take place in the main Sunday Service.

- Baptism should be done with one or three-fold administration of water or immersion.

- Oil for anointing should be liquid oil that has been blessed. Anointing with oil not only follows the practice of the early church but also is a component of some traditional initiation ceremonies.

- The service is for both Adult and Infant Baptism. Section 14 is to be used for infants; the parents and godparents must affirm the baptism vows.

- Adults to be baptised are to be admitted to Holy Communion as part of this service; likewise children candidates who have reached age of discernment (9-10).

- Adult candidates are to be presented to the Bishop for confirmation and commissioning as soon as possible.

ORDER OF SERVICE

1   *Hymn*

    Minister   The Lord be with you.
    People   **And also with you.**

2   *The rest of the congregation sits. The minister asks the godparents and parents of infant candidates:*

    Have these children been baptised in water in the name of the Father, Son, and the Holy Spirit?
    Answer   **No.**

    The minister asks the adult candidates:

    Have you been baptised in water in the name of the Father, Son, and the Holy Spirit?
    Answer   **No.**

The candidates sit -- the minister continues:

3 *Minister*   John came baptising in the desert region and preaching a baptism of repentance for the forgiveness of sins. The whole Judean countryside and all the people of Jerusalem went out to him; confessing their sin, they were baptised by him in the river Jordan *(Mark 1:4-5)*. "Repent and be baptised, everyone of you, in the name of Jesus Christ, so that your sins may be forgiven. And you will receive the gift of the Holy Spirit" *(Acts 2:38)*. So as we come to this service of Baptism, let us reverently confess our sins to almighty God.

A time of silence may be kept.

4 *All*   **Almighty God, creator of all, you marvellously made us in your image; but we have corrupted ourselves and damaged your likeness by rejecting your love and hurting our neighbours. We have done wrong and neglected to do right. We are sincerely sorry and heartily repent of our sins. Cleanse us and forgive us by the sacrifice of your Son; remake us and lead us by your Spirit the Comforter. We ask this through Jesus Christ our Lord. Amen.**

5 *Minister*   Almighty God, whose steadfast love is as great as the heavens are high above the earth, remove your sins from you as far as the east is from the west, strengthen your life in his kingdom and keep you upright to the last day; through Jesus Christ our merciful high priest. **Amen.**

6 *Prayer for the Day*

7 *Hymn*

8 MINISTRY OF THE WORD

Not more than three passages from scripture are read, the last of which is always the Gospel. The reader shall introduce the Old Testament or Epistle with these or other appropriate words.

Reader   The Old Testament Reading /Epistle is taken from ..... Chapter ..... beginning to read at verse .....

At the end of the reading the reader says:

This is the Word of the Lord

People   **Thanks be to God.**

THE GOSPEL. One of the following may be chosen:

Matthew 26:24-27   *Luke 24:45-53*

Mark 1:1-11   *John 3:1-8*

All stand for the Gospel, which is introduced with these or other appropriate words:

Minister   We stand to hear the Good News of our salvation, as it is written in the Gospel according to St..., Chapter..., beginning to read at verse....

After the Gospel,

Minister   This is the Gospel of Christ.

People   **Thanks be to Christ our Saviour.**

9   *Notices*

10 *Hymn*

11 *Sermon*

12 EXHORTATION ON BAPTISM

The minister may give the exhortation below, on the meaning of baptism.

13 *Minister*   Brothers and sisters in Christ, in the Gospel of John, Jesus tells us, "No one can enter the kingdom of God unless he is born of water and the Spirit." Because all of us have been born with a sinful nature and continually sin in many ways, we need to be born again. Baptism is the outward sign of this new birth whereby we are united with Christ in his death on the cross for the forgiveness of sins and his resurrection to new life. In St. Matthew's Gospel Jesus commanded his disciples to go and make disciples of all nations, baptising then in the name of the Father, Son, and the Holy Spirit. In the same way Peter after preaching the Gospel on the day of Pentecost said, "Repent and be baptised in the name of Jesus Christ for the forgiveness of sins and you shall receive the gift of the Holy Spirit. For the promise is to you and your children and all that are far away, everyone whom the Lord calls to him."

It is therefore in obedience to Christ's command that we ourselves have been baptised and these people will be baptised today. So let us thank the Lord for our baptism and pray for these candidates as they now go to be baptised.

14 *All*   **Almighty Father we thank you for calling us to know you and to put our trust in you through your Son, Jesus Christ our Saviour. Deepen our knowledge and strengthen our faith in you. Pour out your Spirit on these people that they may be born again of water and the Spirit and added to the family of your Church; through Jesus Christ the pioneer of our salvation.**

15 PRESENTATION OF CANDIDATES

When the baptiser is the instructor, this section is omitted.
The candidates, parents and godparents stand:

Instructor   I present these candidates for baptism.

The minister facing the adult candidates, asks the instructor:

Minister   Have you sufficiently prepared these candidates for baptism?

Instructor   **Yes, I have sufficiently taught them the Christian faith and found them fit and ready for baptism.**

The minister turns to the parents and godparents and again asks the instructor:

Minister   Have you sufficiently prepared the parents and godparents for the vows they are about to take on behalf of these children.

Instructor   **Yes I have.**

For infant candidates, the following act of commitment is used. If there are no infant candidates the minister continues with the next section.

16 COMMITMENT OF PARENTS AND GODPARENTS

Minister   The Bible tells us that when the Philippian jailer was saved, "he and all his family were baptised".
The Anglican Church baptises children who are not able to answer for themselves on the basis of the faith and repentance of their parents and godparents and on the understanding that they will be brought up as Christians in the fellowship of the Church.
We therefore ask you to commit yourself to this responsibility by answering these questions.

Question   Are you prepared to take baptismal vows on behalf of these children?
Answer   **I am.**

Question   Will you teach these children the Christian faith by your word and example?
Answer   **I will.**

Question   Will you guide and encourage these children in Christian living?
Answer   **I will.**

Question   Will you pray for them regularly and bring them to Sunday worship?
Answer   **I will.**

Question   As soon as they are sufficiently prepared and ready, will you bring them for confirmation?
Answer   **I will.**

17 *An adult candidate may be given an opportunity to give a brief testimony.*

18 BAPTISMAL VOWS
A candle may be lit for every candidate.
The minister says to the candidates, parents and godparents:

You have come here to be baptised. You should therefore answer sincerely before God and this congregation the questions which I now put to you.

Minister   Do you turn to Christ?
Answer   **I turn to Christ.**

Minister	Do you repent of all your sins?
Answer	**I repent of all my sins.**

Minister	Do you renounce Satan, all his works and all the evil powers of this world?
Answer	**I renounce them all.**

Minister	Do you renounce the desires of your sinful nature and all forms of idolatry?
Answer	**I renounce them all.**

Minister	Do you believe and trust in God the Father, who made the world?
Answer	**I believe and trust in him.**

Minister	Do you believe and trust in his Son Jesus Christ, who redeemed humankind?
Answer	**I believe and trust in him.**

Minister	Do you believe and trust in his Holy Spirit, who gives life to the people of God?
Answer	**I believe and trust in him.**

19 THANKSGIVING OVER WATER

The minister approaches the place of baptism and candidates stand around; the congregation stands.

Minister	O give thanks to the Lord for he is good;
People	**For his steadfast love endures for ever.**

Minister	For the blessing of water;
People	**We thank you Lord.**

Minister	For your Son Jesus Christ who was himself baptised in the river Jordan;
People	**We thank you Lord.**

Minister	Hear our prayers as we obey your Son's command to go and baptise in the name of the Father, Son, and the Holy Spirit;
People	**Hear us O Lord.**

Minister	Sanctify this water for baptising your servants;
People	**Sanctify.**

Minister	Bless those who are to be baptised in it;
People	**Bless them**

Minister	May they be cleansed from all their sins;
People	**Be cleansed.**
Minister	May they be united with Christ in his death and resurrection;
People	**Be united.**
Minister	May they be born again by the Spirit to eternal life;
People	**Be born again.**
Minister	May they be joined into the fellowship of the Body of Christ;
People	**Be joined.**
Minister	Christ has defeated Satan and all evil powers!
People	**Alleluia!**

20 BAPTISM

Candidates are brought to the minister for baptism.

Minister   Name this *person. (The names are stated.)*

The minister immerses the candidate or pours water on the candidate's head, saying:

NN, I baptise you in the name of the Father, Son, and the Holy Spirit. **Amen.**

21 *SIGN OF THE CROSS*

The minister marks each candidate with the sign of the cross saying:

Since you have passed from death to new life in Christ I mark you with the sign of the cross. **Amen.**

Ululations may be made and choruses sang after all the candidates have been baptised.

22 *ANOINTING (OPTIONAL)*

The priest anoints each candidate with oil on the forehead saying:
I anoint you in the name of the Anointed One.

23 *WELCOME*

After all the candidates have been baptised (and anointed), they face the congregation. The whole congregation stands and says to them:

We welcome you into the Body of Christ:
you are a new creation,
the old has passed away, the new has come.
Do not be ashamed to confess the faith of Christ
crucified.
Fight bravely under his banner against sin,
the world and the devil,
and continue his faithful soldiers and servants to the
end of your lives. Amen.

If the candidates are few, the priest may choose to present one at a time and each time, the congregation offers the welcome statement.

24 *The adult candidates, who have just been baptised, stand.*

| *Minister* | We were all baptised by one Spirit, |
| *People* | **into one body.** |

| *Minister* | We who are many are one body, |
| *People* | **for we share one bread.** |

| *Minister* | Let us then welcome these our brothers and sisters as fellow partakers of the Lord's Supper. |
| *Communicants* | **We welcome you to share with us the Lord's Supper. Happy are those invited to the marriage feast of the Lamb. Alleluia!** |

25 | *Minister* | The peace of the Lord be always with you. |
| *People* | **And also with you.** |

The candidates are greeted by the members of the congregation.

26 *If the service ends here, an offertory hymn is sang and after offetory the minister ends with the following blessing and, a recessional hymn.*

| *Minister* | May Almighty God protect you from the powers of darkness, grant you daily repentance of sins and lead you to walk in the light, through Jesus Christ the light of the world, and victor over Satan. |
| *People* | **Amen.** |

27 *If the service is proceeding to Holy Communion, the sharing of peace is followed by offertory, and the minister continues from the prayer of thanksgiving.*

Conditional Baptism

NOTES

- It is to be administered only where there is doubt as to whether someone has not been baptised in the Name of the Father, Son, and the Holy Spirit.

- In conditional baptism the service runs the same except for the actual baptism clause which should run thus:

Minister   *N,* if you have not already been baptised, I baptise you in the name of the Father, Son and the Holy Spirit. **Amen.**

Emergency Baptism

- Emergency baptism is to be administered in cases where a person is in the risk of dying unbaptised. If it is an adult, it must be ascertained that he is interested in baptism and that he has accepted Jesus Christ as his Lord and Saviour.

- This baptism may be conducted by a full communicant Christian other than the priest.

- The water of baptism is to be administered thus:

    N, I baptise you in the name of the Father, Son, and the Holy Spirit. *People:* **Amen.**

- After such a baptism, the priest is to be informed immediately afterwards.

- In the event that the person lives after all, *he* is to present himself to the priest who is to ascertain that the baptism was rightly and rightfully administered. The person is to testify and thereafter the priest completes the rite by marking him with the sign of the cross and then prays for him.

- In case of any uncertainty, the priest is to make enquiries.

- Where it is not certain that baptism was properly administered, the priest is to use the conditional baptism clause.

- But where it is clear that proper baptism was not administered, the service of baptism is to be used, unaltered.

Admission to Holy Communion

- This service is to be conducted by the parish minister in the context of a Holy Communion Service.

- It is for children who have been baptised and who have attained the age of reason (9-10 years) and who have received instruction in the meaning of the sacraments.

- The candidates should be taught not necessarily to recite phrases but to understand, internalise the teaching hence be able to explain it from an inward personal conviction. The minister may choose to pick candidates at random and ask them questions.

ORDER OF SERVICE

1   *The service starts with the usual service of Holy Communion (sections 1-24). This is to be followed by:*

PRESENTATION AND EXAMINATION OF CANDIDATES

2   *The candidates stand and the instructor, parents and sponsors together say:*

We present these candidates for admission to Holy Communion.

Minister　Are these candidates ready for admission to Holy Communion?

Instructor　**Yes, I have taught them the meaning of the sacraments of Baptism and Holy Communion, and I am satisfied that they are ready for admission.**

3   *The minister turns to the candidates.*

Minister　What do you understand as the meaning of your Baptism?

Answer　**I was baptised into Christ and died to sin. I have been made clean by him and now live for him. I share his Spirit and am a member of his Church.**

Minister	What do you understand as the meaning of Holy Communion?
Answer	**We remember that Christ died for us. As we receive the bread and wine, we feed on his body and blood in our hearts by faith with thanksgiving.**
Minister	What is required of those who come to Holy Communion?
Answer	**They should make sure that they have truly turned from their sins and live for Christ, that they trust him alone for salvation and love their neighbours.**

4   RENEWAL OF BAPTISMAL VOWS

The minister turns to the candidates in the presence of parents and godparents and says:

Minister	You have been presented here for admission to Holy Communion. You should therefore answer sincerely on your own before God and this congregation the questions which I now put to you, which your parents and godparents answered on your behalf at your baptism.
Minister	Do you turn to Christ?
Answer	**I turn to Christ.**
Minister	Do you repent of all your sins?
Answer	**I repent of all my sins.**
Minister	Do you renounce Satan, his works and all the evil powers of this world?
Answer	**I renounce them all.**
Minister	Do you renounce the desires of your sinful nature and all forms of idolatry?
Answer	**I renounce them all.**
Minister	Do you believe and trust in God the Father, who made the world?
Answer	**I believe and trust in him.**
Minister	Do you believe and trust in his Son Jesus Christ who redeemed human kind?
Answer	**I believe and trust in him.**

| *Minister* | Do you believe and trust in his Holy Spirit, who gives life to the people of God? |
| *Answer* | **I believe and trust in him.** |

5   *The minister turns to the congregation and says:*

| *Minister* | This is the faith of the Church. |
| *All* | **This is our faith.** |

| *Minister* | We believe and trust in one God, |
| *All* | **Father, Son and the Holy Spirit.** |

6   *ADMISSION*

Candidates to be admitted to Holy Communion stand.

| Minister | We are all baptised by one Spirit, |
| *Answer* | **into one body.** |

| *Minister* | We who are many are one body, |
| *Answer* | **for we share one bread.** |

The minister says to each candidate as he shakes their hands:

I, and the communicants of this parish, admit you to be a partaker of Holy Communion, in the name of the Father, Son, and the Holy Spirit.

| *All* | **Amen.** |

7   *Minister*   Let us welcome these our brothers and sisters as fellow partakers with us of the Lord's Supper.

Communicants   **We welcome you to share with us in the Lord's Supper. Happy are those invited to the marriage feast of the Lamb. Alleluia!**

8   *The parents and godparents of the candidates give the candidates a hand of welcome. The rest of the communicants extend this welcome during the sharing of the peace.*

9   *Minister*   May Almighty God continually protect you from the powers of darkness and grant you daily repentance of sins. May he fill your life with thanksgiving as often as you receive the body and blood of his Son Jesus Christ, the bread of life.

| *All* | **Amen.** |

10   *A Hymn may be sang*

The service continues from section 25 of the Service of Holy Communion (Sharing of the Peace). During the administration of Holy Communion, parents and godparents kneel with their respective candidates.

A Revised Catechism

NOTES
- This Catechism is to be taught to all Christians before they are brought to the Bishop for confirmation and Commissioning.
- This order of instruction on Christian faith and doctrine of the Anglican Church should be taught for a period of not less than 6 months.
- Those who do not qualify are to repeat the instruction classes until they understand.
- This Catechism is slightly abridged. The Catechist may also refer to the Confirmation or Baptism training books published by Uzima Press for the Anglican Church of Kenya.
- The Confirmation class is to be taught by the Curate or, in his absence, an instructor, who should be mature, spiritually committed Anglican. He should be sufficiently grounded in theology (whether from a theological college or through Theological Education by Extension).

I   THE CALL OF GOD: THE CHRISTIAN ANSWER

1   What is your baptismal name?
My baptismal name is _____

2   Who gave you that name?
My parents and godparents gave me this name at my baptism.

3   What did God do for you in your baptism?
In my baptism, God called me to himself, and I was made a member of the Body of Christ, a child of God and an inheritor of the kingdom of heaven.

4   What did your godparents promise for you at your baptism?
At my baptism my godparents made three promises to God for me:
First, that I would renounce the devil and fight against evil;
Secondly, that I would hold fast the Christian Faith and put my whole trust in Christ as Lord and Saviour;
Thirdly, that I would obediently keep God's holy will and commandments and serve him faithfully all the days of my life.

5   Are you bound to do as they promised?
Certainly yes, and I will do so by God's help.

II   CHRISTIAN BELIEF

6   Where do you find a summary of this Christian Faith which you are
bound to believe and hold fast?

I find a summary of the Christian Faith in the Apostles' Creed and in
the Nicene Creed.

7   Repeat the Apostles' Creed.

I believe in God,
   the Father Almighty,
creator of heaven and earth.
   I believe in Jesus Christ,
his only Son, our Lord,
who was conceived by the Holy Spirit,
born of the Virgin Mary,
suffered under Pontius Pilate,
was crucified, died and was buried;
   he descended to the dead.
On the third day he rose again;
he ascended into heaven,
he is seated at the right hand of the Father,
and he will come to judge the living
   and the dead.
I believe in the Holy Spirit,
the holy catholic Church,
the communion of saints,
the forgiveness of sins,
the resurrection of the body,
and the life everlasting. Amen.

8   What do you learn from the Creeds?
**From the Creeds, I learn to believe in one God, Father, Son, and
the Holy Spirit, who is the creator and ruler of the universe and
has made all things for his glory.**

9.   What does the Church teach about God the Father?
**The Church teaches that God the Father made me and all
humankind, and that in his love he sent his son to reconcile the
world to himself.**

10 What does the Church teach about God the Son?
The Church teaches that for our salvation, God the Son became man and died for our sins; that he was raised victorious over death and was exalted to the throne of God as our advocate and intercessor; and that he will come as our judge.

11 What does the Church teach about God the Holy Spirit?
The Church teaches that God the Holy Spirit inspires all that is good in humankind; that he came in his fullness at Pentecost to be the giver of life in the Church, and that he enables me to grow in likeness to Jesus Christ.

Thus I learn to believe in one God, Father, Son and the Holy Spirit, and this Holy Trinity I praise and magnify saying: Glory to the Father, Son and the Holy Spirit, as it was in the beginning, is now, and ever shall be, world without end. Amen.

III THE CHURCH AND MINISTRY

12 What is the Church?
The Church is the family of God and the Body of Christ through which he continues his reconciling work among people. Its members on earth enter it by baptism and are one company with those who worship God in heaven.

13 How is the Church described in the Creeds?
The church is described as one, holy, catholic (universal) and apostolic.

14. What do you mean by these words?
By these words I mean that:
1. **the Church is one because, in spite of its division, it is one family under one Father, whose purpose is to unite all people in Jesus Christ our Lord:**
2. **the Church is holy because it is set apart by God for himself, through the Holy Spirit;**
3. **the Church is catholic because it is universal, for all nations and for all time, holding the Christian faith in its fullness;**
4. **the Church is apostolic because it is sent to preach the Gospel to the whole world, and receives its divine authority and teaching from Christ through his apostles.**

15 What orders of ministers are there in the Church?
There are these orders of ministers in the Church: bishops, priests, and deacons.

16 What is the work of a Bishop?
The work of a bishop is to be a chief shepherd and an overseer (ruler) in the church: to guard the faith; to ordain and confirm; and to be the chief minister of the word and sacraments in his diocese.

17 What is the work of a Priest?
The work of a priest is to preach the word of God, to teach, and to baptize; to celebrate the Holy Communion; to pronounce the absolution and blessing in God's name; and to care for the people entrusted by the bishop to his charge.

18 What is the work of a Deacon?
The work of a deacon is to help the priest both in the conduct of worship and in the care of souls.

19 What is the Anglican Church of Kenya?
The Anglican Church of Kenya is catholic and reformed. It proclaims and holds fast the doctrine and ministry of the one, holy, universal and apostolic Church.

20 What is the Anglican Communion?
The Anglican Communion is a family of churches within the universal Church of Christ, maintaining apostolic doctrine and order and in full communion with one another and with the Sees of Canterbury and York.

IV CHRISTIAN OBEDIENCE

21 The third promise made at your Baptism binds you to keep God's commandments all the days of your life. Where has God made these commandments known?
God has made his Commandments known in the Scriptures of Old and New Testaments, especially in the teaching and example of our Lord Jesus Christ.

22 Repeat the Ten Commandments found in the law of Moses:
1. I am the Lord your God who brought you out of Egypt, out of the land of slavery. You shall have no other gods but me.
2. You shall not make for yourself an idol in the form of anything in heaven above or on the earth beneath or in the waters below. You shall not bow down to them or worship them.

3. You shall not misuse the name of the Lord your God.
4. Remember the Sabbath day by keeping it holy. Six days you shall labour and do all your work, but the seventh day is a Sabbath to the Lord your God.
5. Honour your father and your mother, so that you may live long in the land the Lord your God is giving you.
6. You shall not murder.
7. You shall not commit adultery.
8. You shall not steal.
9. You shall not give false testimony against your neighbour.
10. You shall not covet.

23 Repeat the words of our Lord Jesus Christ about God's commandments.
Our Lord Jesus Christ said: "You shall love the Lord your God with all your heart and with all your soul, and with all your mind, and with all your strength. This is the first commandment. The second is this: "You shall love your neighbour as yourself".

24 What then is your duty towards God?
My duty towards God is:
1. To worship him as the only true God, to love, trust, and obey him, and by witness of my words and deeds to bring others to serve him;
2. To allow no created thing to take his place, but to use my time, my gifts, and my possessions as one who must give an account to him;
3. To reverence him in thought, word, and deed;
4. To keep the Lord's day for worship, prayer, and rest from work.

25 What is your duty towards your neighbour?
My duty towards my neighbour is:
1. To love, respect, and help my parents; to obey those in authority over me in all things lawful and good; and to fulfil my duties as a citizen.
2. To hurt nobody by word or deed; to bear no grudge or hatred; to promote peace among people; to be courteous to all; and to be kind to all God's creatures;
3. To be clean in thought, word and deed, controlling my bodily desires through the power of the Holy Spirit who dwells within me; and if called to the state of marriage to live faithfully in it;

4. to be honest and fair in all I do; not to steal or cheat; to seek justice, freedom, and plenty for all people;
5. to keep my tongue from lying, slandering and harmful gossip, and never by my silence to let others be wrongly condemned;
6. to be thankful and generous; to do my duty cheerfully, and not to be greedy or envious.

Thus I acknowledge God's reign among his people, and try to live as a citizen of his kingdom, fighting against evil wherever I find it, in myself or in the world around me.

V THE HOLY SPIRIT IN THE CHURCH

Grace

26. How can you carry out these duties and overcome temptation and sin?
I can do these things only by the help of God and through his grace.

27. What do you mean by God's grace?
By God's grace I mean that God himself acts in Jesus Christ to forgive, inspire, and strengthen me by his Holy Spirit.

28. In what ways do you receive these gifts of God's grace?
I received these gifts of God's grace within the fellowship of the Church when I worship and pray, when I read the Bible, when I receive the sacraments, and as I live my daily life to his glory.

Worship and Prayer

29. What do you mean by the worship of God?
To worship God is to respond to his love, first by joining in the church's offering of praise, thanksgiving, and prayer, and by hearing his holy word; secondly by acknowledging him as the Lord of my life, and by doing my work for his honour and glory.

30. Why do we keep Sunday as the chief day of public worship?
We keep Sunday as the chief day of public worship because it was on the first day of the week that our Lord Jesus rose from the dead.

31. What is prayer?
Prayer is the lifting up of heart and mind to God. We adore him, we confess our sins and ask to be forgiven; we thank him, we pray for others and for ourselves, we listen to him and seek to know and do his will.

32. Repeat the Lord's Prayer.

> **Our Father in heaven,**
> **hallowed be your name,**
> **your kingdom come,**
>   **your will be done,**
> **on earth as in heaven.**
> **Give us today our daily bread.**
> **Forgive us our sins,**
>   **as we forgive those**
>   **who sin against us.**
> **Lead us not into temptation**
> **but deliver us from evil.**
>   **For the kingdom,**
>   **the power and the**
>   **glory are yours,**
>   **now and for ever. Amen.**

The Bible

33. What is the Bible?
The Bible, in both the Old and the New Testaments is the record of God's revelation of himself to humankind through his people Israel, and above all in his Son, Jesus Christ.

34. How was the Bible given to us?
The Bible was given to us by the Holy Spirit who first inspired and guided the writers, and then led the Church to accept their writings as Holy Scriptures.

35. How should we read the Bible?
We should read the Bible with the desire and prayer that through it God will speak to us by His Holy Spirit, and enable us to know him and do his will.

The Gospel, Sacraments and other ministries of Grace

36. What do you mean by a sacrament?
By a sacrament I mean the use of material things as signs and pledges of God's grace, and as a means by which we receive his gifts.

37. What are the two parts of a sacrament?
The two parts of a sacrament are the outward and visible sign, and the inward and spiritual grace.

38. How many sacraments has Christ in the Gospel, appointed for his Church?

Christ in the Gospel has appointed two sacraments for his Church, as needed by all for fullness of life, Baptism, and Holy Communion.

39. What other sacramental ministries of grace are provided in the Church?

Other sacramental ministries of grace are confirmation, ordination, holy matrimony, the ministry of absolution, and the ministry of healing.

40. What is Baptism?

Baptism is the sacrament in which, through the action of the Holy Spirit, we are buried with Christ and arise to new life in him (A commitment to the new life).

41. What is the outward and visible sign in Baptism?

The outward and visible sign in Baptism is water in which the person is baptised; *In the Name of the Father, and of the Son, and of the Holy Spirit.*

42. What is the inward and spiritual gift in Baptism?

The inward and spiritual gift in Baptism is union with Christ in his death and resurrection, the forgiveness of sins, and a new birth into God's family, the Church.

43. What is required of persons to be baptized?

It is required that persons to be baptized should turn from sin, believe the Christian Faith, and give themselves to Christ to be his servants.

44. Why then are infants baptized?

Infants are baptized because, though they are not yet old enough to make their promises for themselves, others, making the promises for them, can claim their adoption as children of God.

45. What is *Confirmation?*

Confirmation is the ministry by which, through prayer with the laying on of hands by the bishop, the Holy Spirit is received to complete what he began in Baptism and to give strength for the Christian service and witness.

46. What is required of persons to be confirmed?

It is required that persons to be confirmed should have been baptized, be sufficiently instructed in the Christian faith, be penitent for their sins, and be ready to confess Jesus Christ as Saviour and obey him as Lord.

47. What is Holy Communion?

Holy Communion is the sacrament in which, according to Christ's command, we make continual remembrance of him, his passion, death, and resurrection, until his coming again, and in which we thankfully receive the benefits of his sacrifice.

It is therefore called the Eucharist, the Church's sacrifice of praise and thanksgiving; and also the Lord's Supper, the meal of fellowship which unites us to Christ and to the whole Church.

48. What is the outward and visible sign in Holy Communion?

The outward and visible sign in Holy Communion is bread and wine given and received as the Lord commanded.

49. What is the inward and spiritual gift in Holy Communion?

The inward and spiritual gift in Holy Communion is the body and blood of Christ truly and indeed given by him and received by the faithful.

50. What is meant by receiving the body and blood of Christ?

Receiving the body and blood of Christ means receiving the life of Christ himself, who was crucified, died and rose again, and is now alive for ever more.

51. What are the benefits we receive in Holy Communion?

The benefits we receive are the strengthening of our union with Christ and his Church, the forgiveness of our sins, and the nourishing of ourselves for eternal life.

52. What is required of those who come to Holy Communion?

It is required of those who come to Holy Communion that they have a living faith in God's mercy through Christ, with a thankful remembrance of his death and resurrection; that they repent truly of their sins, intending to lead the new life, and to love all people.

53. What is Ordination?

Ordination is the ministry in which, through prayer with the laying on of hands, our Lord Jesus Christ gives the grace of the Holy Spirit, and authority, to those who are being made bishops, priests or deacons.

54. What is Holy Matrimony?

Holy Matrimony is Christian marriage, in which the man and the woman, entering into a life-long union, take their vows before God and seek his grace and blessing to fulfill them.

55. What is the ministry of Absolution?

It is the ministry by which those who are truly sorry for their sins, and have made free confession of them to God in the presence of the minister, with intention to amend their lives receive through him the forgiveness of God.

56. What is the sacramental ministry of Healing?

It is the ministry by which God's grace is given for the healing of spirit, mind and body, in response to faith and prayer by the laying on of hands, or by anointing with oil.

VI. THE CHRISTIAN HOPE

57. What is the hope in which a Christian lives?

A Christian lives in the certain hope of the advent of Christ, the last judgement, and resurrection to life everlasting.

58. What do we understand by the advent of Christ?

By the advent of Christ we are to understand that God, who through Christ has created and redeemed all things, will also through Christ at his coming again, make all things perfect and complete in his eternal kingdom.

59. What are we to understand by the last judgement?

By the last judgement we are to understand that every person will give an account of their life to God who will condemn and destroy all that is evil and bring his servants into the joy of their Lord.

60. What are we to understand by resurrection?

By resurrection we are to understand that, God, who has overcome death by the resurrection of Christ, will raise from death in a body of glory all who are Christ's, that they may live with him in the fellowship of the saints.

61. What then, is our assurance as Christians?

Our assurance as Christians is that neither death, nor life, nor things present, nor things to come, shall be able to separate us from the love of God which is in Christ Jesus our Lord. Thus, daily increasing in God's Holy Spirit, and following the example of our Saviour Christ, we shall at the last be made like him, for we shall see him as he is.

Confirmation and Commissioning
for Service and Witness

NOTES

* This service is to be used in the context of Holy Communion.
  The service is for 12 year olds and over, who have been instructed in
  the faith, baptised, and admitted to communion.

* The service is to be conducted by the Diocesan bishop.

* A certificate of confirmation and commissioning should be given to
  each candidate and may be presented by the Parish Priest after the
  service.

ORDER OF SERVICE

1 *Processional Hymn*

2 *CALL TO WORSHIP*

       The Lord be with you:
All   **and also with you.**

       The earth is the Lord's and all that is in it:
All   **Let the heavens rejoice and the earth be glad.**

       Our help is in the name of the Lord:
All   **who made heaven and earth.**

       I was glad when they said to me:
All   **let us go to the house of the Lord.**

       Praise the Lord.
All   **The name of the Lord be praised.**

All   **Heavenly Father,**
       by the power of your Holy Spirit
       you give to your faithful people
       new life in the water of baptism.
       You commission them to serve you in the world.
       Guide and strengthen us by that same Spirit,
       that we who are born again
       may serve you in faith and love
       and grow into the full stature of your Son Jesus Christ,
       who is alive and reigns with you and the Holy
       Spirit, one God, now and for ever. Amen.

3 *Hymn*

4 *PRESENTATION*

Minister, sponsors and parents together say:

> **Father in God, we bring you these**
> **candidates who have been baptised,**
> **that you may confirm and**
> **commission them for service and witness**
> **to Christ and his Church.**

Bishop Take care that these people you have
presented to us have been instructed,
and that they fully understand their baptismal
vows and are willing to serve Christ and his Church.

Minister, sponsors and parents:

> **We have instructed and examined them and find**
> **them worthy.**

5 *The candidates stand before the Bishop.*

Bishop Let us pray for these candidates that God may help them so
that they may fulfil the vows they have just made before
God and this congregation.

Almighty God, you give gifts to humankind, and appoint
some to be apostles, prophets, evangelists, pastors and
teachers, to prepare all God's people for the work of
Christian service in order to build the Body of Christ; we
now pray for these your servants who have come to be
confirmed and commissioned. Grant them sincerity of
heart that they may fulfil the promises they are about to
make. Fill them with the truth of your doctrine and clothe
them with holiness of life that by word and good example
they may faithfully serve you to the glory of your name;
through our Saviour Jesus Christ. **Amen.**

6 *MINISTRY OF THE WORD*

*Either two or three passages from scripture are read, the last of which is
always the Gospel.*

Joshua 24:14-24	*Romans 12:1-3*	*Matthew 28:16-20*
Isaiah 49:1-6	*1 Corinthians 9:15-23*	*Luke 4:14-21*

7   *Hymn*

8   *Sermon*

9   *MAKING OF PROMISES*

The candidates stand before the Bishop.

Bishop   You stand in the presence of God and his Church; with your own mouth and from your own heart you must declare your allegiance to Christ and your rejection of all that is evil.

Therefore I ask these questions:

Do you turn to Christ?

Answer   **I turn to Christ.**

Do you repent of all your sins?

Answer   **I repent of all my sins.**

Do you renounce Satan, his works and all the evil powers of this world?

Answer   **I renounce them all.**

Do you renounce the desires of your sinful nature and all forms of idolatry?

Answer   **I renounce them all.**

Bishop   I now call upon you to declare before God and his Church that you accept the Christian faith into which you were baptised, and in which you live, grow and serve.

Do you believe and trust in God the Father, who made this world?

Answer   **I believe and trust in him.**

Do you believe and trust in his Son Jesus Christ who redeemed humankind?

Answer   **I believe and trust in him.**

Do you believe and trust in his Holy Spirit who gives life to the people of God?

Answer   **I believe and trust in him.**

The Bishop turns to the congregation and says:

This is the faith of the Church.

All   **This is our faith.**

We believe and trust in one God,
Father, Son and the Holy Spirit.

*The Bishop turns to the candidates and continues with either section 10
or/and section 11.*

Either

10 *Bishop* So that all may know your intention and resolve, I ask you:

Will you be willing to tell your neighbours about the love of
Christ?

Answer **I will.**

Will you pray and support your church, the bishops, clergy
and all other church workers?

Answer **I will do so, God being my helper.**

Will you read the Bible regularly and fashion your life
after it?

Answer **I will diligently do so.**

Will you endeavour to meet with other Christians for
fellowship and stir up the gift of God that is in you?

Answer **I will endeavour to do so.**

Will you make every effort to attend Sunday worship and in
particular the celebration of Holy Communion?

Answer **I will do so.**

Will you pursue justice, truth and the reconciliation of
God's people?

Answer **I will do so whenever opportunities arise.**

Will you endeavour to feed the hungry, give water to the
thirsty, welcome the needy, clothe the naked, visit the sick
and those in prison?

Answer **I will do so with the help of God.**

Will you support and pray for the lonely, the orphans,
widows and all the voiceless?

Answer **I will support and pray for them.**

Will you endeavour to be a good steward of God's creation
and care for the environment?

Answer **I will endeavour to do so.**

Will you be a faithful citizen of your nation, and regularly pray for its leaders.

Answer **I will.**

Will you be alert and watchful, and firmly resist your enemy the devil?

Answer **I will do so with the help of God.**

Or/and

11 *Bishop* So that all may know your intention and resolve, what is your pledge?

Answer **I, about to be commissioned
for service and witness to Christ
and his Church, do pledge to keep and walk in
God's commandments all the days of my life,
and to read the Bible and pray regularly.
I pledge to proclaim Christ in season and out
of season, to obey him and to live in
the fellowship of all true believers throughout the
world. I pledge to be active in church,
to give to the work of the church,
to help the needy, support the poor, and
to be a good steward of all that the Lord
gives me. I pledge to uphold truth and justice,
and to seek reconciliation among all
people; Christ being my helper.**

Bishop Do you who are gathered here agree that these people be confirmed and commissioned for the mission of Christ and his Church?

All **We agree.**

12 *CONFIRMATION*

The Bishop stretches his hand over the candidates and says:

The Lord says: "You are my witnesses, and my servants whom I have chosen."

Answer **We are indeed.**

Give thanks to the Lord and call upon his name.

Answer **I will thank him, praise him and call upon his name
always.**

The Bishop lays hands on the head of each candidate saying:
Strengthen, O Lord, your servant *N*, with your Holy Spirit.
Empower *him* for your service and sustain *him* all the days
of *his* life.

All **Amen.**

13 *COMMISSIONING*

*All candidates stand and face the congregation and the Bishop stretches his
hands over them and says:*
Now that you have been confirmed, I commission you to go
into the world. This is your mission:
Where there is hatred, sow love.
Where there is injury, pardon
Where there is doubt, faith
Where there is despair, hope.
Where there is darkness, light.
Where there is sadness, joy.

And then he prays:
O divine Master,
grant that they may not so much seek
to be consoled, as to console;
to be understood, as to understand;
to be loved, as to love.
For it is in giving that we receive,
it is in pardoning that we are pardoned,
it is in dying that we are born to eternal life. **Amen.**

14 *All* **O Lord, without whom our Labour is lost;**
we beseech you to prosper all
works in your Church undertaken
according to your holy will. Grant
your workers a pure intention, a
patient faith, sufficient success on
earth, and the blessedness of
serving you in heaven; through Jesus
Christ our Lord. Amen.

15 *Bishop* On behalf of the Anglican communicants in this
Parish of ..., and in the Diocese of ... and the Anglican
Church of Kenya and the entire Anglican Communion

throughout the world, I welcome you to become full communicants and commissioners for Christ in the Anglican Church, in the name of the Father, Son, and the Holy Spirit. **Amen.**

16   *The Bishop addresses the congregation:*

Will you welcome and support these whom we have confirmed and commissioned into the service and witness of Christ and his Church.

All   **In the name of Christ we welcome them and pledge our support.**

17   THE SHARING OF PEACE

Bishop   The peace of the Lord be always with you.
All   **And also with you.**

Bishop   Let us welcome the candidates with a sign of peace.

The congregation moves forward to greet the candidates. Suitable hymns may accompany this gesture. Communion follows at Section 26 of the Holy Communion service.

Admitting Christians From Other Churches

- This service is to be conducted in the context of Holy Communion by a parish priest, and may be conducted prior to the sharing of peace. If the candidates are not confirmed, the parish priest is to admit them to communion. Subsequently they are to be prepared and registered for the service of confirmation and commissioning.

- It is meant for those who wish to join the membership of the Anglican Church of Kenya. Before one can be admitted, he is to be examined by the parish priest and the church council as part of administrative and pastoral routine.

- If *he* has not been baptised properly, that is, with water and in the threefold formula, he is to undergo the catechetical training that subsequently leads to baptism.

- For those properly baptised, the service is to take the following order.

ORDER OF SERVICE

1 *The priest addresses the congregation:*

Dear brothers and sisters, the persons here standing desire to become members of the Anglican Church of Kenya.

He reads the persons' names and the churches they are leaving, and then continues:

But before I admit them, I will ask them to make certain important declarations pertaining to their faith in God, in whose threefold names they were baptised.

Do you believe in God the Father, the Son and the Holy Spirit and accept the Christian faith as contained in the Apostles' Creed?
I believe in God the Father, the Son and the Holy Spirit and accept the Christian faith as contained in the Apostles' Creed.

Do you acknowledge the Anglican Church of Kenya to be a true part of the one, holy, universal and apostolic church?
I do.

Do you accept its ministry of bishops, priests, and deacons, and believe its sacraments of Baptism and Holy Communion to be those which Christ appointed?
I do.

Will you be a loyal member of the Anglican Church of Kenya, accepting its teaching and discipline in all things truthful, and share in its worship, work, and witness?
I will.

Almighty God who gives you the will to do all these things, grant you grace and power to perform them, that he may complete the good work he has begun in you, through Jesus Christ our Lord. **Amen.**

2 *The priest extends a hand of admission to (each of) the candidate(s) saying:*

N, I admit you into the Anglican Church of Kenya, and into the fellowship of the Anglican Communion. In the name of the Father, Son, and the Holy Spirit. **Amen.**
And he may add a charge and a blessing, for instance:

Let your light shine before people, that they may see your good works, and glorify your Father who is in heaven. Go out to love and serve the Lord.
In the name of Christ, Amen.

3 *The candidates kneel and the priest prays for them:*
O God our Father, who sent your only Son Jesus to die for us and to reconcile us with you, we thank you for these your servants whom we have admitted to the fellowship of believers of this congregation and the Anglican Communion. May they experience your presence whenever they come to worship you here and in all the other congregations of the Anglican Church. Help us all to bring the best of our talents in the Lord's vineyard and for the extension of his kingdom here and beyond. Help us so that we may daily bring honour and glory to your holy name, in all that we do, and in all that we say. Through Jesus Christ our Lord and Saviour. **Amen.**

4 *The congregation may join in this statement of welcome, or a song that serves a similar purpose.*

We welcome you into our fellowship.
We are members together of the Body of Christ;
We are children of the same heavenly Father;
We are inheritors together of the Kingdom of God.
We welcome you.

A few people may come forward and shake hands with them.

5 *The service continues from the Sharing of the Peace.*

Service of Holy Communion

NOTES

- Where the rubric specifies that the congregation should kneel, it is understood that sitting is also allowed.

- Hymns, choruses and choir items may be inserted as may be deemed appropriate.

- Sufficient bread and wine should be placed on the Holy Table so that reconsecration is not necessary. Whatever has been consecrated should all be consumed.

- The Prayer of Thanksgiving (Section 27) is a single prayer. It is recommended that the congregation stands throughout this prayer to emphasize its unity.

- Special seasonal thanksgiving to be included in the Prayer of Thanksgiving (section 27) are written in the appendix. Extemporary prayers are also encouraged.

- The breaking of bread is in section 29.

SCRIPTURE SENTENCES FOR USE IN SECTION 2
One of these or other appropriate sentences shall be said by the minister in section 2.

God rained down upon them manna to eat, and gave them the grain of heaven. *(Psalm 78:24)*

You shall have a song as in the night when a holy feast is kept; and gladness of heart, as when one sets out to the sound of the pipe to go to the mountain of the Lord, to the Rock of Israel. *(Isaiah.30:29)*

Why spend money and get what is not bread, why give the price of your labour and go unsatisfied? Listen to me and you will have good food to eat. *(Isaiah 55:2)*

Jesus said to them, "I am the bread of life; he who comes to me shall not hunger, and he who believes in me shall never thirst". *(John 6:35)*

Christ our paschal lamb has been sacrificed. Let us therefore celebrate the festival, not with the old leaven of malice and evil, but with the unleavened bread of sincerity and truth. *(1 Corinthians 5:8)*

Our ancestors all ate the same supernatural food and all drank the same supernatural drink, for they drank from the same supernatural Rock which followed them, and the Rock was Christ. *(1 Corinthians 10:3-4)*

CHRISTMAS
She will bear a son and you shall call his name Jesus, for he will save his people from their sins. *(Matthew 1:21)*

EASTER
When he was at table with them, he took the bread and blessed it, broke it, and gave it to them. And their eyes were opened and they recognized him. *(Luke 24:30)*

PENTECOST
For by one Spirit we were all baptised into one body–Jew or Greek, slave or free and all were made to drink of one Spirit.
(1 Corinthians 12:13)

ORDER OF SERVICE

1 *At the entry the people stand and a hymn is announced.*

2 *The minister reads a scripture sentence.*

3 *The minister welcomes the people using these or other appropriate words:*

Minister	The Lord be with you.
People	**And also with you.**

Minister	The earth is the Lord's and all that is in it:
People	**Let the heavens rejoice and the earth be glad.**

Minister	Our help is in the name of the Lord:
People	**Who made heaven and earth.**

Minister	I was glad when they said to me:
People	**"Let us go to the house of the Lord."**

Minister	Praise the Lord:
People	**The name of the Lord be praised.**

The following acclamations should be added according to season.

CHRISTMAS

Minister	The Prince of Peace is born:
People	**O come let us adore him!**

EASTER

Minister	Christ is risen:
People	**He is risen indeed! Alleluia!**

PENTECOST

Minister	The Spirit is here:
People	**The promise of God.**

Minister	Let us pray.

4   *People kneel. One of the following prayers for purity is said by all.*
Either

All **Almighty God,**
You bring to light
Things hidden in darkness,
And know the shadows of our hearts;
Cleanse and renew us by your Spirit,
That we may walk in the light
And glorify your name,
Through Jesus Christ,
The Light of the world. Amen.

Or

All **Almighty God,**
To whom all hearts are open,
all desires known,
and from whom no secrets are hidden:
cleanse the thoughts of our hearts
by the inspiration of your Holy Spirit,
that we may perfectly love you,
and worthily magnify your holy name;
through Christ our Lord. Amen.

5   *THE COMMANDMENTS*

*People remain kneeling. Then follows the reading of the Ten Commandments,
or the New Testament interpretation of the Law, or the Summary of the Law.*

Minister	Hear the commandments of God and take them to heart.
	I am the Lord your God who brought you out of the house of bondage. You shall have no other gods but me.
People	**Amen. Lord have mercy and give us grace to keep this law.**

Minister	You shall not make for yourself a graven image, or any likeness of anything that is in heaven above, or on the earth beneath, or what is in the water under the earth; you shall not bow down to them or serve them.
People	**Amen. Lord have mercy and give us grace to keep this law.**
Minister	You shall not take the name of the Lord your God in vain for the Lord will not hold him guiltless who takes his name in vain.
People	**Amen. Lord have mercy and give us grace to keep this law.**
Minister	Remember the Sabbath day, to keep it holy. Six days you shall labour, and do all your work; but the seventh day is a Sabbath of the Lord your God; in it you shall not do any work, you, or your son, or your maidservant, or your cattle, or the sojourner who is within your gates; for in six days the Lord made heaven and earth, the sea, and all that is in them, and rested the seventh day; therefore the Lord blessed the Sabbath day and hallowed it.
People	**Amen. Lord have mercy and give us grace to keep this law.**
Minister	Honour your father and your mother that your days may be long in the land which the Lord your God gives you.
People	**Amen. Lord have mercy and give us grace to keep this law.**
Minister	You shall not kill.
People	**Amen. Lord have mercy and give us grace to keep this law.**
Minister	You shall not commit adultery.
People	**Amen. Lord have mercy and give us grace to keep this law.**
Minister	You shall not steal.
People	**Amen. Lord have mercy and give us grace to keep this law.**
Minister	You shall not bear false witness against your neighbour.
People	**Amen. Lord have mercy and give us grace to keep this law.**

Minister		You shall not covet your neighbour's house; you shall not covet your neighbour's wife, or his manservant, or his maidservant, or his ox, or his ass, or anything that is your neighbour's.
People		**Amen. Lord have mercy and write these laws in our hearts, we pray.**

OR

THE NEW TESTAMENT INTERPRETATION OF THE LAW
This section may be shared by two leaders: one to read the Old Testament version and the other, the New Testament rendering of the law.

6   *Minister*   Our Lord Jesus Christ said, if you love me, keep my commandments; blessed are those who hear the word of God and keep it. Hear therefore, what God has commanded his people:

I am the Lord your God: you shall have no other gods but me.
You shall love the Lord your God with all your heart, with all your soul, with all your mind and with all your strength.

People   **Amen. Lord have mercy and give us grace to keep this law.**

Minister   You shall not make for yourself any idol.
God is spirit and those who worship him must worship him in spirit and in truth.

People   **Amen. Lord have mercy and give us grace to keep this law.**

Minister   You shall not dishonour the name of the Lord your God.
You shall worship him with awe and reverence.

People   **Amen. Lord have mercy and give us grace to keep this law.**

Minister   Remember the Lord's day and keep it holy.
Christ is risen from the dead: set your minds on things that are above, not on things that are on the earth.

People   **Amen. Lord have mercy and give us grace to keep this law.**

Minister	Honour your father and your mother. If anyone does not provide for his relatives, and especially for his own family, he has disowned the faith and is worse than an unbeliever.
People	**Amen. Lord have mercy and give us grace to keep this law.**
Minister	You shall not commit murder. Everyone who is angry with his brother shall be liable to judgement.
People	**Amen. Lord have mercy and give us grace to keep this law.**
Minister	You shall not commit adultery. Anyone who looks at another lustfully has already committed adultery with *her* in *his* heart.
People	**Amen. Lord have mercy and give us grace to keep this law.**
Minister	You shall not steal. Let the thief labour, doing honest work with his hands, so that he may be able to give to those in need.
People	**Amen. Lord have mercy and give us grace to keep this law.**
Minister	You shall not be a false witness. Let everyone speak the truth.
People	**Amen. Lord have mercy and give us grace to keep this law.**
Minister	You shall not covet anything which belongs to your neighbour. It is more blessed to give than to receive. Love your neighbour as yourself, for love is the fulfilling of the law.
People	**Amen. Lord have mercy and write these laws in our hearts, we pray.**

OR SUMMARY OF THE LAW

7 *Minister*   Our Lord Jesus Christ said: The first and great
                 commandment is this:
                 "Hear, O Israel, the Lord our God is the only Lord.
                 You shall love the Lord your God with all your heart,
                 with all your soul, with all your mind and with all your
                 strength." The second is this: 'Love your neighbour as
                 yourself.' There is no other commandment greater
                 than these.

   People   **Amen. Lord have mercy and write these laws in our
                 hearts, we pray.**

THE GLORIA AND 'KYRIE ELEISON' (LORD HAVE MERCY)
Either version of the GLORIA may be sung or said:

   Minister   We stand to glorify the Lord.

EITHER

8 *This first version of the GLORIA may be accompanied by regular clapping.*

   Minister   Glory to the Father
   People   **Glory to the Son**

   Minister   Glory to the Spirit
   People   **For ever Three in One**

   Minister   Be glorified at home
   People   **Be glorified in church**

   Minister   Be glorified in Kenya
   People   **Be glorified in Africa**

   Minister   Be glorified on earth
   People   **Be glorified in heaven**

   Minister   Glory to the Father
   People   **Glory to the Son**

   Minister   Glory to the Spirit
   People   **For ever Three in One**

   Minister   Alleluia
   People   **Amen.**

9 *All*   **Glory to God in the highest,**
             and peace to his people on earth.
             Lord God, heavenly King,
             Almighty God and Father,
             We worship you, we give you thanks,
             we praise you for your glory.
             Lord Jesus Christ, only Son of the Father,
             Lord God, Lamb of God,
             you take away the sin of the world:
             have mercy on us;
             you are seated at the right hand of the Father:
             receive our prayer.
             For you alone are the Holy One,
             you alone are the Lord,
             you alone are the Most High, Jesus Christ,
             with the Holy Spirit,
             in the glory of God the Father.
             Amen.

OR DURING LENT ONLY

10 *During Lent the petitions 'Lord have Mercy' are recommended instead of the Gloria. At other seasons, the Gloria is used.*

Minister	Lord have mercy
People	**Lord have mercy**
Minister	Christ have mercy
People	**Christ have mercy**
Minister	Lord have mercy
People	**Lord have mercy**

People remain standing.
Prayer for the Day, introduced with these or other appropriate words:

11 *Minister*   As we stand, let us pray the prayer appointed for today.

MINISTRY OF THE WORD

People sit.
Not more than three passages from Scripture are read, the last of which is always the Gospel.

12 *The Old Testament:*
    Reader   The Old Testament reading is taken from…, chapter…
               beginning to read at verse… .

After the reading,

    Reader   This is the word of the Lord
    People   **Alleluia, Praise be to God.**

Silence may be kept. Choir may sing.

13 *The Epistle:*
    Reader   The Epistle is taken from …, chapter… beginning to
               read at verse… .

After the reading,

    Reader   This is the word of the Lord
    People   **Alleluia, Praise be to God.**

14 *Silence may be kept. Hymn.*

15 *The Gospel*
All stand for the reading, which is introduced with these or other appropriate words:

    Minister   We stand to hear the good news of our salvation, as it is
                written in the Gospel according to Saint…, chapter…,
                beginning to read at verse….

After the Gospel

    Minister   This is the Gospel of Christ
    People   **Alleluia. Praise be to Christ our Saviour.**

16 Silence may be kept. Hymn.

17 *Sermon*

18 *THE NICENE CREED, introduced with the words:*

    Minister   We stand together with Christians throughout the
                centuries, and throughout the world today, to affirm
                our faith in the words of the Nicene Creed.

      All   **We believe in one God,**
                the Father, the Almighty,
                maker of heaven and earth,

of all that is, seen and unseen.
We believe in one Lord, Jesus Christ,
the only Son of God,
eternally begotten of the Father,
God from God, Light from Light,
true God from true God,
begotten, not made,
of one Being with the Father.
Through him all things were made.
For us and for our salvation
he came down from heaven;
by the power of the Holy Spirit
he became incarnate of the Virgin Mary,
and was made man.
For our sake he was crucified under Pontius Pilate;
He suffered, died, and was buried.
On the third day he rose again
in accordance with the Scriptures;
he ascended into heaven
and is seated at the right hand of the Father.
He will come again in glory
to judge the living and the dead,
and his kingdom will have no end.
We believe in the Holy Spirit,
the Lord, the giver of life,
who proceeds from the Father and the Son.
With the Father and the Son he is worshipped
and glorified.
He has spoken through the Prophets.
We believe in one holy, catholic,
and apostolic Church.
We acknowledge one baptism for the
forgiveness of sins.
We look for the resurrection of the dead,
and the life of the world to come. Amen.

INTERCESSIONS

Prayerful songs may be sang between intercessions. People may be encouraged to join in open prayer. The leading of the intercessions may be shared among the people.

Minister   Let us pray

People sit or kneel
EITHER - THIS LITANY

19 *Leader*   May the bishops and leaders of our churches have
                  wisdom and speak with one voice.
    People   **Amen. Lord have mercy.**

    Leader   May the leaders of our country rule with righteousness.
    People   **Amen. Lord have mercy.**

    Leader   May justice be our shield and defender.
    People   **Amen. Lord have mercy.**

    Leader   May the country have peace and the people be blessed.
    People   **Amen. Lord have mercy.**

    Leader   May the flocks and the herds prosper and the fish
                  abound in our lakes.
    People   **Amen. Lord have mercy.**

    Leader   May the fields be fertile and the harvest plentiful.
    People   **Amen. Lord have mercy.**

    Leader   May we and our enemies turn towards peace.
    People   **Amen. Lord have mercy.**

    Leader   May the love of the Father touch the lonely,
                  the bereaved and the suffering.
    People   **Amen. Lord have mercy.**

    Leader   May the path of the world be swept of all dangers.
    People   **Alleluia. The Lord of Mercy is with us.**

OR   THESE PRAYERS OF INTERCESSION

20 *Leader*   Let us pray for the Church.

                  Almighty God, our heavenly Father,
                  bless and guide all our bishops, pastors, other
                  church workers and all your faithful people.
                  Grant wisdom to our archbishop…,
                  and to our bishop…,
                  that under them we may be led in the
                  unity of your Holy Spirit. May all who confess your

holy name continue to witness by serving their neighbours, loving their enemies and working together for
the extension of your kingdom in and beyond our land.
Graciously hear our prayer:

People **We beseech you O Lord.**

Leader Let us pray for our nation.

Merciful Father, protect and guide our President... and
all who are in authority under him, that we may be
governed in the way of peace, love and unity.
May our leaders exercise your authority without fear or
favour, so that justice may roll down like
waters and righteousness like an ever-flowing stream.
Graciously hear our prayer:

People **We beseech you O Lord.**

Leader Let us pray for the needs of the world.

Loving Father, your Son grew in wisdom and stature,
in favour with God and man: as he brought your good
news to the poor, we now bring
to you those who are suffering from
hunger, poverty and sickness, and
who are under oppression and
exploitation. Your kingdom come,
your will be done in transforming
their lives and in inspiring us to share
your gospel, so that friends and
strangers may be saved.
Graciously hear our prayer:

People **We beseech you O Lord.**

Leader Let us thank God for the lives of those who have
departed in Christ.

Gracious Father, we heartily thank you for our faithful
ancestors and all who have passed through death to the
new life of joy in our heavenly home.
We pray that, surrounded by so great a cloud of
witnesses, we may walk in their footsteps and be fully
united with them in your everlasting kingdom.
Grant the prayers of your family, Father:

People **Through Jesus Christ, our mediator.**

PRAYERS OF PENITENCE
People remain kneeling

21 *Minister*   Hear the words of challenge and comfort our Saviour
Christ says to all who follow him.

If anyone would come after me, let him deny himself,
take up his cross and follow me. For whoever would
save his life will lose it; and whoever loses his life for
my sake will save it. *(Luke 9:23-24)*

Come to me all of you who are tired of carrying
your heavy loads, and I will give you rest.
(Matthew 11:28)

So, all of you who repent of your sins, who love your
neighbours and intend to lead a new life, following the
way of Jesus, come with faith and take this holy
sacrament to strengthen you.

Let us reverently confess our sins to Almighty God.

22 *All*   **Almighty God, creator of all,**
you marvellously made us in your image;
but we have corrupted
ourselves and damaged your likeness
by rejecting your love
and hurting our neighbours.
We have done wrong and neglected to do right.
We are sincerely sorry and heartily repent of our sins.
Cleanse us and forgive us by the sacrifice of your Son;
Remake us and lead us by your Spirit, the Comforter.
We ask this through Jesus Christ our Lord. Amen.

23 *Minister*   Almighty God, whose steadfast love is as great as the
heavens are high above the earth, remove your sins
from you as far as the east is from the west, strengthen
your life in his kingdom and keep you upright to the
last day; through Jesus Christ our merciful High Priest.
Amen.

24 *All*   Thank you Father, for forgiveness; We come to your
              table as your children, not presuming but assured,
              not trusting ourselves but your Word; we hunger
              and thirst for righteousness, and ask for our hearts
              to be satisfied with the body and blood of your Son,
              Jesus Christ the righteous. Amen.

MINISTRY OF THE SACRAMENT

25 *Sharing of Peace.*

People stand

Minister   The peace of the Lord be always with you.
People   **And also with you.**

Minister   Let us offer one another a sign of peace.

*People greet each other with a handshake or other appropriate
gestures.*

26 *The Holy Table is prepared for communion. A hymn is sang, during
which the offering is collected. Presiding minister and his assistants may
wash hands. If there is no offertory the minister moves directly to section 27.
When there is offertory, the minister and people may respond in the following
or other appropriate manner.*

Minister   All things come from you O Lord.
People   **And of your own have we given you.**

Prayer of Thanksgiving.

People remain standing.

27 *Minister*   We remain standing for thanksgiving and
                  remembrance.

              Is the Father with us?
People   **He is.**

Minister   Is Christ among us?
People   **He is.**

Minister   Is the Spirit here?
People   **He is.**

Minister   This is our God.
People   **Father, Son and the Holy Spirit.**

Minister	We are his people.
People	**We are redeemed.**
Minister	Lift up your hearts.
People	**We lift them to the Lord.**
Minister	Let us give thanks to the Lord our God.
People	**It is right to give him thanks and praise.**
Minister	It is right and our delight to give you thanks and praise, great Father, living God, supreme over the world. Creator, Provider, Saviour and Giver. From a wandering nomad you created your family; for a burdened people you raised up a leader; for a confused nation you chose a king; for a rebellious crowd you sent your prophets. In these last days you have sent us your Son, your perfect image, bringing your kingdom, revealing your will, dying, rising, reigning remaking your people for yourself. Through him you have poured out your Holy Spirit, filling us with light and life.

Special thanksgiving shall be said at this point when appropriate (Sections 39-47)

	Therefore with angels, archangels, faithful ancestors and all in heaven, we proclaim your great and glorious name, forever praising you and saying:
All	**Holy, holy, holy Lord,** **God of power and might,** **Heaven and earth are full of your glory.** **Hosanna in the highest.**

THE BREAKING OF BREAD IS AT SECTION 29.
The presiding minister performs the traditional actions of taking the bread and the cup.

People remain standing.

Minister	Almighty God, owner of all things, we thank you for giving up your Son to die on the cross for us who owe you everything. Pour your refreshing Spirit on us as we remember him in the way he commanded, through these gifts of your creation. On the same night that he was betrayed he

took bread and gave you thanks; he broke it and gave it
to his disciples, saying, 'Take, eat, this is my body
which is given for you; Do this in remembrance of me'.

People **Amen. His body was broken for us.**

Minister In the same way, after supper he took the cup and gave
you thanks; he gave it to them saying: Drink this, all of
you, this is my blood of the new covenant, which is shed
for you and for many, for the forgiveness of sins. Do this
as often as you drink it, in remembrance of me.

People **Christ has died**
Christ is risen
Christ will come again.

Minister We are brothers and sisters through his blood.

People **We have died together,**
we will rise together,
we will live together.

Minister Therefore, heavenly Father, hear us as we celebrate this
covenant with joy, and await the coming of our Saviour,
Jesus Christ. He died in our place, making a full
atonement for the sins of the whole world, the perfect
sacrifice, once and for all. You accepted his offering by
raising him from death, and granting him great honour
at your right hand on high.

People **Amen. Jesus is Lord.**

Minister This is the feast of victory

People **The lamb who was slain has begun his reign. Alleluia.**

THE COMMUNION

People kneel

28 *Minister* As our Saviour taught us, we are bold to pray:

All **Our Father in heaven,**
hallowed be your name,
your kingdom come,
your will be done,
on earth as in heaven.
Give us today our daily bread.

Forgive us our sins,
as we forgive those
who sin against us.
Lead us not into temptation
but deliver us from evil.
For the kingdom,
the power and the
glory are yours,
now and for ever. Amen.

29 *Minister*   We break this bread to share in the body of Christ.
   People   **Though we are many we are one body, for we all**
   share one bread.

Minister   The cup of blessing which we bless,
People   **is a sharing in the blood of Christ.**

Minister   Draw near with faith and receive.
People   **Christ is the host and we are his guests.**

Minister   Christ is alive for ever.
People   **We are because he is.**

The celebrant and his assistants receive the bread and wine.
The congregation is led by the choir in a musical recitation of the
AGNUS DEI.

Lamb of God, you take away the sin of the world,
Have mercy on us.
Lamb of God, you take away the sin of the world,
Have mercy on us.
Lamb of God, you take away the sin of the world,
Give us your peace.

The celebrant then holds the bread, and one of his assistants holds the wine
and they declare to the people:

30 *Minister*   The body of our Lord Jesus Christ which was broken
   for you, keep your body and soul in eternal life.
   Take and eat this, in remembrance that Christ died for
   you, and feed on him in your hearts, by faith, with
   thanksgiving.

Assistant   The blood of our Lord Jesus Christ, which was shed for
   you, keep your body and soul in eternal life.

Drink this, in remembrance that Christ's blood was
shed for you and be thankful.

31 *As the bread and wine are distributed, the minister or his assistant may say
to each communicant:*

Minister   The body of Christ keep you in eternal life.
Assistant   The blood of Christ keep you in eternal life.

Each time, the communicant replies, **Amen,** *and then receives.*

*If the bread and the wine are used up they are replaced by more from the
Holy Table without any additional prayers.*
*Reconsecration is necessary only if the bread and wine on the Holy Table run
out.*

During Communion prayerful songs may be sang.

AFTER COMMUNION
The congregation may observe a brief moment of silence.
People stand. One of the following prayers is said.

EITHER

32 *All*   **Almighty God, eternal Father, we have sat at your feet,
learnt from your word, and eaten from your table.
We give you thanks and praise for accepting us into
your family.
Send us out with your blessing, to live and to witness for
you in the power of your Spirit,
through Jesus Christ, the First Born from the dead.
Amen.**

      OR

33 *All*   **God Most High, we thank you for welcoming us,
teaching us and feeding us. We deserve nothing from
you but in your great mercy, you have given us
everything in your Son Jesus Christ.
We love you and give ourselves to you to be sent out for
your work; Grant us your blessing, now and for
ever. Amen.**

      OR
34 *All*   **O God of our ancestors, God of our people, before
whose face the human generations pass away;
We thank you that in you we are kept safe for ever,**

And that the broken fragments of our history are
gathered up in the redeeming act of your dear Son,
remembered in this holy sacrament of bread and
wine. Help us to walk daily in the Communion of
saints, declaring our faith in the forgiveness of sins
and the resurrection of the body.
Now send us out in the power of your Holy Spirit to live
and work for your praise and glory. Amen.

THE BLESSING
One of the following two blessings may be used.

EITHER

35 *People accompany their first three responses with a sweep of the arm
towards the cross behind the Holy Table, and their final response with a
sweep towards heaven.*

Minister	All our problems,
People	**We send to the cross of Christ.**

Minister	All our difficulties,
People	**We send to the cross of Christ.**

Minister	All the devil's works,
People	**We send to the cross of Christ.**

Minister	All our hopes,
People	**We set on the risen Christ.**

Minister   Christ the Sun of Righteousness
Shine upon you and scatter the
darkness from before your path:
And the blessing of God Almighty, Father,
Son and Holy Spirit, be among you,
and remain with you, always.

OR/AND

36 *Minister*   Let us pray.

People kneel or sit.

Minister   The peace of God, which passes all
understanding, keep your hearts and
minds in the knowledge and love of
God, and of his Son Jesus Christ our
Lord;

And the blessing of God Almighty,
the Father, the Son and the Holy Spirit,
be among you, and remain with you always. **Amen.**

DISMISSAL

37 *One of the following may be used.*

EITHER

Minister	Go in peace to love and serve the Lord.
People	**In the name of Christ. Amen.**

OR

Minister	Go out into the world, rejoicing in the power of the Spirit.
People	**Thanks be to God.**

OR

Minister	Jesus said, "As the Father has sent me, even so I send you". Go forth in peace.
People	**Thanks be to God.**

38 *Recessional Hymn.*

Appendix to Service of Holy Communion

SPECIAL THANKSGIVINGS

These are to be inserted into the Prayer of Thanksgiving before: "Therefore with angels and archangels... ."

1 *ADVENT*

EITHER

And now we give you thanks and praise because he came as man when the day of our deliverance had dawned, and will come again in power and triumph to judge the world and to consummate all things.

OR

And now we give you thanks because you prepared the way of your Son by the preaching of your prophet John the Baptist, who proclaimed him as the Lamb of God who takes away the sin of the world.

2 *CHRISTMAS*

EITHER

And now we give you thanks because you gave your only Son to be born at this time for us, who through the power of the Holy Spirit was made man, being born of the Virgin Mary: in him there was neither spot nor sin, and in him we are cleansed from all sin.

OR

And now we give you thanks because in the Incarnation of the Eternal Word, a new light has dawned upon the world, and those who sat in darkness and under the shadow of death have seen the great light.

3 *EASTER DAY*

EITHER

And now we praise you for the glorious resurrection of your Son, the lamb who was offered for us and has taken away the sin of the world: by his death he has destroyed death, and by his rising to new life he has restored to us eternal life.

OR

And now we give you thanks because you raised him gloriously from the dead: through him you have given us the resurrection hope, for our life will be changed, not taken away; when our mortal flesh is laid aside, we will enter our everlasting dwelling place to live with him.

4   *ASCENSION DAY*

EITHER

And now we give you thanks because you have highly exalted your Son, and have given him the name above every name, that at the name of Jesus every knee shall bow, and every tongue confess that Jesus Christ is Lord.

OR

And now we give you thanks because, after his resurrection, your dearly beloved Son ascended into heaven, where he now prepares a place for us and will receive us in his eternal glory.

5   *PENTECOST*

EITHER

And now we give you thanks because the coming of the Holy Spirit upon the apostles inspired them to speak in tongues and gave them courage to preach the Gospel to all nations: by their preaching we have come to a true knowledge of you.

OR

And now we give you thanks because your Holy Spirit inspired the scriptures and leads us into all truth: he gives us power to proclaim your gospel to all nations and to serve you as a royal priesthood.

6   *TRINITY SUNDAY*

And now we give you thanks because you have revealed to us your glory as the glory of your Son and of the Holy Spirit: three Persons, equal in majesty, undivided in splendour, yet One Lord, One God, ever to be trusted and adored.

7 *ALL SAINTS' DAY*

And now we give you thanks for the hope to which you call us in your Son, that following in faith of all your saints, we may run with perseverance the race that is set before us, looking to Jesus the Pioneer and Perfecter of our faith.

8 *DEDICATION OF A CHURCH*

And now we give you thanks for this house of prayer, dedicated to your glory, where your people, the true temple of the Holy Spirit, gather together in worship.

9 *ORDINATION, CONSECRATION OR ENTHRONEMENT*

And now we give you thanks because within the royal priesthood of your Church you ordain pastors and consecrate bishops, to tend and guide your flock, to proclaim the good news of salvation and to celebrate the sacraments of the new covenant.

Ordination of Deacons

NOTES:

- Notices about this service should be made on three consecutive Sundays prior to the ordination day in all the parishes in the diocese. The announcement should go thus: "I wish to bring notice of the service of Ordination of Deacons on *(date)* at *(venue)*, by the Rt Rev *NN*; for the following people: *(candidates are named)*. If any of you knows a just cause why any of these people should not be ordained to the diaconate, you are to make it known..., *(and during the ordination day, this notice is published by the bishop who also adds the clause)*: "...or else for ever hold your peace".

- Hymns and choruses may be inserted as the Bishop may deem appropriate.

- The service is designed to be used in the context of Holy Communion.

- Declarations may be signed earlier and not necessarily during the service.

- Where the candidate is only one the wording shall be changed accordingly where it might matter.

- After each ordination a climax may be observed by short ululation or any other acceptable form of applause.

ORDER OF SERVICE

1 *Hymn*

2 *CALL TO WORSHIP*

The Lord be with you.
And also with you.

The earth is the Lord's and all that is in it.
Let the heavens rejoice and the earth be glad.

Our help is in the name of the Lord.
Who made heaven and earth.

I was glad when they said to me.
Let us go to the house of the Lord.

Praise the Lord.
The name of the Lord be praised.

Collect for Ordination

Bishop   Almighty and everlasting God, who according to your
various graces equips and sends your people for various
ministries, come now we pray and fill this place with your
inspiring presence as we ordain and send out these servants
for the sacred ministry they believe you have called them to.
May your name be glorified by what we do now and
hereafter. Through Jesus Christ our mediator and high priest.
Amen.

All   **Almighty God to whom all hearts are open, all desires
known and from whom no secrets are hidden: cleanse
the thoughts of our hearts by the inspiration of your Holy
Spirit, that we may perfectly love you and worthily
magnify your holy name, through Christ our Lord. Amen.**

3   *PRESENTATION*

*A hymn may be sang as candidates come forward for presentation by a priest
and a lay-person. The candidates are presented to the Bishop thus:*

Bishop in the service of God, we present to you *(name the
ordinands)* **that you may ordain them Deacons.**

4   *Bishop*   Be careful that the persons you present to us are: truly
called, have uprightness of life, are sober, self controlled, of
good social conduct, and are well learned in the word of
God, so that they may be able to exercise their ministry to
the honour of God and the building up of his Church.

The ministry of a deacon entails pastoral service and
concern for all people but particularly the sick, the poor, the
helpless and the lonely. Also, assisting the bishop and parish
priest in administering the church's sacraments of Holy
Communion and baptism; exercising the ministry of the
Word including preaching and teaching; studying the
scriptures and modelling *his* life accordingly. A deacon is to
carry out all such other duties as *he* may be called upon so
to do from time to time by the priest or the bishop under
whom *he* is serving. The deacon is supposed to exercise this
ministry with gladness and zeal.

Presenter: **We have enquired about them and have examined
them; to the best of our assessment, they are fit for
this ministry.**

5   *The ordinands face the congregation and the Bishop says to the people:*

Beloved in the Lord, those whose duty it is to enquire about these persons and examine them are satisfied that the same are of sound learning and godly lives, and believe them to be duly called to serve God in this ministry. Nonetheless, if any of you has a just cause why any of them should not be ordained, let him or her come forward now and make it known. *(Pause), or* else forever hold your peace.

Bishop   Is it therefore your wish that we ordain these persons?
People   **That is our wish.**

6   *DECLARATIONS*
To be conducted by the Diocesan Chancelor or the Administrative Secretary.

7   *Bishop*   Beloved in the Lord, it is written in the Gospel of Luke that the Lord Jesus watched and prayed a whole night before appointing and sending the twelve apostles. It is also written in the Acts of Apostles that the disciples in Antioch fasted and prayed before laying hands on Paul and Barnabas and sending them out. So also ourselves, as we follow the example of our Lord Jesus Christ and his apostles, we must pray before accepting and sending *these brothers and sisters,* to do the work the Holy Spirit has called *them* to do.

8   *LITANY*

May be led by various people.

God the Father, creator of the universe and all that is there.
Have mercy on us.

God the Son, the Saviour of the world.
Have mercy on us.

God the Holy Spirit the comforter of humanity.
Have mercy on us

Holy, blessed and glorious Trinity.
Have mercy on us.

From all satanic plottings against your Church.
O Lord deliver us.

From malice and hatred, from all forms of corruption and worldliness.
O Lord deliver us.

From all fear of persecution and the dread of death.
O Lord deliver us.

From disordered and sinful affections and from the deceits of the world, the flesh and the devil,
O Lord deliver us.

From drought and floods, from earthquakes and other disasters, from wicked people who plan evil against us, from gangsters, robbers, murderers, hijackers and kidnappers, from carjackers and reckless drivers, from slanderers and rumour mongers.
O Lord deliver us.

Protect and direct your holy Church to the source of truth; govern and encourage her to speak the truth in love, both in season and out of season.
Hear us O Lord.

Endow your servants (*name them*) now to be ordained deacons, with your Holy Spirit and let them serve you faithfully and courageously without fear or favour.
Hear us, O Lord.

Enlighten your ministers with knowledge and understanding, that by their teaching and their lives, they may proclaim your Word.
Hear us O Lord.

That by the indwelling of the Holy Spirit they may be encouraged to persevere to the end.
Hear us O Lord.

For their homes and families, that they may be adorned with all Christian virtues.
Hear us O Lord.

Give your people grace to hear and receive your Word, and bring forth the fruit and the gifts of the Spirit.
Hear us O Lord.

For the nations of the world, that they may peacefully co-exist, and that a spirit of respect and forbearance may grow among nations and peoples.
We beseech you O Lord.

For the poor, the persecuted and the suffering; for prisoners and the detained, refugees and all in danger; that they may be relieved and protected.
We beseech you O Lord.

For the terminally ill and all who are living with dreadful scourges, that they may be comforted in their suffering.
May they place all their hope in you and hence find peace that passes all understanding.
We beseech you O Lord.

For doctors and scientists in the medical research who spend many hours in various laboratories of the world in search of cures for diseases.
Grant them patience, endurance and success.

For the little children and babies: born and unborn, that their tender lives may be protected and their rights guarded.
We beseech you O Lord.

Guide and govern your holy Church, fill it with love and truth, and grant it that unity which is your will, binding it together with your Spirit.
We beseech you O Lord.

Give courage to our bishops, clergy, and all church leaders, that they may courageously proclaim the good news of the Kingdom, and fearlessly challenge injustices in the nation.
We beseech you O Lord.

Direct and guide all church based organizations that work for peace, justice and reconciliation, and for the wholistic development of God's people; that they may achieve their mission goals, for the glory and honour of your holy name.
We beseech you O Lord.

Bring into the way of truth, all who have erred and are deceived and those who have been tossed to and fro by every wind of doctrine.
We beseech you O Lord.

Strengthen those who stand, comfort and help the fainthearted, raise up the fallen and finally beat down Satan under your feet. **We beseech you O Lord.**

Guide our President and other leaders of this country into ways of justice, peace and unity. Grant that there will be peace within our borders, that all the people in this region may live in harmony and enjoy good neighbourliness. **Hear us O Lord.**

For political tolerance among people of different political persuasions, for greater respect for one another's opinions and convictions, for greater thirst after truth and justice for all, that political thuggeries and assassinations may come to an end, that people may enjoy fullness of life as God intended for them. **Hear us O Lord.**

Guide and bless those who administer the law; that honesty and truth may be upheld, and that they may proclaim justice without fear or favour except the fear of God. **Hear us O Lord.**

Help and comfort the lonely, the bereaved, the oppressed and the voiceless. **Help and comfort them.**

Protect our Archbishop, bishops and ministers from threats and intimidations of all kinds. **Lord protect them.**

Heal the sick in body and mind, provide for the widows and the orphans, the homeless, the hungry and the destitute. **Lord have mercy.**

Pour your blessing on all human labour, that your people may enjoy good output, be well fed and live in economic comfort. **Hear us O Lord.**

Preserve and guard the integrity of creation against exploitation; that forests, lakes, game reserves and other natural and environmental resources may be safeguarded against misuse or abuse. **Hear us O Lord.**

For all of us here gathered in your name and for your service; for the forgiveness of our sins, and for the grace of the Holy Spirit to amend our lives. **Hear us O Lord.**

The congregation is led in a prayerful hymn.

9   MINISTRY OF THE WORD

The reader may first say:
The Old Testament reading/Epistle is taken from..., chapter...,
beginning to read at verse....

After the reading,

This is the Word of the Lord.
Alleluia, praise be to God.

Silence may be kept.

OLD TESTAMENT: *Isaiah 6:1-8, or Jeremiah 1:4-9.*
PSALM: 84, or 119:33-40.
At the end of the psalm:

Glory to the Father, Son and the Holy Spirit.
As it was in the beginning, is now and ever shall be. Amen.

EPISTLE: 1 Timothy 3:8-13; or Acts 6:2-7; or 2 Corinthians 3:1-6.
GOSPEL: Luke 12:35-40; or, Luke 22:24-27 *(to be read by an ordinand).*

*All stand for the Gospel reading which is introduced with these or other
appropriate words:*

We stand to hear the good news of our salvation, as it is written in
the Gospel according to Saint..., chapter... beginning to read at verse....

After the Gospel:

This is the Gospel of Christ.
Alleluia, praise be to Christ our Saviour.

Silence may be kept.

10   Hymn

11   Notices

12   Sermon

13   THE NICENE CREED

We stand together with Christians throughout the centuries, and
throughout the world today, to affirm our faith in the words of the
Nicene Creed.

All   We believe in one God,
the Father, the almighty,
  maker of heaven and earth,
of all that is, seen and unseen.
  We believe in one Lord, Jesus Christ,
the only Son of God,
eternally begotten of the Father,
God from God, Light from Light,
  true God from true God,
begotten, not made,
of one Being with the Father.
Through him all things were made.
  For us and for our salvation
he came down from heaven;
by the power of the Holy Spirit
he became incarnate of the Virgin Mary,
  and was made man.
For our sake he was crucified under Pontius Pilate;
  He suffered, died, and was buried.
On the third day he rose again
in accordance with the Scriptures;
  he ascended into heaven
and is seated at the right hand of the Father.
He will come again in glory
  to judge the living and the dead,
and his kingdom will have no end.
  We believe in the Holy Spirit,
the Lord, the giver of life,
who proceeds from the Father and the Son.
With the Father and the Son he is worshipped
  and glorified.
He has spoken through the Prophets.
  We believe in one holy, catholic,
and apostolic Church.
We acknowledge one baptism for the
  forgiveness of sins.
We look for the resurrection of the dead,
and the life of the world to come. Amen.

14 *Hymn/Offertory*

15 THE EXAMINATION

The ordinands stand before the Bishop who examines them. Each ordinand must respond for him/herself, and must speak with clarity of voice.

Bishop   Have you inwardly examined yourself with the help of the Holy Spirit and are you truly convinced that you should take up the responsibilities pertaining to the office of a deacon?

Answer   **I have done so and I am truly convinced that I should take these responsibilities.**

Bishop   Do you believe that all Scripture is inspired by God and is useful for teaching the truth, rebuking error, correcting faults and giving instructions for right living, so that the person who serves God may be fully qualified and equipped to do every kind of good deed?

Answer   **I do believe so.**

Bishop   Will you faithfully study, preach, and teach from the Holy Scriptures in season and out of season?

Answer   **Yes, with God's help.**

Bishop   Will you faithfully model your life according to the teachings of Jesus Christ and will you be a good example in word and deed to the people you serve and the community at large?

Answer   **Yes, with God's help.**

Bishop   Will you, in all things just and lawful, obey the bishop of the diocese and his successors, and all those to whom the charge of the church government is entrusted?

Answer   **Yes I will.**

16   *The ordinands kneel before the Bishop who then prays*

Almighty God and Father, we thank you and give you
all the glory, for out of your everlasting love and mercy,
you sent your only Son Jesus Christ who,
being in very nature God, did not consider equality with
God something to be grasped but humbled himself to death,
even death on a cross. He has taught us that the way
to greatness is in servanthood.

The bishop outstretches his arm over the candidates and prays

Send now O Lord, your Holy Spirit on these your servants whose desire it is, to follow in your footsteps as they embark on the ministry to which we believe you have called them. May they serve with faithfulness and zeal, and ever be keen to listen and obey your voice when you exhort them as much as when you rebuke them. Grant that the good work you have began in them will be carried on to completion, for the sake of him before whom every knee shall bow and every tongue confess that He is Lord, to the glory of God the Father. **Amen.**

17   *The ordinands return to their seats. One at a time they kneel before the Bishop, who places his hand on the candidate's head and says,*

N, may the Holy Spirit stir up the gift of God that is in you, for the ministry to which he has called you. May he equip you with all wisdom, strength and power necessary for the execution of the duties pertaining to the diaconate. In the name of the Father, Son, and the Holy Spirit. **Amen.**

Each one is then vested according to custom.

18   *Presentation of the Bible, the ordinands standing.*

N, Receive the holy scriptures. This is the authority given to you this day, to rebuke, to strengthen, to encourage and comfort God's people and to proclaim in season and out of season, the good news of the Kingdom.

19   *The ordinands are each presented with their licence which they lift up as the Bishop says:*

Receive this licence to authorize you to serve as a deacon in the diocese of ...; and the Anglican Church of Kenya, in the name of the Father, Son and the Holy Spirit. **Amen.**

20   COMMISSIONING

Bishop   Jesus said, "Go into all the world and make people my disciples, baptising them in the name of the Father, Son, and the Holy Spirit, and teaching them to obey every-thing I have commanded you".
I commission you to preach the gospel, heal the sick, com-fort the troubled, feed the hungry and love the loveless.

And surely the Lord will be with you always to the very end of the age. In the name of the Father, Son and the Holy Spirit. **Amen.**

21 *A song of praise*

22 *Presentation to the laity*

Bishop I present to you, these servants of God whom we have just ordained deacons. Will you support and uphold them in prayer as they render service to God and his Church?

Answer: **We will support and uphold them.**

23 *Presentation to the clergy*

Bishop I present to you these servants of God whom we have just ordained deacons. Do you receive them into your fellowship?

Answer: **We receive them gladly**

24 *Ululations and joyous spontaneous singing may follow while members of the congregation, and the clergy greet the newly ordained.*

25 SERVICE OF HOLY COMMUNION

The order of service of Holy Communion follows from the Prayer of Penitence.

26 POST COMMUNION

Either
Protect us Lord in all our doings with your most gracious favour, and further us with your continual help; that in all works begun, continued and ended in you, we may glorify your holy name, and finally by your mercy obtain everlasting life; Through Jesus Christ our Lord. **Amen.**

Or
Almighty God who of your own will has called different people in your service and have endowed them with different spiritual gifts, help these brethren whom you have called and whom we have this day set apart for your service in your church, that they may by their faith and life be true witnesses of the mysteries of the Gospel, through Jesus Christ our Lord and Saviour. **Amen.**

27 *THE BLESSING*

Christ the sun of righteousness shine upon you and scatter the darkness from before your path; and the blessing of God almighty, Father, Son and the Holy Spirit be among you, and remain with you always. **Amen.**

Or

The peace of God, which passes all understanding, keep your hearts and minds in the knowledge and love of God and of his Son Jesus Christ; and the blessing of God almighty, Father, Son and the Holy Spirit, be among you, and remain with you always. **Amen.**

28 *Recessional Hymn*

Ordination of Priests

NOTES:

- Notices about this service should be made on three consecutive Sundays prior to the ordination day in all the parishes in the diocese. The announcement should go thus: "I wish to bring notice of the service of ordination of priests on (*date*) at (*venue*), by the Rt Rev *NN*; for the following people: (*candidates are named*). If any one of you knows a just cause why any of these people should not be ordained to priesthood, you are to make it known...", *(and during the ordination day, this notice is published by the bishop who also adds the clause):* " ...or else for ever hold your peace".

- This service is designed for use in the context of Holy Communion.

- Hymns and choruses may be inserted at any stage as the Bishop may deem appropriate.

- Where only one candidate is being ordained, the wording may be changed appropriately where it might matter.

- After each ordination a climax may be observed by short ululations or other acceptable form of applause.

ORDER OF SERVICE

1   *Processional Hymn*

2   *CALL TO WORSHIP*

The Lord be with you.
And also with you.

The earth is the Lord's and all that is in it.
Let the heavens rejoice and the earth be glad.

Our help is in the name of the Lord;
Who made heaven and earth.

I was glad when they said to me;
Let us go to the house of the Lord.

Praise the Lord.
The name of the Lord be praised.

Collect for Ordination

Bishop   Almighty and everlasting God, Who according to your various graces equip and send your people for various ministries, come now we pray and fill this place with your inspiring presence as we ordain and send out these servants for the sacred ministry. May your name be glorified by what we do now and hereafter. Through Jesus Christ our mediator and high priest. **Amen.**

All   **Almighty God to whom all hearts are open, all desires known and from whom no secrets are hidden: cleanse the thoughts of our hearts by the inspiration of your holy Spirit, that we may perfectly love you and worthily magnify your holy name through Christ our Lord, Amen.**

3   *PRESENTATION*

The presenters, at least a priest and a lay person, present the ordinands to the Bishop thus:

Bishop in the service of God, on behalf of the clergy and the people of ... Diocese, we present to you these candidates, that you may ordain them priests. They are: *(Read out their names).*

Bishop   Take care that the persons you present to us are by their learning and godly lives suitable to exercise the ministry of priesthood to the honour of God and the building up of his Church.

Presenters: **We have enquired about them and have examined them; to the best of our assessment, they are fit for the office.**

The ordinands face the congregation and the Bishop, seated, says,

Brothers and sisters, those whose duty it is to enquire about these persons and examine them are satisfied that the same are of sound learning and godly lives, and believe them to be duly called to serve God in this ministry. Nonetheless, if any of you has a just cause why any of them should not be ordained, let him or her come forward now and make it known; *(Pause),* or else forever hold your peace.

Bishop	Is it therefore your wish we ordain these people?
People	**That is our wish.**

4   *EXHORTATION TO THE ORDINANDS*

The ordinands stand, facing the Bishop, who says:

As a priest you will be called to be a servant and shepherd among the people to whom you will be sent. You are to proclaim the word of the Lord, call hearers to repentance, and in Christ's name announce absolution, and the forgiveness of sins. You will baptise and admit to communion, and prepare the candidates for confirmation and com-missioning. You will preside at the celebration of the Eucharist, and further lead the people in prayer and worship, to intercede for them, to bless them in the name of the Lord, and to teach and encourage by word and example. You will minister to the sick and prepare the dying for their death. You will extend the ministry of pastoral care and counselling to those who require it. You must set the Good Shepherd always before you as the pattern of your calling, caring for the people committed to your charge and joining with them in a common witness to the world.

In the name of our Lord we bid you remember the greatness of the trust committed to your charge. You are to teach and to admonish, to feed and to provide for the Lord's family, to search for his children, lost in the wilderness of this world's temptations and to guide them through its confusion, so that they may be saved.
Since you cannot bear the weight of this ministry in your own strength but only by the grace and power of God, you are to pray earnestly for the Holy Spirit to daily enlarge and enlighten your understanding of the Scriptures as you seek to fashion your life and that of your flock on the word of God.

In order that we may know your mind and purpose, and that you may be strengthened in your resolve to fulfil your ministry, you must answer the questions we now put to you.

5   *EXAMINATION*

Bishop	Do you truly believe that God has called you to the office and work of a priest in his church?
Answer:	**I do believe he has called me.**

Bishop	Do you now in the presence of God and his Church wholly commit yourself to this trust and responsibility?
Answer:	**I do.**
Bishop	Do you accept the Holy Scriptures as revealing all things necessary for eternal salvation through faith in Jesus Christ?
Answer:	**I do.**
Bishop	Will you endeavour to minister the word of God and sacraments of the new covenant, that the reconciling love of Jesus Christ may be known and received?
Answer:	**By the help of God I will.**
Bishop	Will you accept the discipline of the Church and give due respect to those in authority?
Answer:	**I will.**
Bishop	Will you be diligent in prayer, in reading the Holy Scriptures, and in all studies that will deepen your faith and fit you to uphold the truth of the Gospel against error?
Answer:	**By the help of God I will.**
Bishop	Will you do your best to fashion your life and that of your household in accordance with the teachings of Christ so that you may be a wholesome example to your people?
Answer:	**By the help of God I will.**
Bishop	Will you promote unity, peace and harmony among all people and especially among those whom you serve?
Answer:	**By the help of God I will.**
Bishop	Will you undertake to be a faithful pastor to all whom you are called to serve, labouring together with them and with your fellow ministers to build up the family of God?
Answer:	**I will.**
Bishop	Will you persevere in prayer, both in public and in private, asking God's grace both for yourself and for others, offering all your labours to God through the mediation of Jesus Christ, and in the sanctification of the Holy Spirit.
Answer:	**I will.**

Bishop	Will you then in the strength of the Holy Spirit, continually stir up the gift of God that is in you, to make Christ known to all the people?
Answer:	**By the help of God I will.**
Bishop	Will you in all things just and lawful obey the Bishop of the Diocese, his successors and all those to whom the charge of the church government is entrusted?
Answer:	**Yes I will.**
Bishop	Almighty God who has given you the will to undertake all these things, give you all the strength to perform them; that he may complete that work which he has begun in you; through Jesus Christ our Lord. **Amen.**

6   *DECLARATIONS*
To be conducted by the Diocesan Chancellor or the Administrative Secretary.

7   *Bishop*   Brothers and sisters in Christ, it is written in the Gospel of Luke that the Lord Jesus watched and prayed a whole night before appointing and sending the twelve apostles. It is also written in the Acts of Apostles that the disciples in Antioch fasted and prayed before laying hands on Paul and Barnabas and sending them out. So also ourselves, as we follow the example of our Lord Jesus Christ and his apostles, we must pray before accepting and sending these servants, to do the work the Holy Spirit has called them to do.

8   *LITANY*
May be led by various people

God the Father, creator of the universe and all that is there,
Have mercy on us.

God the Son, the Saviour of the world,
Have mercy on us.

God the Holy Spirit the comforter of humanity,
Have mercy on us.

Holy, blessed and glorious Trinity,
Have mercy on us.

From all satanic plottings against your Church,
O Lord deliver us.

From malice and hatred, from all forms of corruption and worldliness,
O Lord deliver us.

From all fear of persecution and the dread of death,
O Lord deliver us.

From disordered and sinful affections and from the deceits of the world, the flesh and the devil.
O Lord deliver us.

From drought and floods, from earthquakes and other disasters, from wicked people who plan evil against us, from gangsters, robbers, murderers, hijackers and kidnappers, from carjackers and reckless drivers, from slanderers and rumour mongers.
O Lord deliver us.

Protect and direct your holy Church to the source of truth; govern and encourage her to speak the truth in love, both in season and out of season.
Hear us O Lord.

Enlighten your ministers with knowledge and understanding, that by their teaching and their lives, they may proclaim your Word.
Hear us O Lord.

Endow your servants (*name them*), now to be ordained priests in your church, with the Holy Spirit that they may faithfully fulfil the duties of this ministry, build up your Church and glorify your name.
Hear us O Lord.

That by the indwelling of the Holy Spirit they may be encouraged to persevere to the end.
Hear us O Lord.

For their homes and families, that they may be adorned with all Christian virtues.
Hear us O Lord.

Give your people grace to hear and receive your word, and bring forth the fruit and the gifts of the Spirit.
Hear us O Lord.

Hear us as we remember the priests in this diocese who have died in the peace of Christ *(pause in silence)....*
Grant us with them a share in your eternal kingdom.

For all in the communion of your Church, who have died in Christ; that we may walk in their footsteps and be fully united with them in your everlasting kingdom.
Hear us O Lord.

For the nations of the world that they may peacefully co-exist, and that a spirit of respect and forbearance may grow among nations and peoples.
We beseech you O Lord.

For the poor, the persecuted and the suffering; for prisoners and the detained, refugees and all in danger; that they may be relieved and protected.
We beseech you O Lord.

For the terminally ill and all who are living with dreadful scourges, that they may be comforted in their suffering. May they place all their hope in you and hence find peace that passes all understanding.
We beseech you O Lord.

For doctors and scientists in the medical research who spend many hours in various laboratories of the world in search of cures to diseases.
Grant them patience, endurance and success.

For the little children and babies: born and unborn, that their tender lives may be protected and their rights guarded.
We beseech you O Lord.

Guide and govern your holy Church, fill it with love and truth, and grant it that unity which is your will, binding it together with your Spirit.
We beseech you O Lord.

Give courage to our bishops, clergy, and all church leaders, that they may courageously proclaim the Good News of the Kingdom, and fearlessly challenge injustices in the nation.
We beseech you O Lord.

Direct and guide all church based organizations that work for peace, justice and reconciliation, and for the wholistic development of God's people; that they may achieve their mission goals, for the glory and honour of your holy name.
We beseech you O Lord.

Bring into the way of truth, all who have erred and are deceived and those who have been tossed to and fro by every wind of doctrine.
We beseech you O Lord.

Strengthen those who stand, comfort and help the fainthearted, raise up the fallen and finally beat down Satan under your feet.
We beseech you O Lord.

Guide our President and other leaders of this country into ways of justice, peace and unity. Grant that there will be peace within our borders, that all the people in this region may live in harmony and enjoy good neighbourliness.
Hear us O Lord.

For political tolerance among people of different political persuasions, for greater respect for one another's opinions and convictions, for greater thirst after truth and justice for all, that political thuggeries and assassinations may come to an end, that people may enjoy fullness of life as God intended for them.
Hear us O Lord.

Guide and bless those who administer the law; that honesty and truth may be upheld, and that they may proclaim justice without fear or favour except the fear of God.
Hear us O Lord.

Help and comfort the lonely, the bereaved,
the oppressed and the voiceless.
Help and comfort them.

Protect our Archbishop, bishops and ministers from
threats and intimidations of all kinds.
Lord protect them.

Heal the sick in body and mind, provide for the widows
and the orphans, the homeless, the hungry and the
destitute.
Lord have mercy.

Pour your blessing on all human labour, that your
people may enjoy good output, be well fed and live in
economic comfort.
Hear us O Lord.

Preserve and guard the integrity of creation against
exploitation; that forests, lakes, game reserves and other
natural and environmental resources may be safeguarded against misuse or abuse.
Hear us O Lord.

For all of us here gathered in your name and for your
service; for the forgiveness of our sins, and for the
grace of the Holy Spirit to amend our lives.
Hear us O Lord.

Bishop   Almighty God, grant that we shall receive what we
have earnestly asked in faith, that in all the services we
render to you and in your name, we may find fulfilment, and that your people may be well-nourished,
to the glory and honour of your holy name. **Amen.**

9   *Hymn*

10   *MINISTRY OF THE WORD*

The reader may first say:
The Old Testament reading/The Epistle is taken from..., chapter...,
beginning to read at verse....

After the reading,

This is the Word of the Lord.
Alleluia, praise be to God.
Silence may be kept.

OLD TESTAMENT: *Jeremiah 1:1-9 or Ezekiel 33:1-9; Isaiah 6:1-8.*

PSALM: *43; or 132: 8-19.*
At the end of the Psalm:
Glory to the Father Son and the Holy Spirit....

EPISTLE: *2 Cor 4:1-7; or Ephesians 4:1-16; or 2 Timothy 4:1-5; 1 Peter 5:1-4.*

GOSPEL: *Luke 5:1-11; or Matthew 9: 35-38; or John 10:11-18 (to be read by an ordinand).*

All stand for the reading which is introduced with these or other appropriate words:

We stand to hear the Good News of our salvation, as it is written in the Gospel according to Saint..., chapter... beginning to read at verse....

After the Gospel:

This is the Gospel of Christ.
Alleluia, praise be to Christ our Saviour.

Silence may be kept.

11 *Hymn*

12 *Notices*

13 *Sermon*

14 *NICENE CREED*

Minister	We stand together with Christians throughout the centuries, and throughout the world today, to affirm our faith in the words of the Nicene Creed.

All We believe in one God,
the Father, the Almighty,
   maker of heaven and earth,
of all that is, seen and unseen.
   We believe in one Lord, Jesus Christ,
the only Son of God,
eternally begotten of the Father,
God from God, Light from Light,
   true God from true God,
begotten, not made,
of one Being with the Father.
Through him all things were made.
   For us and for our salvation
he came down from heaven;
by the power of the Holy Spirit
he became incarnate of the Virgin Mary,
   and was made man.
For our sake he was crucified under Pontius Pilate;
   He suffered, died, and was buried.
On the third day he rose again
in accordance with the Scriptures;
   he ascended into heaven
and is seated at the right hand of the Father.
He will come again in glory
   to judge the living and the dead,
and his kingdom will have no end.
   We believe in the Holy Spirit,
the Lord, the giver of life,
who proceeds from the Father and the Son.
With the Father and the Son he is worshipped
   and glorified.
He has spoken through the Prophets.
   We believe in one holy, catholic,
and apostolic Church.
We acknowledge one baptism for the
   forgiveness of sins.
We look for the resurrection of the dead,
and the life of the world to come. Amen.

15 *PRAYER FOR THE ORDINANDS*

The ordinands kneel and the Bishop gives the congregation time to commend them to God in silent prayer. Afterwards he may invite a priest to pray (either extemporary, or using the prayer below).

O God almighty, ageless and eternal, you have never failed to appoint for yourself ministers to shepherd your people, to preach forgiveness and reconciliation, and to lead them in offering holy sacrifices of praise, worship and adoration. Look at these your servants whom you have called and set apart for this very noble ministry. Fill them with the Holy Spirit for the office and work of a priest in this diocese. Grant that they shall be faithful ministers of your Word and the holy sacraments. Give them grace to endure the rigours of the office they now go to take. Sustain them and provide for their every need according to your perfect will for their lives. Bless their families and grant that they shall be supportive of the minister in their midst.

Now Lord, our hands are cold unless they receive the warmth from above; our charge is empty unless it is charged from above. Come therefore and lay your hands on these people, granting them a fresh charge to go and exercise in the name of God, the duties pertaining to this office. Hear these our prayers O ageless God, for the sake of Jesus Christ our Lord and Saviour. **Amen.**

16 *VENI CREATOR. The congregation joins in this or another song that serves a similar purpose of invoking the Holy Spirit.*

Come, Holy Ghost, our souls inspire
And lighten with celestial fire;
Thou the anointing Spirit art,
Who dost thy sevenfold gifts impart;

Thy blessed unction from above
Is comfort, life, and fire of love,
Enable with perpetual light
The dullness of our blinded sight.

Anoint and cheer our soiled face
With the abundance of thy grace,
Keep far our foes, give peace at home;
Where thou art guide no ill can come.

Teach us to know the Father, Son,
And thee, of both to be but one;
That through the ages all along
This may be our endless song.

17 *ORDINATION*

The ordinands go back to their seats. One at a time, they kneel before the Bishop who, assisted by the priests lays hands on the candidate and prays:

N, may the Holy Spirit stir up all the gifts of God that are in you for the ministry. May he equip you with all wisdom, strength and power necessary for the execution of the duties pertaining to priesthood. We lay our hands on you to confirm your ordination to this ministry. In the name of the Father, Son, and the Holy Spirit. **Amen.**

The newly ordained priest is vested according to custom. After all have been ordained, they kneel in a row before the Bishop. With his arm stretched over the candidates, and with the congregation standing, the Bishop prays:

Spirit of the Living God, descend upon these your servants as you did to the apostles on the day of Pentecost. Set their hearts aflame for the mission to which you have called them. May they serve faithfully, zealously and courageously at all times. Grant this for the sake of Jesus Christ our Saviour and mediator. **Amen.**

18 *ANOINTING: (This section is optional)*
The Bishop may anoint each ordinand with oil saying:

As the Father anointed his Son with the Spirit, so may Jesus Christ preserve you, to sanctify his people and to offer sacrifices of praise and thanksgiving. We anoint you with this oil, in the name of the Father, Son, and the Holy Spirit. **Amen.**

19 *Presentation of the Bible.*

N, Receive the holy scriptures. This is your authority to rebuke, to strengthen, to encourage and comfort God's people and to proclaim in season and out of season, the good news of the Kingdom.

20 *Presentation of the chalice and paten.*

Receive this chalice and paten, and regularly administer Christ's holy sacraments; In the name of the Father, Son, and the Holy Spirit. **Amen.**

21 *Presentation to the People and clergy.*

The newly ordained stand in a line facing the congregation.
The congregation stands and the Bishop says:

People of God, we present to you these servants of God whom we have just ordained priests. Will you support and uphold them in their ministry?

All   **We will support and uphold them.**

22   *The Bishop presents the newly ordained to the clergy:*

Clergy of *this* diocese, we present to you these newly ordained priests. Do you receive them into your fellowship?

Clergy   **We receive them gladly.**

Bishop   Will you encourage them in their ministry?
Clergy   **We will encourage them.**

Bishop   Offer them then a hand of fellowship.

23   *Joyful songs and/or choruses are sang during which the newly ordained are greeted by the members of the congregation and the clergy. The newly ordained then take their place among the House of Clergy.*

24   OFFERTORY

25   *Hymn. The service of Holy Communion continues from paragraph 26.*

Ordination of Bishops

NOTES:

- This service is to take place in the diocesan Cathedral, unless otherwise desired.

- The service is presided over by the Archbishop but if need arise, his place may be taken by the Dean, or the senior-most bishop.

- At least two other bishops are to lay hands on the bishop-elect together with the Archbishop.

- Installation does not necessarily have to be a component of this service. It can be conducted later by the Vicar General and the Archdeacons and Canons of the Diocese. Where this is the case, the Bishop gives his charge immediately after the ordination. Then follows the Service of Holy Communion beginning from Prayer of Thanksgiving.

- Where Installation is to take place immediately after ordination, the Provincial Chancellor reads the Archbishop's certificate of Installation. Otherwise when installation comes later, the certificate is read by the Administrative Secretary. The service then would begin from Paragraph 21 of *INSTALLATION*.

- The Service is to be conducted in the context of Holy Communion.

- A procession may be organized.

ORDER OF SERVICE

1   *As the procession approaches the entrance, the people stand and the Archbishop says aloud:*

Blessed be God the Father, Son and Holy Spirit.
And blessed be his kingdom now and forever. Amen.

2   *Hymn*

3   *CALL TO WORSHIP*

The Lord be with you.
And also with you.

The earth is the Lord's and all that is in it.
Let the heavens rejoice and the earth be glad.

Our help is in the name of the Lord.
Who made heaven and earth.

I was glad when they said to me.
Let us go to the house of the Lord.

Praise the Lord.
The name of the Lord be praised.

The following collect is used.

Eternal Father,
through your Holy Spirit you have appointed
many ministries in the Church:
bless your servant *N* now called to be a bishop.
Maintain him in your truth,
renew him in your holiness
and make him your ever faithful servant;
through Jesus Christ our Lord.
Amen.

All join in the confession

Almighty God to whom all hearts are open,
all desires known and from whom no secrets are hidden:
cleanse the thoughts of our hearts
by the inspiration of your holy Spirit,
that we may perfectly love you
and worthily magnify your holy name
through Christ our Lord, Amen.

4   *PRESENTATION*

People stand.

The Bishop-elect, dressed in cassock/alb is presented by representatives of the electoral college, preferably a lay person, a priest and a bishop.

They say:

Your Grace, the Electoral College of the Anglican Church of Kenya, was led by the Holy Spirit to elect Reverend *NN*, to be bishop and shepherd in the Diocese of ....

5   *The Bishop-elect faces the congregation and the Archbishop asks the whole congregation:*

Brothers and sisters, is it your wish that *NN* be ordained Bishop of this diocese?

People　**That is our wish.**

Archbishop　In view of your wish I now direct the Provincial Chancellor to read the mandate of the election and appointment.

6　*After the mandate has been read the presenters sit with the Bishop-elect.*

7　*MINISTRY OF THE WORD*

The reader may first say:

The Old Testament reading/The Epistle, is taken from..., chapter..., beginning to read at verse....

After the reading,
This is the Word of the Lord.
Alleluia, praise be to God.

Silence may be kept.

OLD TESTAMENT: Jeremiah 1: 1-10; or Joshua 1:1-9; or Ezekiel 33:1-9; 34:1-16; or Isaiah 6:1-8.

PSALM 99; 40:1-14, or 100.

At the end of the Psalm:
Glory to the Father Son and the Holy Spirit....

EPISTLE: Acts 20:17-32; or 2 Timothy 1:6-14; or 1 Timothy 3:1-7.

GOSPEL: John 21:15-17; or John 13: 2-17.

All stand for the Gospel reading which is introduced with these or other appropriate words:

We stand to hear the Good News of our salvation, as it is written in the Gospel according to Saint..., chapter... beginning to read at verse....

After the Gospel:

This is the Gospel of Christ.
Alleluia, praise be to Christ our Saviour.

Silence may be kept.

8   *Hymn*

9   *Sermon*

10 *NICENE CREED*

    Leader: We stand together with Christians throughout the centuries and throughout the whole world, to affirm our faith in the words of the Nicene Creed.

    All   **We believe in one God,**
the Father, the Almighty,
  maker of heaven and earth,
of all that is, seen and unseen.
  We believe in one Lord, Jesus Christ,
the only Son of God,
eternally begotten of the Father,
God from God, Light from Light,
  true God from true God,
begotten, not made,
of one Being with the Father.
Through him all things were made.
  For us and for our salvation
he came down from heaven;
by the power of the Holy Spirit
he became incarnate of the Virgin Mary,
  and was made man.
For our sake he was crucified under Pontius Pilate;
  He suffered, died, and was buried.
On the third day he rose again
in accordance with the Scriptures;
  he ascended into heaven
and is seated at the right hand of the Father.
He will come again in glory
  to judge the living and the dead,
and his kingdom will have no end.
  We believe in the Holy Spirit,
the Lord, the giver of life,
who proceeds from the Father and the Son.
With the Father and the Son he is worshipped
  and glorified.

He has spoken through the Prophets.
We believe in one holy, catholic,
and apostolic Church.
We acknowledge one baptism for the
forgiveness of sins.
We look for the resurrection of the dead,
and the life of the world to come. Amen.

11   *The presenters lead the Bishop-elect to the vestry to put on the rochet and then present him before the Archbishop and say:*

Your Grace, we bring to you the Reverend *NN*, that he may be consecrated Bishop.

12   *OATHS*
      The Archbishop calls upon the Provincial Chancellor to lead the Bishop-elect in taking the oaths.
      The Provincial Chancellor leads the Bishop-elect in taking the oath of obedience and other oaths.

13   *After the oaths,*

Archbishop: Brothers and sisters in Christ, it is written in the Gospel of Luke that the Lord Jesus watched and prayed a whole night before appointing and sending the twelve apostles. It is also written in the Acts of Apostles that the disciples in Antioch fasted and prayed before laying hands on Paul and Barnabas and sending them out. So also ourselves, as we follow the example of our Lord Jesus Christ and his apostles, we must pray before accepting and sending *N*, to do the work the Holy Spirit has called *him* to do.

14   LITANY:

To be led by various people.
God the Father, creator of the universe and all that is there.
Have mercy on us.

God the Son, the Saviour of the world.
Have mercy on us.

God the Holy Spirit the comforter of humanity.
Have mercy on us.

Holy, blessed and glorious Trinity.
Have mercy on us.

From all satanic plottings against your Church.
O Lord deliver us.

From malice and hatred, from all forms of corruption and worldliness.
O Lord deliver us.

From all fear of persecution and the dread of death.
O Lord deliver us.

From disordered and sinful affections and from the deceits of the world, the flesh and the devil.
O Lord deliver us.

From drought and floods, from earthquakes and other disasters, from wicked people who plan evil against us, from gangsters, robbers, murderers, hijackers and kidnappers, from carjackers and reckless drivers, from slanderers and rumour mongers.
O Lord deliver us.

Protect and direct your holy Church to the source of truth; govern and encourage her to speak the truth in love, both in season and out of season.
Hear us O Lord.

Enlighten your ministers with knowledge and understanding, that by their teaching and their lives, they may proclaim your Word.
Hear us O Lord.

That by the indwelling of the Holy Spirit they may be encouraged to persevere to the end.
Hear us O Lord.

For their homes and families, that they may be adorned with all Christian virtues.
Hear us O Lord.

Give your people grace to hear and receive your word, and bring forth the fruit and the gifts of the Spirit.
Hear us O Lord.

Hear us as we remember the bishops who have died in the peace of Christ *(pause in silence)*....
Grant us with them a share in your eternal kingdom.

For all in the communion of your Church, who have died in Christ; that we may walk in their footsteps and be fully united with them in your everlasting kingdom.
Hear us O Lord.

Pour your Holy Spirit upon your servant *(Bishop) N*; fill him with humility of a good servant. Give him courage to become a powerful prophet, love to become a good shepherd, and wisdom to solve the problems of his flock.
We beseech you O Lord.

For the nations of the world that they may peacefully co-exist, and that a spirit of respect and forbearance may grow among nations and peoples.
We beseech you O Lord.

For the poor, the persecuted and the suffering; for prisoners and the detained, refugees and all in danger; that they may be relieved and protected.
We beseech you O Lord.

For the terminally ill and all who are living with dreadful scourges, that they may be comforted in their suffering. May they place all their hope in you and hence find peace that passes all understanding.
We beseech you O Lord.

For doctors and scientists in the medical research who spend many hours in various laboratories of the world in search of cures for diseases.
Grant them patience, endurance and success.

For the little children and babies: born and unborn, that their tender lives may be protected and their rights guarded.
We beseech you O Lord.

Guide and govern your holy Church, fill it with love and truth, and grant it that unity which is your will, binding it together with your Spirit.
We beseech you O Lord.

Give courage to our bishops, clergy, and all church leaders, that they may courageously proclaim the Good News of the Kingdom, and fearlessly challenge injustices in the nation.
We beseech you O Lord.

Direct and guide all church based organizations that work for peace, justice and reconciliation and for the wholistic development of God's people; that they may achieve their mission goals, for the glory and honour of your holy name.
We beseech you O Lord.

Bring into the way of truth, all who have erred and are deceived and those who have been tossed to and fro by every wind of doctrine.
We beseech you O Lord.

Strengthen those who stand, comfort and help the faint-hearted, raise up the fallen and finally beat down Satan under your feet.
We beseech you O Lord.

Guide our President and other leaders of this country into ways of justice, peace and unity. Grant that there will be peace within our borders, that all the people in this region may live in harmony and enjoy good neighbourliness.
Hear us O Lord.

For political tolerance among people of different political persuasions, for greater respect for one
another's opinions and convictions, for greater thirst after truth and justice for all, that political thuggeries and assassinations may come to an end, that people may enjoy fullness of life as God intended for them.
Hear us O Lord.

Guide and bless those who administer the law; that honesty and truth may be upheld, and that they may proclaim justice without fear or favour except the fear of God.
Hear us O Lord.

Help and comfort the lonely, the bereaved, the oppressed and the voiceless.
Help and comfort them.

Protect our Archbishop, bishops and ministers from threats and intimidations of all kinds.
Lord protect them.

Heal the sick in body and mind, provide for the widows and the orphans, the homeless, the hungry and the destitute.
Lord have mercy.

Pour your blessing on all human labour, that your people may enjoy good output, be well fed and live in economic comfort.
Hear us O Lord.

Preserve and guard the integrity of creation against exploitation; that forests, lakes, game reserves and other natural and environmental resources may be safeguarded against misuse of abuse.
Hear us O Lord.

For all of us here gathered in your name and for your service; for the forgiveness of our sins, and for the grace of the Holy Spirit to amend our lives.
Hear us O Lord.

Archbishop   Almighty God, grant that we shall receive what we have earnestly asked in faith, that in all the services we render to you and in your name, we may find fulfilment, and that your people may be well-nourished, to the glory and honour of your holy name. **Amen.**

15.   *Bishop-elect kneels. The Congregation is led in a prayerful hymn.*

EXHORTATION AND EXAMINATION OF THE BISHOP-ELECT BY THE ARCHBISHOP.

16.   *The Archbishop exhorts the Bishop-elect thus:*

My dear *brother N*, as a bishop you are called to lead in serving and caring for the people of God and to work with them in the oversight of the Church. As a chief pastor you are to share with your fellow bishops a special responsibility to maintain and further the unity of the Church, and particularly be a focus of unity in the diocese.

You are to maintain the church's discipline, guard her faith and promote her mission in the world.

It is your duty to watch over and pray for all those committed to your charge. You are to know your people and be known by them. You are to ordain and to commission new ministers, guiding those who serve with you and enabling them to fulfil their ministry. You are to baptise and to confirm, to preside at the Holy Communion, and to lead the offering of praise and worship. You are to be merciful, but with firmness; to minister discipline, but with mercy.

You are to have a special care for the outcasts, and a passion for lost souls. To all who turn to Christ, you are to declare the forgiveness of sins.

Remember, the work you are called for is God's work and must be done in God's name and for his glory. You are therefore to serve humbly, cheerfully and in keeping with Christ's example for, although he was in very nature God, he did not consider equality with God something to be grasped but took the very nature of a servant and obeyed unto death, even death on a cross. As a result of this obedience, God gave him the name that is above any other name, that at the name of Jesus every knee should bow and every tongue confess that Jesus Christ is Lord, to the glory of God the Father.

17. *Archbishop examines the Bishop-elect:*

In order that we may know your mind and purpose, and that you may be strengthened in your resolve to fulfil your ministry, you must answer the questions we now put to you.

Archbishop Are you convinced, that God has called you to the office and work of a bishop in his Church?
Answer **I believe that God has called me.**

Archbishop Do you accept the holy scriptures as revealing all things necessary for eternal salvation through faith in Jesus Christ?
Answer **Yes, I do accept them.**

Archbishop Will you accept the discipline of the Church, and faithfully exercise authority within it?
Answer **By the help of God, I will.**

Archbishop	Will you be diligent in prayer, in reading the Bible, and in all studies that will deepen your faith and knowledge of the Word of God, and enable you to uphold the truth of the Gospel against error?
Answer	**By the help of God, I will.**
Archbishop	Will you strive to fashion your own life and that of your household according to the way of Christ?
Answer	**By the help of God, I will.**
Archbishop	Will you promote unity, love and reconciliation among all Christians, and especially among those whom you serve?
Answer	**By the help of God, I will.**
Archbishop	Will you then be a faithful witness of Christ to those among whom you live, and lead your people to obey our Saviour's command to make disciples of all nations?
Answer	**By the help of God, I will.**

18.   ORDINATION

The escorting representatives take the Bishop-elect to the vestry for the episcopal robes.

The Bishop-elect kneels before the Lord's table. A moment of silence is observed after which the congregation joins in a prayerful hymn e.g. Veni Creator as follows.

Come, Holy Ghost, our souls inspire
And lighten with celestial fire;
Thou the anointing Spirit art,
Who dost thy sevenfold gifts impart;

Thy blessed unction from above
Is comfort, life, and fire of love,
Enable with perpetual light
The dullness of our blinded sight.

Anoint and cheer our soiled face
With the abundance of thy grace,
Keep far our foes, give peace at home;
Where thou art guide no ill can come.

Teach us to know the Father, Son,
And thee, of both to be but one;
That through the ages all along
This may be our endless song.

The bishops surround the Bishop-elect. The Archbishop stretches out his hand towards the Bishop-elect and prays thus:

We praise and glorify you, Almighty Father, because you have formed throughout the world a holy people for your own possession, a royal priesthood, a universal Church. We praise and glorify you because you have given us your only Son Jesus Christ to be the Apostle and High Priest of our faith, and the Shepherd of our souls.

We praise and glorify you that by his death he has overcome death; and that having ascended into heaven he has given his gifts abundantly to your people, making some apostles; some evangelists; some pastors and teachers; to equip them for the work of ministry and to build up his Body.

And now we give you thanks that you have called this your servant *N,* whom we ordain in your name, to share this ministry entrusted to your Church by the great shepherd, Jesus Christ our Lord. **Amen.**

19.   *Archbishop and other bishops lay hands on the Bishop-elect.*
        The Archbishop prays:

Send your Holy Spirit Lord on your servant *N,* and empower him for the office and work of a Bishop.

And then:

N, Remember that you stir up the gift of God which is given you, for God has not given us a spirit of fear but of power, love and self control. Like a good shepherd, tend the flock of Christ committed to your care. In the name of the Father, Son, and the Holy Spirit. **Amen**

A short doxology may be inserted here. See Appendix for suggestion.

20.   *Presentation of a Bible by the Archbishop*

Receive the Holy Scriptures, tend the flock of Christ committed to your charge, guard and defend them in his truth and be a faithful steward of his holy word and sacraments. Amen.

21. *After this, other symbols of office are given: the ring, pectoral cross and the staff.*

Ring

Receive this ring, to serve as a reminder of your marriage to Christ and his Church.

Pectoral cross

Receive this cross, to serve as a constant reminder of your call to carry the cross of Christ as a symbol of your ministry.

When applicable, the Archbishop may request the outgoing Bishop of the diocese to give the pastoral staff to the new Bishop as a way of passing on the mantle. The staff may be given with these or similar words:

Receive this staff to serve as a constant reminder of your call to be a shepherd to the flock that Christ has put in your care, not by persuasion but by self will, just as the Lord wills, not for selfish gain or for money but voluntarily. *(And may the Lord bless you as you pastor the people of this diocese who have been under my care.)* In the name of the Father, Son, and the Holy Spirit. **Amen.**

End of the Service of Ordination. The Archbishop and bishops give the new bishop a hand of fellowship as they welcome him to the House of Bishops. More songs of jubilation may be sung.

22 INSTALLATION
As the singing is going on, the new Bishop is taken to the vestry by the archdeacons and the canons of the diocese to complete robing. When the procession enters, all people stand.

23 *Hymn*

24 *The Provincial Chancellor (or the Administrative Secretary) reads the Arcbishop's certificate of Installation). See note 5.*

25 *The Bishop takes his oath of office in the following words:*

I *NN,* by divine providence, Bishop of the Diocese of ..., hereby promise that I will respect, uphold and protect truth, justice and freedom in this diocese, and in all things strive to be a good example to everyone, God being my helper.

(Congregational applause)

26 *Archdeacons and the canons of the diocese escort the Bishop to his seat and say the following:*

We the Archdeacons and Canons of this diocese, on behalf of all the Christians do welcome you, our bishop, to occupy your seat of authority.

The congregation applauds with a standing ovation and then they sit. The Bishop sits.

27 *The Archbishop may ask all the active clergy of the diocese to shake hands with their new Bishop as a sign of their canonical obedience to him. First, he says:*

Dear clergy of ... Diocese, I present to you your new bishop, the Right Rev *NN*. Do you accept him?

Clergy **We the clergy of ... Diocese do accept the Rt Rev *NN*, to be our Bishop and senior shepherd.**

28 *The bishop stands. The Archbisop presents him to the laity thus:*

Dear Christians of ... Diocese, I present to you your new bishop and father in God. Do you accept him?

Christians **We accept him gladly.**

Will you support and uphold him in prayers?

Christians **We pledge to support and uphold him.**

29 *People stand and the choir leads in either of the doxologies below. It is to be sang promptly.*

Praise God from whom all blessings flow
Praise him all creatures here below
Praise him above, ye heavenly host
Praise Father, Son, and Holy Ghost.
Amen.

OR

Take My life and let it be
Consecrated Lord to thee
Take my moments and my days
Let them flow in ceaseless praise
Amen.

30 *Bishop* The peace of the Lord be always with you.
And also with you.

Let us offer one another a sign of peace.

Ululation and joyous singing as people share the peace.

31 *Hymn*

32 *Offertory. During this time choirs may also present.*

33 *Speeches.*

34 *BISHOP'S CHARGE:*
    Archbishop invites the new Bishop to address the gathering from his seat of authority. A song may be sang before and after the Bishop has given his address.

35 *HOLY COMMUNION*

    A short service of Holy Communion is conducted beginning from Prayer of Thanksgiving (item 27).

Laying the Foundation Stone of a Church

NOTES

- This service is to be conducted at the site, preferably when the building is about four feet high.

- This service is for use with permanent buildings only.

ORDER OF SERVICE

1 *A hymn is sang, preferably,* **The Church's One Foundation** *or another appropriate one.*

2 *The Parish priest and the wardens invite the Bishop:*

> **Reverend father in God, on behalf of the Christians of this church and parish as a whole, we request you to lay the foundation stone of this church.**

Bishop It is my pleasure to do so.

The Lord be with you.

All **And also with you.**

3 *The Bishop may say these or similar words:*

Brothers and sisters in Christ, we are gathered here for the purpose of laying the foundation stone of this church *(he may mention the name of the church)* which is being built for the sole purpose of worship to God. Let us pray that this good work will be brought to completion, that the builders will be protected against accidents, and that the Christians will be able to raise the money needed for the work of construction.

4 *Hymn*

5 *The following scripture selections are used.*

Who is able to build a house for God when heaven itself, the highest heaven cannot contain him? *(2 Chronicles 2:5-6).*

Unless the Lord builds the house, its builders labour in vain. *(Psalms 127:1).*

When the builders laid the foundation of the temple of the Lord, the priests in their vestments and with trumpets, and the Levites with cymbals, took their places to praise the Lord as prescribed by David, king of Israel. With praise and thanksgiving, they sang to the Lord:

All join   **The Lord is good;**
His love to *us* lasts for ever.

And all the people gave a great shout of praise to the Lord because the foundation of the house of the Lord was laid. *(Ezra 3:10-11)*

All   **Alleluia, Amen!**

Other Readings: Isaiah 8:13-15; Matthew 21:42-44; Ephesians 2:19-22; 1 Peter 2:4-8.

6   *Hymn*

7   *MINISTRY OF THE WORD*
   (as in the lectionary, or other appropriate ones)
   Old Testament
   Psalm
   Epistle
   Gospel

8   *Notices*

9   *Sermon*

10   *APOSTLES' CREED*

   I believe in God, the Father Almighty,
   creator of heaven and earth.
   I believe in Jesus Christ,
   his only Son, our Lord,
   who was conceived by the Holy Spirit,
   born of the Virgin Mary,
   suffered under Pontius Pilate,
   was crucified, died and was buried;
   he descended to the dead.
   On the third day he rose again;
   he ascended into heaven,
   he is seated at the right hand of the Father,
   and he will come to judge the living
   and the dead.
   I believe in the Holy Spirit,
   the holy catholic Church,
   the communion of saints,
   the forgiveness of sins,
   the resurrection of the body,
   and the life everlasting. Amen.

11   *A hymn is sang during which the Bishop proceeds with the clergy to the place of the foundation stone. Bishop prays thus:*

Almighty God and creator of all, you created the birds of the air; with only their beaks they entwine a shelter for themselves. We thank you for endowing us more richly than the birds of the air. Strengthen our resolve to serve you with greater dedication in unity with one another as members of the body of Christ. And all, for the glory of Jesus Christ our Lord. **Amen.**

OR

Almighty God, your Son Jesus Christ is the living stone chosen by you and of great worth to you. Build us up as living stones into a spiritual temple and form us into a holy priesthood to offer spiritual sacrifices acceptable to you. **Amen.**

12   *PRAYER FOR PROTECTION:*

Defend and protect from all danger, O Lord, all who will be involved in the construction of this church. Give the architects, the engineers, masons, carpenters, and all concerned, your architectural wisdom, that this church may be built in a way that it will not endanger the lives of worshippers, and that it will be a sure testimony of your love, beauty, truth and faith in you whom we worship in spirit and in truth. **Amen.**

13   *PRAYER FOR BUILDING PROVISIONS*

Touch the hearts of your people, that they may give generously towards the building and completion of this church. Touch their silver and their gold, that they may willingly give the same for the purchase of the materials needed, the wages of the workers, and all other related expenses, until as in Moses's time, the workers report that the people are bringing more than is needed for the work. May the completion of this church testify to the unity of these Christians and their outstanding love and zeal for your work. We pray and thank you in Jesus name. **Amen.**

14 *Then this prayer as the stone is being placed:*

Establish this stone
Which we place here in your name.
Give us the continual presence of your Spirit,
That this work undertaken for your service
May be completed to your praise and glory,
Through Jesus our Lord who lives and reigns
With you and the Holy Spirit,
One God, now and for ever. Amen.

15 *Bishop:* *These are the words of the Lord God;*
I am laying a foundation stone in Zion,
A precious corner-stone, well founded;
He who has faith will not waver.
I shall use justice as a plumbline
And righteousness as a plummet. *(Isaiah 28:16-17)*

To the glory of God, we lay this
Foundation stone of *N* Church,
In the name of the Father, Son, and of the
Holy Spirit. **Amen.**

16 *The writing on the stone is read aloud. People clap and sing.*

17 *FINAL PRAYER*

Guide us Lord in all our doings in your gracious favour,
And further us with your continuing help, that in all our works,
begun, continued and ended in you, we may glorify your holy name;
and by your mercy attain everlasting life,
Through Jesus Christ our Lord. **Amen.**

18 *BLESSING*

May God who laid a chief cornerstone in Zion
bless you at the laying of this foundation stone;
may he cause this work to be built up for you and for his name.

And the blessing of God Almighty,
Father, Son and the Holy Spirit
Be upon you and remain with you always. **Amen.**

19 *Recessional hymn.*

Consecration of a Church

NOTES

- The Anglican Church of Kenya flag should be hoisted in the morning.

- The service is conducted by the Diocesan Bishop.

- A procession may be organized.

ORDER OF SERVICE

1 *Hymn, during which the Bishop leads the procession round the church and then stops at the main door. The Bishop knocks at the door with the staff three times and symbolically opens with a key. The door is opened from the inside.*

2 *Bishop*   The Peace of God be in this house
  Congregation   **Alleluia, Alleluia, Alleluia.**

3 *COLLECT FOR DEDICATION*

Lord God,
Your Son blessed with his presence,
the feast of the dedication in Jerusalem:
as we thank you for the many blessings
given to those who have worshipped here
we pray that all who seek you in this place will find you
and become a living temple acceptable to you;
through Jesus Christ our Lord. **Amen.**

4 *Bishop leads the congregation into the church. Meanwhile the church choir leads the music. Everyone sits and the Bishop, standing by the holy table says aloud:*

    Bishop   "When the ark of the covenant of the Lord came into the camp, all Israel gave a mighty shout until the earth resounded."
    People   **Alleluia, Alleluia, Alleluia!**

5 *The Gloria is said or sung.*

EITHER:

  Bishop   Glory to the Father;
  People   **Glory to the Son.**

Bishop	Glory to the Spirit;
People	**For ever Three in One.**

People	**Be glorified at home;**
Bishop	Be glorified in Church.

Bishop	Be glorified in Kenya;
People	**Be glorified in Africa.**

Bishop	Be glorified on earth;
People	**Be glorified in heaven.**

Bishop	Glory to the Father;
People	**Glory to the Son.**

Bishop	Glory to the Spirit;
People	**For ever Three in One.**

Bishop	Alleluia;
People	**Amen.**

OR:

THE TRADITIONAL GLORIA

**Glory to God in the highest,
And peace to his people on earth.
   Lord God, heavenly King,
Almighty God and Father,
we worship you, we give you thanks,
We praise you for your glory.
Lord Jesus Christ, only Son of the Father,
   Lord God, Lamb of God,
You take away the sin of the world:
have mercy on us;
You are seated at the right hand of the Father:
receive our prayer.
   For you alone are the Holy One,
you alone are the Lord,
You alone are the Most High,
Jesus Christ, with the Holy Spirit,
In the glory of God the Father. Amen.**

DEDICATION AND CONSECRATION

6 *Bishop, standing at the Holy Table facing the congregation says:*

From the days of old the Lord God has been touching the hearts of his people, creating in them a desire to build or set aside holy places for worship. With joy and thanksgiving we have met here today to consecrate and dedicate this building to God and for the glory of His name.

Bishop   Let us pray.

Ever Living Father, watchful and caring, our source and our end: all that we are and all that we have is yours. Accept us now, as we dedicate this place to which we come to praise your name, to ask your forgiveness, to know your healing power, to hear your Word, and to be nourished by the body and the blood of your Son. Be present always, to guide, to judge, to forgive, to illuminate and to bless your people. **Amen.**

7 CONSECRATION OF THE BAPTISMAL FONT
Bishop and clergy proceed to the baptismal font. Meanwhile a hymn may be sang. The Bishop may request various people to read different portions.

Reading: Titus 3:5-7:

Reader   He saved us, not because of any good deeds that we ourselves had done but because of his own mercy through the Holy Spirit who gives us new birth and new life by washing us. God poured out the Holy Spirit abundantly on us through Jesus Christ our Saviour, so that by his grace we might be put right with God and come into possession of the eternal life we hope for.

Bishop   There is one Lord, one faith, one baptism.
People   **One God Father of all.**

Consecration Prayer:

Bishop   Father we thank you that through the waters of baptism we die to sin and are made new in Christ. Grant through your Spirit that those baptised here may enjoy the liberty and splendour of the children of God. We consecrate this font in the name of the Father, Son, and the Holy Spirit. **Amen.**

8 CONSECRATION OF THE LECTERN
Reading: 1 Timothy 4:13.

Reader   All Scripture is inspired by God and is profitable for teaching, for reproof, for correction and for training in righteousness, that the people of God may be complete, equipped for every good work.

Bishop   Your Word is a lamp to our feet.
People   **It is the light that illuminates our way.**

Consecration prayer:

Bishop   Lord we beseech that those who will be reading the holy scriptures would have faith in your Word and read it carefully; and that all who hear it will not only understand it but also receive it in their hearts and bear the fruit of the Holy Spirit in their lives. We consecrate this lectern in the name of the Father, Son, and the Holy Spirit. **Amen.**

9 CONSECRATION OF THE PULPIT
Reading: 2 Timothy 4:1,2

Reader   I solemnly urge you to preach the message, to insist upon proclaiming it in season and out of season, to convince, reproach and encourage, as you teach with all patience.

Bishop   May the words of my mouth, and the meditations of our hearts,
People   **Be acceptable to you O Lord, our rock and our redeemer.**

Consecration prayer:

Bishop   Father in every way you have spoken through the voices of prophets, pastors and teachers, purify the lives and the lips of those who speak here, that your Word only may be heard. We consecrate this pulpit in the name of the Father, Son, and the Holy Spirit. **Amen.**

10 CONSECRATION OF THE PRAYER DESK
Reading: 1 Timothy. 2:1-2

Parish Priest: First of all then I urge that supplications and prayers, intercessions and thanksgivings be made for all *the people,* for all kings and for all who are in high positions, that we may lead a quiet and peaceable life, godly and respectful in every way.

Bishop Lord hear our prayers;
People **And let our cry come to you.**

Consecration prayer:

Bishop We pray for all who will be leading worship in this church, that they will always lead your people in prayers, psalms and thanksgiving such as will bring glory to your heavenly throne, where our mediator Jesus Christ unceasingly prays for us. We consecrate this prayer desk in the name of the Father, Son, and the Holy Spirit. **Amen.**

11 *CONSECRATION OF THE ALTAR RAIL*
Reading: Psalm 27:4

Reader I have asked the Lord for one thing; one thing only do I want: to live in the Lord's house all my life, to marvel there at his goodness, and to ask for his guidance.

Bishop One day spent in your temple,
People **Is better than a thousand anywhere else.**

Consecration prayer:

Bishop We pray that all those who will kneel on this altar rail for confirmation, Holy Communion, Holy Matrimony, thanksgiving or any other acceptable purpose will rise up with spiritual enrichment and go out to serve you and to live in honour of your name. We consecrate this altar rail in the name of the Father, Son, and the Holy Spirit. **Amen.**

12 *CONSECRATION OF THE LORD'S TABLE*
Reading: Psalm 23:5

Reader You prepare a banquet for me, where all my enemies can see me; you welcome me as an honoured guest and fill my cup to the brim.

Bishop We who are many are one body,
People **For we share one bread.**

Consecration Prayer:

Bishop   Bless this table O Lord, and sanctify it for use at Holy
Communion, prayers and offerings of your people. We
consecrate this table in the name of the Father, Son, and
the Holy Spirit. **Amen.**

13 *CONSECRATION OF THE COMMUNION VESSELS*
An anthem may be sang while the communion vessels are brought forward.
Reading: 2 Timothy 2:20-21.

Reader   In a large house there are dishes and bowls of all kinds:
some are made of silver and gold, others of wood and
clay; some are for special occasions, others for ordinary
use. If anyone makes himself clean he is dedicated and
useful to his master, ready to be used for every good deed.

Bishop   With this plate and this cup,
People   **We show forth Christ's death until he comes in glory.**

Consecration prayer:

Bishop   O Lord our God, grant that all who will be coming to
partake the Holy Communion will have dedicated
themselves to you in righteousness; and thus receive all
the benefits that proceed from Christ's sufferings. We
consecrate these communion vessels in the name of the
Father, Son, and the Holy Spirit. **Amen.**

14 *DEDICATION OF PEWS/SEATS*
Reading: Jeremiah 26:2-3a:

Reader   Stand in the courtyard of the Lord's house and speak to
all the people of the towns of Judah who come to
worship in the house of the Lord. Tell them everything I
command you; do not omit a word. Perhaps they will
listen and each will turn from his evil way.

Bishop   Blessed are those who hunger and thirst for righteousness.
People   **For they shall be filled.**

Consecration prayer:

Bishop   Bless O Lord, all who will be using these pews/seats
during worship and other purposeful functions. Grant that
those who hear your word shall take heed and accept the

godly instructions pronounced inside this building, and that many more shall be revived and edified.
We consecrate all these pews/seats, in the name of the Father, Son, and of the Holy Spirit. **Amen.**

15 DEDICATION OF COLLECTION VESSELS

Bishop   All things come from you Lord;
People   **And of your own do we give you.**

Consecration prayer:

Bishop   O Lord, owner of all things; provider and giver, we acknowledge that all what we are and all what we have belong to you, and that you are pleased with all who give generously with gratitude and cheer.
We consecrate these collection vessels which shall be used in receiving the offerings of your peoople . In the name of the Father, Son, and the Holy Spirit.   **Amen.**

16 CONSECRATION OF CHURCH BELL

Reader   Ding dong, ding dong, on a Sunday morning, what a melodious sound it is. Across the valleys and ridges, it reminds us yet again, the hour is here, to come and join in the praise and worship of our Living God. And so we come, young and old, men and women, in response to the bell.

Consecration prayer:

Bishop   Accept O Lord, our offering of this bell, which we dedicate today. Grant that in this generation and in those that are to come, its voice may continually call your people to praise and worship.
We concecrate this bell in the name of the Father, Son, and the Holy Spirit. **Amen.**

17 CONSECRATION OF THE CROSS

Reader   We will glory in the cross our Lord Jesus Christ in whom is our salvation, our life and resurrection.

Bishop   Christ for us became obedient unto death:
People: **Even death on a cross.**

Consecration prayer:

Bishop   O gracious God, who in your mercy ordained that your Son should suffer death on a cross of shame: We thank you that it has become for us the sign of his triumph and the banner of our salvation; and we pray that this cross may draw our hearts to him, who leads us to the glory of your kingdom; where you live and reign for ever and ever. **Amen.**

18 CONSECRATION OF CHURCH BIBLE

Reader   Whatever was written in former days was written for our instruction, that by steadfastness and by the encouragement of the Scriptures we might have hope.

Bishop   God's word is like the snow and the rain,
Response   **That come down from the sky to water the earth.**

Consecration prayer:

Bishop   We thank you Father for sending us your beloved Son Jesus Christ to show us the way to the Father. Grant that our hearts shall burn within us whenever the scriptures are read and expounded. May we be challenged, encouraged and exhorted as we seek to fashion our lives according to your word.
We dedicate this Bible in the name of the Father, Son, and the Holy Spirit. **Amen.**

19 CONSECRATION OF MUSICAL INSTRUMENTS

Reader   Praise him with trumpets and the tambourines.
Praise him with harps and lyres.
Praise him with drums and the piano.
Praise him with harps and flutes.
Praise him with loud cymbals and the *kayamba.*

Bishop   Praise God in his Temple!
Response   **Praise his strength in heaven.**

Consecration prayer

Bishop   O Lord, before whose throne trumpets sound, and saints and angels sing the songs of Moses and the Lamb: Accept these instruments *(name them) for* worship in

this church, that with the voice of music we may
proclaim your praise and tell it abroad.
We consecrate these instruments in the name of the
Father, Son, and the Holy Spirit. Amen.

20   *The Lord's Prayer*

Bishop   As our Saviour taught us, we are bold to pray:

All   **Our Father in heaven,**
              hallowed be your name,
              your kingdom come,
              ** your will be done,**
              on earth as in heaven.
              Give us today our daily bread.
              Forgive us our sins,
              ** as we forgive those who sin against us.**
              Lead us not into temptation
              but deliver us from evil.
              For the kingdom, the power, and the
              ** glory are yours,**
              now and for ever. Amen.

21   *LITANY OF THANKSGIVING FOR A CHURCH*

Bishop   Let us thank God whom we worship in the beauty
              of holiness.
              Eternal God, the heavens cannot contain you,
              much less the walls of temples made with hands.
              Graciously receive our thanks for this place and accept
              the work of our hands, offered to your honour and
              glory; for the church universal of which these visible
              buildings are a symbol.
People   **Receive our thanks Lord.**

Bishop   For your presence whenever two or three are gathered
              in your name,
People   **We thank you Lord.**

Bishop   For making us your children by adoption through grace,
              and refreshing us day by day with the bread of life;
People   **We thank you Lord.**

Bishop   For the knowledge of your will and the grace to do it;
People   **We thank you Lord.**

Bishop	For the fulfilling of our desires and petitions as you see best for us;
People	**We thank you Lord.**
Bishop	For the pardon of our sins and restoration to the company of your faithful people;
People	**We thank you Lord.**
Bishop	For the blessing of our vows and the crowning of our years with your goodness;
People	**We thank you Lord.**
Bishop	For the faith of those who have gone before us and for our encouragement by their perseverance;
People	**We thank you Lord.**
Bishop	Yours O Lord is the Kingdom;
People	**And you are exalted as head over all. Amen.**

22   *A prayerful hymn may be sang while the congregation is still seated.*

23   *CONSECRATION PRAYERS FOR THE WHOLE BUILDING*
The congregation stands. The bishop recites the following scripture adaptation:

O Lord our God, in all heaven and earth, there is no God like you. Not even all heaven is large enough to hold you. So how can this building that we have built be large enough? Lord God, we are your servants. Listen to our prayers and grant the requests that we will be making to you from this house.

Watch over this building day and night, that none may profane it. Hear the prayers of your people when they come to this place and pray.

May from this house be proclaimed the conviction of those who are guilty and the declaration of forgiveness to all those who sincerely repent and confess their sins.

In times of calamities, famine, floods or drought; when your people fight one another or enemies attack; when epidemics and incurable diseases afflict us, or doctors and scientists fail to discover the cause and the cure, and we come and pray in this house, listen to us, forgive us, heal us and save us O Lord.

Grant that from this church shall come men and women who shall powerfully witness for Jesus Christ so that the world may know you and obey you.

May the prayers of your people Lord rise up to you like the fragrance of incense; and may our praise and worship be a daily offering to you. Cleanse our hearts as we dedicate our souls for your service. Increase our faith and grant the sincere needs of our hearts, that we may praise you all the days of our lives. Through Jesus Christ our mediator and Saviour. **Amen.**

Bishop   God the Father, Son, and the Holy Spirit, sanctify this place.

People   **Which we set aside for the worship of your name.**

CONSECRATION STATEMENT

Bishop   Because of our faith in Jesus Christ, we consecrate the whole of this building to the Almighty God. It shall be called... . In the name of the Father, Son, and the Holy Spirit. **Amen.**

24   *People clap, ululate and shake hands. The choir then leads in an appropriate hymn of praise to mark this climax. Further spontaneous expressions of joy may ensue.*

25   *Notices*

26   *Sermon*

27   *Offertory*

28   *Bishop reads the certificate of consecration and gives it to the Vicar, together with the keys to the church.*

29   *RECESSIONAL HYMN*

30   *Outside the church the Bishop unveils the plaque and the Vicar reads it. The congregation responds with ululation and clapping. The Bishop blesses the Anglican Church of Kenya flag.*

31   *BLESSING (this or other, to be given by the Bishop).*

May the Lord bless you and keep you,
The Lord make his face to shine upon you
and be gracious to you.
The Lord turn his face towards you
and give you peace.
And the blessing of God Almighty,
Father, Son, and the Holy Spirit,
be among you and remain with you always. **Amen.**

Wedding Service
(Holy Matrimony)

NOTES

- This service is for Christian couples who are intending to live together for the first time as husband and wife. It may also be used by those who are widowed and wish to remarry.

- For couples that have been living together through customary or civil arrangements, and now wish to have their marriage blessed in Church, the *Blessing of Marriage* service is to be used.

- First the banns of the persons to be wedded must be published in their respective churches three consecutive Sundays prior to the wedding, in the following form:

  I wish to give notice of wedding between *NN* and *NN*, *(state where each comes from)*. If anyone of you has any just cause why the two may not be joined in marriage, you are to declare. This is the first *(second, or third)* notice.

- At the day and time appointed for the wedding service, the persons to be married come into the church with their witnesses.

- Acceptable symbols other than a ring may be used where this is the cultural style.

- During this service, the bride should be to the right and the bride groom to the left.

- Other forms of prayers and blessings related to this service may be found in the last section of this book.

ORDER OF SERVICE

1 *Bridegroom's procession enters first led by the priest, and then likewise the bridal procession. Music is played to their taste.*
   People remain standing.

   Priest   The Lord be with you.
   People   **And Also with you.**

2 *Hymn*

3 *The priest facing the people and the persons to be married (with the man to*

the left and the woman to the right) addresses the congregation saying:
Dearly beloved, we have come together at this time before God, to witness and celebrate the union in marriage, of *NN* and *NN*, and pray for His blessings upon them now and in the years ahead.

Marriage is a gift of God and a means of grace. God himself ordained it when, in the Garden of Eden he created our first parents, Adam and Eve, and joined them for a life-long companionship. Jesus blessed this manner of life when he responded to a wedding invitation in Cana of Galilee where he performed his first miracle.

It is God's intention in marriage that husband and wife commit themselves to each other in love and in so doing reflect Christ's relationship with his Church.

In marriage, husband and wife belong to each other and they commit themselves to one another in absolute fidelity, love and respect.

They are to comfort and fulfil each other's needs, emotional and physical. Marriage makes possible the full expression of love between husband and wife.

Marriage provides an environment into which children may be born and brought to maturity in the knowledge and fear of the Lord for the well being of the family and the community at large.

This is a solemn state of life and is not to be undermined. Those who enter marriage must respect and uphold each other faithfully and lovingly, to the honour of God and the glory of his name.

It is to this manner of life that *N* and *N* come now to be joined. If any of you can show just cause why they should not be joined, you must declare it now *(pause)*, or forever hold your peace.

4   *The Priest says to the persons to be married:*

Priest   *N* and *N,* you are about to exchange marriage vows. As you have heard, marriage is a solemn state and it's not to be taken lightly; therefore I charge you before God who is judge of all and before whom nothing can be hidden, that if any of you has a just reason why you two should not be joined together, you are to state it now.

Bridegroom: **I, *N*, declare that I do not know any reason why I may not be joined to *N*, in holy matrimony.**

Bride: **I, *N*, declare that I do not know any reason why I may not be joined to *N*, in holy matrimony.**

5   *MAKING PROMISES*
     The priest says to the bridegroom:

        N, will you take *N,* to be your wife, and be united with her in the covenant of marriage? Will you love her? Will you cherish her, honour her, comfort and protect her; and forsaking all others, be faithful to her, as long as you both shall live?

Answer: **I will.**

The Priest says to the bride:

        N, will you take *N,* to be your husband, and be united with him in the covenant of marriage? Will you love him? Will you cherish him, honour him, comfort and protect him; and forsaking all others, be faithful to him as long as you both shall live?

Answer: **I will.**

6   *The Priest asks:*

    Priest   Who presents *N* and *N* for marriage?

Presenters from each side present their son/daughter to the Priest with the following words:

7   Presenters   We present our daughter/son *N,* before the Lord, to be married.

8   *MAKING VOWS*
     The Priest leads them in making the vows. Facing each other, the bridegroom takes the bride's right hand and tells her:

        I *N*, take you *N*, to be my wife,
        to have and to hold from this day forward;
        for better for worse,
        for richer for poorer,
        in sickness and in health,
        to love and to cherish and to honour in the Lord,
        till we are separated by death,
        according to God's holy law;
        and this is my solemn vow.
        Amen.

9   *They loose hands. The bride takes the bridegroom's right hand in hers and
     makes the vow:*

I *N*, take you *N*, to be my husband,
to have and to hold from this day forward;
for better for worse, for richer for poorer,
in sickness and in health,
to love and to cherish and to honour in the Lord,
till we are separated by death, according to God's
holy law; and this is my solemn vow.
Amen.

They loose hands.

10   *The Priest receives the rings and prays:*

Priest   Bless O Lord, these *rings* to be a reminder of the vows
          by which *N* and *N* now affirm their commitment to each
          other; through Jesus Christ our Lord. **Amen.**

11   *The bridegroom puts the ring on the third finger of the bride's left hand, or
     the symbol in its appropriate place, and says:*

Groom   **N, I give you this *ring* as a symbol of our marriage.
         With the help of God, I shall love you and honour
         you with all that I am and all that I have, all the
         days of my life. In the name of the Father, Son and
         the Holy Spirit. Amen.**

Likewise the bride to the bridegroom:

Bride   **N, I give you this *ring* as a symbol of our marriage.
         With the help of God, I shall love you and honour
         you with all that I am and all that I have, all the
         days of my life. In the name of the Father, Son, and
         the Holy Spirit. Amen.**

12   *The priest joins the right hands of the couple and says:*

Now that *N*, and *N*, have committed themselves to each other by
solemn vows, with the joining of hands and the giving and receiving
of *rings* in the presence of God and you all, I pronounce them
husband and wife, in the name of the Father, Son, and the Holy
Spirit. **Amen.**

Priest   Those whom God has joined together,
People   **No one should separate.**

Priest	God the maker of marriages,
People	**Unite their hearts in one.**

Ululation and clapping as the couple hugs. A doxology may follow.

13   *The couple faces the congregation. The priest says:*

Priest	Brothers and sisters in the Lord, *N* and *N* are going to begin a new life of partnership in marriage. The two will require your love, support and encouragement as they seek to uphold this honourable state. Do you promise to do your best to uphold them in their marriage covenant?
People	**We will uphold them.**

15   *The couple may choose to say this or other suitable prayer of commitment.*

O God our Father and author of marriage, we rejoice on this our wedding day. True to each other help us to stay, safely guarding all the solemn vows we have taken today. Never should the memories of this day grow dim with each passing day.

Progressing through life with its many hurdles, may selfless love be our banner; seeking ever to promote the other;

Rejoicing in our strengths and bearing with each other's weaknesses.

In all our days together, may we draw strength and comfort from you and from each other.

Guide us as we begin this new life; we know not what lies ahead. You are our refuge and underneath are your everlasting arms.

Bless our marriage Lord, and grant us many happy years together until we come to the wedding banquet of the Lamb. **Amen.**

16   *Ululation, and a song.*

17   *The priest, standing before the couple, may use the following prayer of invocation.*

	May the Lord bless your marriage,
All	**Bless your marriage.**

*	*May he bless you with children,*
All	***Bless you with children.***

	May he give you joy and happiness,
All	**Joy and happiness.**

May love and forgiveness be the banner in your marriage,

All   **Forgiveness and love.**

May you be actively involved in the life of the Church,

All   **Be actively involved.**

May he bless the work of your hands,

All   **The work of your hands.**

May he bless your herds and flocks,

All   **Your herds and flocks.**

May your fields yield abundantly,

All   **Yield abundantly.**

May Christ be the head of your home,

All   **To bless your going out and your coming in.**

*   *This part is optional*

18   *AND/OR (The couple kneel)*

Priest   Eternal God, creator and preserver of all humankind, giver of all spiritual grace and author of everlasting life, send your blessing upon *N*, and *N*, whom we bless in your name, that as Isaac and Rebecca lived faithfully together, so *N* and *N* may surely perform and keep the vow and covenant made between them, may ever remain in perfect love and peace together and live according to your laws: through Jesus Christ our Lord. **Amen.**

Then this blessing:

God bless you and keep you. May he look upon you and fill you with all blessings that spring from his gracious favour, that you may have a wonderful life together, and in the world to come share in the life everlasting; through Jesus Christ our Lord. **Amen.**

19   As our Saviour taught us, we are bold to pray:

All   **Our Father in heaven,**
hallowed be your name,
your kingdom come,
   your will be done,
on earth as in heaven.

Give us today our daily bread.
Forgive us our sins,
as we forgive those
who sin against us.
Lead us not into temptation
but deliver us from evil.
For the kingdom,
the power, and the
glory are yours,
now and for ever. Amen.

PSALMS
One of the following psalms may be said or sang.

20   *Psalm 128*
Blessed is everyone who fears the Lord:
  and walks in the confine of his way.
You will eat of the fruit of your labours;
happy shall you be and all shall go well with you.
Your wife within your house:
  shall be as a fruitful vine,
your children around your table,
  like the fresh shoots of the olive.
Behold thus shall the man be blessed;
  who lives in the fear of the Lord.
May the Lord so bless you from Zion;
that you see Jerusalem in
  prosperity all the days of your life.
May you see your children's children and in
  your home let there be peace.

Glory to the Father, Son and the Holy Spirit.
As it was in the beginning, is now and ever shall be. Amen.

21   *Psalm 121*
I lift up my eyes to the hills–where does my help come from?
My help comes from the Lord, the Maker of heaven and earth.
He will not let your foot slip–he who watches over you will not
    slumber; Indeed, he who watches over Israel will neither
slumber nor sleep.
The Lord watches over you–the Lord is your shade at your
    right hand; The sun will not harm you by day, nor the
moon by night.

The Lord will keep you from all harm–he will watch over your life; The Lord will watch over your coming and going both now and forever more.

Glory to the Father, Son and the Holy Spirit.
As it was in the beginning, is now and ever shall be. Amen.

22 *Psalm 67*

Let God be gracious to us and bless us; and make his face shine
  upon us, that your ways may be known on earth:
Your liberating power among all nations. Let the people praise
  you O God:
Let all the people praise you. Let the nations be glad and sing;
  for you judge the people with integrity and govern the
nations upon earth.
Let the people praise you O God: Let all the people praise you.
Then the earth will yield its fruitfulness, and God our God will
bless us.
  God shall bless us and all the ends of the earth will fear him.
Glory to the Father, Son and the Holy Spirit.
As it was in the beginning, is now and ever shall be. Amen.

23 *MINISTRY OF THE WORD*
The lessons(s) may be selected from these or other appropriate texts.
Genesis 1:26-28; 2:4-9; Song of Solomon 2:10-13; 8:6-7;
Colossians 3:12-17; Matthew 7:21-27; 19:3-12; John 2:1-11.

24 *Hymn*

25 *Sermon*

26 *Signing of certificates, as offering is taken.*

27 *People sit. The couple kneel.*

  Priest   Let us pray.

28 *Prayer for the blessing of children.*

  We praise you, Father for creating us in
  your own image and for your gracious gift
  whereby humankind is increased,
  give to *N,* and *N,* the blessing of children,
  and grant them the wisdom and grace to bring them up in the
  discipline and instruction of the Lord,
  to the praise and honour of Jesus Christ our Lord. **Amen.**

29 *Blessing*

God the Father, God the Son, God the Holy Spirit,
bless, preserve, and keep you; the Lord mercifully with his favour
look upon you and fill you with all spiritual benediction and grace,
that you may faithfully live together in this life and in the age to
come have life everlasting. **Amen.**

30 *SHARING OF PEACE*

Priest   The peace of the Lord be always with you.
All   **And also with you.**

People greet one another.

Priest (to the couple)
              N and *N,* Go in Peace and in Christ begin you marriage.
All   **Thanks be to God.**

31 *Wedding march, or recessional hymn, as the bridal procession leaves the
Church.*

Blessing of Marriage

NOTES

- This service is for Christian couples who may have been married either through customary or civil arrangements, and now wish to have their marriage blessed in church.

- In the case of customary marriage, first the banns must be published in the couple's respective church(es) three consecutive Sundays prior to the wedding day in the following form:

  I wish to give notice of the blessing of marriage between *NN* and *NN*. If anyone of you has any just cause why this marriage may not be blessed in church, you are to declare it. This is the first (*second, or third*) notice.

- In case any impediment is presented, the service shall not continue until matters have been sorted out through legal procedures in accordance with the African Christian Marriage Act.

- Symbols other than a ring may be used where this is the acceptable cultural style.

- For the civil married, after the blessing of the rings (or other symbols) the priest goes on from section 13 "The couple kneels ...." There is no signing of certificates as this is presumed to have already taken place.

- During this service, the wife should be to the right and the husband to the left of the priest.

ORDER OF SERVICE

1   *At the entrance, a hymn, psalm or anthem may be sang or instrumental music played.*
    Procession into the church is led by the Priest and the couple to be blessed walks together without holding hands, to the chancel steps.

2   *Hymn*

3   *Priest*   The Lord be with you
    All   **And also with you**

4   *People remain standing. The priest addresses the congregation:*

Dearly beloved, we have come together at this time before God, to witness and celebrate the blessing of marriage, of *NN* and *NN*, and pray for His blessings upon them now and in the years ahead.

Marriage is a gift of God and a means of grace. God himself ordained it when, in the Garden of Eden he created our first parents, Adam and Eve, and joined them for a life-long companionship. Jesus blessed this manner of life when he responded to a wedding invitation in Cana of Galilee where he performed his first miracle.

It is God's intention in marriage that husband and wife commit themselves to each other in love and in so doing reflect Christ's relationship with his Church.

In marriage, husband and wife belong to each other and they commit themselves to each other in absolute fidelity, love and respect. They are to comfort and fulfil each other's needs, emotional or physical. Marriage makes possible the full expression of love between husband and wife.

Marriage provides an environment into which children may be born and brought to maturity in the knowledge and fear of the Lord for the well being of the family and the community at large.

This is a solemn state of life and is not to be undermined. Those who enter marriage must respect and uphold each other faithfully and lovingly, to the honour of God and the glory of his name.

It is to this manner of life that *N* and *N* come now to be joined. If any of you can show just cause why they should not be joined, you must declare it now *(pause)*, or forever hold your peace.

MAKING OF PROMISES

The couple stands before the Priest who leads them in the making of promises.

5 *Priest (to the man):*

> *N*, will you before God and this congregation declare that *N*, is your wife, and that it is your desire to live together with her in the biblical covenant of marriage?

Man **Yes, I will.**

Priest Will you also declare that you will at all times love her, cherish her, honour her, comfort and protect her, and forsaking all others, be faithful to her as long as you both shall live?

Man: **Yes, I will.**

6   *Priest (to the woman):*

                  N, will you before God and this congregation declare that *N,* is your husband, and that it is your desire to live with him in the biblical covenant of marriage?

Woman: **Yes, I will.**

Priest   Will you also declare that you will at all times love him, cherish him, honour him, comfort and protect him, and forsaking all others, be faithful to him as long as you both shall live?

Woman: **Yes, I will.**

7   *The priest leads them in making the vows. The congregation may respond appropriately by clapping, ululation e.t.c. each time a vow is made.*

8   *Husband faces wife and takes her by her right hand and says the following:*

**I, *N*, declare before God and this congregation
assembled here that you *N*, are my beloved wife,
to have and to hold; for better for worse,
for richer for poorer, in sickness and in health,
to love and to cherish and to honour in the Lord,
till we are separated by death, according to God's holy law;
and this is my solemn vow. In the name of the Father, Son,
and the Holy Spirit. Amen.**

9   *The woman still facing her husband and taking his right hand in hers, says:*

**I *N*, declare before God and this congregation
assembled here that you *N*, are my beloved husband,
to have and to hold; for better for worse,
for richer for poorer, in sickness and in health,
to love and to cherish and to honour in the Lord,
till we are separated by death, according to God's holy law;
and this is my solemn vow. In the name of the Father, Son,
and the Holy Spirit. Amen.**

10 *They loose hands. The priest takes the rings (or other marriage symbols) and blesses them as follows:*

Priest   Bless O Lord, these *rings* to be a reminder of the vows by which *N,* and *N,* now reaffirm themselves to each other; through Jesus Christ our Lord. Amen.

11 *The husband places the ring on the third finger of his wife's left hand, or the symbol in its appropriate place, and says:*

Husband   N, I give you this ring as an outward mark that you are my wife. With all that I am, and all that we have, I honour you. In the name of the Father, Son, and of the Holy Spirit. Amen.

12 *The woman likewise and similarly affirms:*

Wife   N, I give you this ring as an outward mark that you are my husband. With all that I am, and all that we have, I honour you. In the name of the Father, Son, and the Holy Spirit. **Amen.**

13 *The couple kneels and join their right hands.*

Priest   Now that N and N have before God, and this congregation, renewed their vows of commitment to one another in marriage, I now bless their union. In the name of the Father, Son, and the Holy Spirit. **Amen.**

Priest   Those whom God has joined together,
People   **No one should separate.**

Priest   God the maker of marriages,
People   **Unite their hearts in one.**

14 *Clapping, ululation and other forms of appropriate applause.*

15 *Notices   (During this time entertainment through song and dance is welcome, if time allows.)*

16 *Hymn*

17 *Sermon*

18 *Signing of Certificates/Offertory*

19 *LITANY OF BLESSINGS FOR THE COUPLE*
    The congregation may stand. The couple stand facing the Priest.

Priest   Lord we thank you for the marriage estate and the beauty of family life.
People   **We thank you Lord.**

Priest   For N, and N, and the blessing of their marriage.
People   **We thank you Lord.**

Priest	For publicly declaring their love for each other.
People	**We thank you Lord.**
Priest	**Bless their children and their children's children.*
People	***Bless them Lord.***
Priest	May love and forgiveness be the banner in their marriage.
People	**Forgiveness and love.**
Priest	May they be actively involved in the life of the Church.
People	**Be actively involved.**

20 *OR/AND this prayer*

Priest Everlasting God, who created Adam and Eve and ordered that a man shall leave his father and mother, be joined to his wife and the two shall become one flesh; pour your blessings upon *N* and *N*, and grant that they shall be to one another a constant source of comfort, joy and strength. May *this man* love *his wife* completely and selflessly, and may *this woman* reciprocate the love with submission and reverence. **Grant them the joy of parenthood, and the commitment to bring up their children in the fear of God, and for the glory of his name.* **Amen.**

* *This portion may be left out if and when not applicable.*

Priest As our Saviour taught us, we are bold to pray:

All **Our Father in heaven,**
hallowed be your name,
your kingdom come,
your will be done,
on earth as in heaven.
Give us today our daily bread.
Forgive us our sins,
as we forgive those who sin against us.
Lead us not into temptation
but deliver us from evil.
For the kingdom, the power and the
glory are yours,
now and for ever. Amen.

22 *FINAL BLESSING*

Priest   God the Father, God the Son and God the Holy Spirit,
bless, preserve and keep you; the Lord mercifully look upon
you with favour, and fill you with all grace that you may
faithfully live together in this life and in the age to come
have everlasting life. And the blessing of God Almighty,
Father, Son, and the Holy Spirit, be upon you and remain
with you always. **Amen.**

23 *Recessional hymn as the couple leaves the church.*

Reaffirmation of Marriage Vows

NOTES

- This service may be used for wedding anniversaries like Silver Jubilee, Golden Jubilee or any other occasion as might seem suitable.

- The service may also be used by couples who have at one time broken up and now wish to come back together with greater commitment.

- The service may be conducted on its own or in the context of Holy Communion, or Morning Worship.

ORDER OF SERVICE

1   *People are already gathered inside the church.*

2   *Hymn, during which the couple, holding hands and followed by their witnesses and children (if they have thus been blessed), process to the church, led by the priest. They remain standing.*

3   *Priest*   The Lord be with you.
    People   **And also with you**

    Priest   Dearly beloved, we are gathered here to join *N,* and *N,* in rejoicing and giving thanks to God for the time they have lived as husband and wife, and to ask for His blessings upon them *and their children.*

4   *People sit. The Priest continues:*

Marriage is a gift of God and a means of grace. God himself ordained it when, in the Garden of Eden he created our first parents, Adam and Eve, and joined them for a life-long companionship. Jesus blessed this manner of life when he responded to a wedding invitation in Cana of Galilee where he performed his first miracle.

It is God's intention in marriage that husband and wife commit themselves to each other in love and in so doing reflect Christ's relationship with his Church.

In marriage, husband and wife belong to each other and they commit themselves to one another in absolute fidelity, love and respect. They are to comfort and fulfil each other's needs, emotional or physical.

Marriage makes possible the full expression of love between husband and wife.

Marriage provides an environment into which children may be born and brought to maturity in the knowledge and fear of the Lord for the well being of the family and the community at large.

This is a solemn state of life and is not to be undermined.

Those who enter marriage must respect and uphold each other faithfully and lovingly, to the honour of God and the glory of his name.

We rejoice with *N*, and *N*, as they give thanks to God for calling them into this state, and as they reaffirm their vows of love and mutual fidelity for the years ahead.

5   *Priest:*   Let us pray:

Our help is in the name of the Lord,
Who made heaven and earth. *(Psalm 124:8)*

Unless the Lord builds the house,
Its builders labour in vain. *(Psalm 127:1)*

Blessed is he who fears the Lord,
Who walks in his ways. *(Psalm 128:1)*

Almighty God, our heavenly Father, who sets the lonely in families and causes them to be fruitful and secure, we beseech you to have mercy upon us as we put our hope in you. Be with us on this joyous occasion, as your Son was with those at the wedding in Cana of Galilee. We pray that you may present to us your best gift, your own presence. We pray this through the same Jesus Christ, our Lord. **Amen.**

6   *The couple stands facing the Priest who conducts the renewal of vows.*

Priest: Do you solemnly promise to keep the vows and the promises you made on your wedding day?

Couple: **We do.**

Priest: Do you solemnly promise, that you will continue to love and uphold each other, and that under all circumstances you will strive to cherish and protect each other?

Couple: **We do.**

Priest: Do you promise to cultivate a Christian environment in your home and to encourage each other in godly living and Christian service?

Couple: **We do.**

7 *Re-dedication of rings or other wedding symbols: the original rings may be re-dedicated. If new ones have been bought, they are dedicated afresh.*

We *re*-dedicate these *rings*, that through them, *N,* and *N,* shall always be reminded of the vows of their covenant of unending love and faithfulness which they took on their wedding day, and which they have reaffirmed today.

We *re*-dedicate these *rings* in the name of the Father, Son, and the Holy Spirit. **Amen.**

(Exchange of rings or other marriage symbols ensues. The priest may look for suitable wording for this).

8 *The couple kneel and join hands. Their children may kneel by their parents side. The Priest prays:*

Most merciful and gracious God, sanctify and bless these your servants, and pour out the riches of your grace upon them that, living faithfully together they may please you and live in happy union with each other to their lives' end; through Jesus Christ our Lord. **Amen.**

9 *The priest may also read this scripture when marriage has been blessed with children.*

Children are a reward from the Lord.
Like arrows in the hands of a warrior
are children born in one's youth.
Blessed is the man whose quiver is full of them
They will not be put to shame when they contend
with their enemies in the gate. *(Psalm.127: 1-3)*

10 *Priest:* Let us pray.

O God our Father who makes and sustains marriages, we beseech you to bestow your blessing upon these your servants whom you have appointed to dwell together under the shelter of the same roof, and cause your mercies to rest upon their household. Bless their going out and their coming in. Prosper them in all their worthy undertakings; and whether in prosperity or adversity, in health or in sickness, let them know that your Fatherly hand is upon them for good. Supply all their needs according to the riches of your grace. (Bless the children of their home.) Grant your mercy to all those who are dear to them wherever they are, and shelter all your children in your love. Through Jesus Christ our Lord. **Amen.**

11 *Blessing*

God the Father,
God the Son,
God the Holy Spirit,
Bless, preserve and keep you;
The Lord pour upon you the riches of his grace,
That you may continue faithful together
And receive the blessings of eternal life.
Through Jesus Christ our Lord. **Amen.**

The couple return to their seats.

12 *A hymn may be sang*

13 *Proverbs 31:10-31 and/or another scriptural reading*

14 *Sermon*

15 *Hymn/Offertory*

16 *If this service is being conducted in the context of Holy Communion, the rest of the service may continue from THE PRAYERS OF PENITENCE or else:*

17 *THE BLESSING*

Burial Service

NOTES

- This Service is not to be used for those who die unbaptised, excommunicated or those who have committed suicide.

- The burial service is best accompanied by pastoral care being exercised for the bereaved before, during and afterwards.

- It is not necessary that any part of this service be conducted inside a place of worship. The whole of it may take place on the burial site. Intercessory prayers may be used at any stage, for instance, at the mortuary, but the service should not be divided except when the body has to be transported to the site of the grave.

- The burial service should not be interrupted once it has began.

- Eulogies should be well organized and strictly controlled.

- The Synod of the Anglican Church of Kenya has advised that the whole burial service should not exceed two hours; feeding should be very minimal, if any.

- A simple and inexpensive burial is advised: burial ceremonies should not overtake the resources of the bereaved.

- Any traditional custom, or way of placing the body, which is not repugnant to Christian faith, can be incorporated in the service. The synod of ACK to offer guidance on this.

- After the burial, the minister or any other authorized church member should escort the bereaved back to their home if possible.

- Follow up visitations are encouraged for purposes of pastoral support and fellowship.

ORDER OF SERVICE

1   *If the minister(s) and the bereaved proceed with the body to the place of the service, some of the following Bible sentences are to be said in an audible voice.*

The grass withers and the flowers fall, because the breath of the Lord blows on them. Surely the people are grass. *(Isaiah 40:7)*

Blessed are those that mourn for they will be comforted. *(Matthew 5:4)*

Precious in the sight of the Lord is the death of his saints. *(Psalm 116:15)* The saying is sure: If we have died with him, we shall also live with him; If we endure, we shall also reign with him; If we deny him, he also will deny us; If we are faithless, he remains faithful – for he cannot deny himself. *(2Timothy 2:11-13)*

For God so loved the world that he gave his only Son, that whoever believes in him should not perish but have eternal life. *(John 3:16)*

Since the children have flesh and blood, he too shared in their humanity so that by his death he might destroy him who holds the power of death – that is, the devil. *(Hebrews 2:14)*

To him who overcomes, I will give the right to sit with me on the throne, just as I overcame and sat down with my Father on his throne. *(Revelation 3:21)*

Tell the next generation that this is God, our God for ever and ever; he himself will guide us up to death. *(Psalm 48:14)*

Be faithful unto death and I will give you the crown of life. *(Revelation 2:10).*

2   *Hymn*

3   *Minister*   We have come together to lay to rest the body of *our brother/sister N,* whom the Lord has called to himself. Yet we believe that since Jesus died and rose again, so it will be for those who die in Christ. For God will bring them to life with Jesus.

    All   **Heavenly Father in your Son Jesus Christ, you have given us a true faith and a sure hope. Strengthen this faith and this hope in us all our days that we may live as those who believe in the communion of saints, the forgiveness of sins, and the resurrection to eternal life. Amen.**

This Litany may be used.

For everything there is a season, and a time for every matter under heaven:

a time to be born,
   and a time to die;
a time to plant,
   and a time to pluck;
a time to weep,
   and a time to laugh;
a time to mourn,
   and a time to dance;
a time to cast away stones,
   and a time to gather them;
a time to embrace,
   and a time to refrain from embracing;
a time to seek,
   and a time to loose;
a time to keep,
   and a time to cast away;
a time to rend,
   and a time to sew;
a time to keep silent,
   and a time to speak.
                    (Ecclesiastes 3:2-8)

5   *The Psalm (either 23 or 121). Or one of these: Psalms 16:1-11; 49:7-15; 73:21-28; 139:1-18.*

Psalm 23
The Lord is my shepherd I shall not be in want;
   He makes me lie down in green pastures:
he leads me beside still waters.
   He restores my soul.
He leads me in paths of righteousness;
   for his name's sake.
Even though I walk through the valley
   of the shadow of death,
I will fear no evil; for you are with me:
   your rod and your staff, they comfort me.
You prepare a table before me:
   in the presence of my enemies;

you anoint my head with oil: my cup overflows.
Surely goodness and mercy shall follow me:
all the days of my life;
and I shall dwell in the house of the Lord
forever. Amen.

Psalm 121
I lift up my eyes to the hills:
where does my help come from?
My help comes from the Lord:
who made heaven and earth.
He who will not let your foot be moved;
he who keeps you will not slumber.
Behold, he who keeps Israel
will neither slumber nor sleep.
The Lord is your keeper:
the Lord is your shade on your right hand.
The sun shall not hurt you by day:
nor the moon by night.
The Lord will keep you from all harm:
he will keep your life.
The Lord will keep your going out and coming in
from this time forth and for evermore. Amen.

6   *Eulogy/Tributes*

7   *Hymn*

8   *Readings:*
One of the following passages is read:

Isaiah 25:6-9
On this mountain the Lord Almighty will
prepare a feast of rich food for all people,
a banquet of aged wine – the best of meats and the finest
of wines.
On this mountain he will destroy the shroud that enfolds
all people,
the sheet that covers all nations.
He will swallow up death for ever.
The sovereign Lord will wipe away the tears from all faces.
He will remove the disgrace of his people
from all the earth.

The Lord has spoken.
In that day they will say, see, this is our God;
  we trusted in him, and he saved us.
This is the Lord, we trusted in him;
  let us rejoice and be glad in his salvation.

9 *I Thessalonians 4:14-18*
We believe that Jesus died and rose again,
  and so we believe that God will bring with Jesus
  those who have fallen asleep in him.
According to the Lord's own word,
we tell you that we who are still alive,
  who are left till the coming of the Lord,
shall not precede those who have fallen asleep.
For the Lord himself will come down from heaven,
  with a loud command, with the voice of the archangel
and with the trumpet call of God,
  and the dead in Christ will rise first.
After that, we who are still alive,
who are left, will be caught up together with them
  to meet the Lord in the air.
And so we will be with the Lord forever.
Therefore encourage each other with these words.

10 *Revelation 20:11-15*
Then I saw a great white throne and him who
was seated on it.
  Earth and sky fled from his presence,
and there was no place for them.
And I saw the dead, great and small,
  standing before the throne, and books were opened.
Another book was opened, which is the book of life.
The dead were judged according to what they had done
  as recorded in the books.
The sea gave up the dead that were in it,
and Death and Hades gave up the dead that were in them,
  and each person was judged according to what he had done.
Then Death and Hades were thrown into the lake of fire.
The lake of fire is the second death.
  If anyone's name was not found written in the book of life,
he was thrown into the lake of fire.

11 *Revelation 21:1-4*
Then I saw a new heaven and a new earth,
for the first heaven and the first earth had passed away,
   and there was no longer any sea.
I saw the Holy City, the new Jerusalem,
coming down out of heaven from God,
   prepared as a bride beautifully dressed for her husband.
And I heard a loud voice from the throne saying,
"Now the dwelling of God is with the people,
   and he will live with them.
They will be his people,
and God himself will be with them and be their God.
   He will wipe every tear from their eyes.
There will be no more death or mourning or crying or pain,
for the old order of things has passed away."

12 *Or one of these passages: John 6:35-40; 14:1-13; Romans 4:1-17; 5; 6:5-14; 8:31-39; 1Cor 15:20-28;*

13 *Hymn*

14 *Sermon*

15 *Offertory (optional)*

PRAYERS OF INTERCESSION

These may be selected as appropriate. See other prayers starting section 34.

16 *Minister*   Let us in silence thank God in our hearts for *N's* life,
each of us remembering what he/she has meant to us.

The minister may prayerfully lead the mourners in a memorial prayer, mentioning some of the most significant things about the departed, and offering thanks to God and then says:

Receive our thanks Lord and grant that we shall treasure the memories of our *loved one*, with sadness and with joy that we were blessed to know *him* and to share in *his* life. Through Jesus Christ our Lord. **Amen.**

Grant Lord that we who are still alive shall constantly be reminded that life is fleetingly short. Help us therefore to daily walk in your footsteps; making the best use of our varied talents and living each day as though it were our last. Give us abundant grace to cope with the difficult episodes in our lives, and soberness as we enjoy the lighter moments. Through Jesus Christ our Lord. **Amen.**

17   Most merciful God, whose wisdom is beyond our understanding, deal graciously with the family of *N* in their grief. May the Holy Spirit the comforter minister to them, that they may not be overwhelmed by their sorrow; grant them the peace that passes all understanding, and strength to meet the day ahead, through Jesus Christ our Lord. **Amen.**

18   Almighty God, through the death of your Son on the cross your love overcame death for us. Through his burial and resurrection from the dead you have restored to us eternal life. We therefore remember those who died believing in Jesus and are buried with him in the hope of rising again. O God of the living and the dead, may those who faithfully trusted in you on earth praise you for ever in the joy of heaven. We ask this in the name of Jesus Christ our Lord. **Amen.**

19   God of all consolation, in your unending love and mercy for us you turn the darkness of death into the dawn of new life. Show compassion to your people in their sorrow. Be our refuge and our strength, to lift us from the darkness of this grief to the peace and light of your presence. **Amen.**

20   Your Son Jesus Christ, by dying for us, conquered death and by rising again restored life. May we then go forward eagerly to meet him and after our life on earth is over be reunited with our brothers and sisters in the land where there will be no death and no sorrow, and where every tear will be wiped away. Through Jesus Christ the conqueror. **Amen.**

21   O Lord, support us all the day long of this turbulent life, until the shades lengthen, and the evening comes, and the busy world is hushed, the fever of life is over, and our work is done. Then, Lord, in your mercy grant us safer lodging, a holy rest, and peace at last, through Jesus Christ our Lord. **Amen.**

As the procession leaves the church, the minister says:

EITHER

22   May the angels lead you into paradise;
May the martyrs come to welcome you
and take you to the holy city, the new

and eternal Jerusalem.
May the choir of angels welcome you
where Lazarus is poor no longer.
May you have eternal rest.
Through Jesus Christ our Lord. **Amen.**

OR

23 Give rest O Christ to your servant with the saints,
where sorrow and pain are no more.
Neither sighing but life everlasting;
You only are immortal,
The creator and maker of all;
And we are mortal, formed of the earth
And to the earth we shall return
as you ordained when you created us saying:
'dust you are, to dust you shall return';
We all go down to the dust,
And weeping at the grave we make our song,
Alleluia, alleluia, alleluia.

24 *Hymn*

25 *PROCESSION TO THE GRAVE*

Hymns or choruses may be sang interspersed with one or more of the following sentences:

I am the resurrection and the life; he who believes in me, will live, even though he dies; and whoever lives and believes in me will never die. (*John 11:25*)

The Lord gave and the Lord has taken away. Blessed be the name of the Lord. *(Job 1:21)*

Multitudes who sleep in the dust of the earth will awake: some to everlasting life, others to shame and everlasting contempt. Those who are wise will shine like the brightness of the heavens, and those who lead many to righteousness, like the stars for ever and ever. (*Daniel 12:2,3*)

I know that my Redeemer lives, and that in the end he will stand upon the earth. And after my skin has been destroyed, yet in my flesh I will see God; I myself will see him with my own eyes – I, and not another. How my heart yearns within me! *(Job 19:25-27)*

This grace was given us in Christ Jesus before the beginning of time, but it has now been revealed through the appearing of our Saviour, Christ Jesus, who has destroyed death and has brought life and immortality to light through the Gospel. (*2 Timothy 1:9b,10*)

For we brought nothing into the world, and we can take nothing out of it. (*1 Timothy 6:7*)

He who overcomes will, like them, be dressed in white. I will never blot out his name from the book of life, but will acknowledge his name before my Father and his angels. *(Revelation 3:5)*

Do not be amazed at this, for a time is coming when all who are in their graves will hear his voice and come out, those who have done good will rise to live, and those who have done evil will rise to be condemned. *(John 5:28)*

In my Father's house are many rooms; If it were not so, I would have told you. I am going there to prepare a place for you. And if I go and prepare a place for you, I will come back and take you to be with me that you also may be where I am. *(John 14:2-3)*

26 *CONSECRATING THE GRAVE*

The minister may consecrate the grave with this prayer:

Minister   Lord Jesus Christ, through your own time in the grave, you made the graves of all believers sacred. May the body of *N,* lie peacefully in the earth, and may *he* participate in your resurrection, through the power of the Holy Spirit. **Amen**

27   *The body is lowered into the grave, after which there is silence:*

28 *COMMITTAL*

Minister   Lord, have mercy upon us.
All   **Christ, have mercy upon us.**
Minister   Lord, have mercy upon us.

Minister   Then I heard a voice from heaven say, "Write: Blessed are the dead who die in the Lord from now on." "Yes," says the Spirit, "they will rest from their labour, for their deeds will follow them". *(Revelation 14:13)*

Therefore, trusting in God's abundant provision of grace and in his gift of righteousness through the one person Jesus Christ, we give the spirit of our *brother* here departed, into the everlasting arms of God to take *him* to himself, while we commit *his* body to the ground:

The minister casts soil over the body, saying:

Earth to earth, ashes to ashes, dust to dust. For all the redeemed of the Lord, our sure hope is in the resurrection to eternal life through Jesus Christ, our Lord, who shall change our perishable body so that it may be raised like his glorious body, according to the working of his mighty strength which he exerted in Christ when he raised him from the dead and seated him at his right hand far above all rule and authority, power and dominion, for ever and ever. **Amen.**

29 *Minister*   They are before the throne of God and serve him day and night in his temple; and he who sits on the throne will spread his tent over them. Never again will they hunger; never again will they thirst. The sun will not beat upon them, nor any scorching heat. For the Lamb at the centre of the throne will be their shepherd; he will lead them to springs of living water; And God will wipe away every tear from their eyes. *(Revelation 7:15-17)*

30 *Minister*   As our Saviour taught us, we are bold to pray:

All   **Our Father in heaven,**
hallowed be your name,
your kingdom come,
your will be done,
on earth as in heaven.
Give us today our daily bread.
Forgive us our sins,
as we forgive those who sin against us.
Lead us not into temptation
but deliver us from evil.
For the kingdom, the power and the
glory are yours,
now and for ever. Amen.

31 *Hymns are sang as the grave is filled.*

32 *Erecting of the cross (optional)*

33 *The Blessing OR The Grace*
    Blessing (one of the following may be used)

> *Minister*   The Lord bless you and keep you;
> the Lord make his face shine upon you and be gracious
> to you; the Lord turn his face towards you and give you
> peace. *(Numbers 6:24-26)*
> And the blessing of God Almighty, the Father, the Son,
> and the Holy Spirit, be among you and remain with you
> always. **Amen.**

OR

> Now to him who is able to do immeasurably more than
> all we ask or imagine, according to his power that is at
> work within us, to him be glory in the church and in
> Christ Jesus throughout all generations, for ever and
> ever! *(Ephesians 3:20-21)*
> And the blessing of God Almighty, the Father, the Son,
> and the Holy Spirit, be among you and remain with you
> always. **Amen.**

OR

> The peace of God, which passes all understanding, keep
> your hearts and minds in the knowledge and love of God,
> and of his Son, Jesus Christ our Lord. *(Philippians 4:7)*
> And the blessing of God Almighty, the Father, the Son,
> and the Holy Spirit, be among you and remain with you
> always. **Amen.**

The Grace, introduced with these words:

> *Lay minister*   Now may our Lord Jesus Christ himself, and God
> our Father, who loved us and gave eternal comfort
> and good hope through grace, comfort our hearts
> and establish them in every good work and word.
> **And may the grace of our Lord Jesus Christ,**
> **the love of God, and the fellowship of the Holy**
> **Spirit, be with us and remain with us, now and**
> **for evermore. Amen.** *(2 Thessalonians 2:16 -17)*

OTHER PRAYERS WHICH MAY BE USED IN VARIOUS
CIRCUMSTANCES OF DEATH

34 *Young child*

O God our Father and Father of our ancestors, who alone understands the mystery of life and death, you know and understand the agony of losing a child. You assured us through your Son, that the angels of the little ones are always in your presence. May this comforting assurance bring added consolation to the parents and relatives of this child as they ponder the loss. You are our refuge and strength in times of sorrow, and not a single tear drop escapes your attention. Grant this child the blessing of eternal life in the land where there will be no more pain or sorrow or death, and where every teardrop will be wiped away. Through Jesus Christ our Saviour. **Amen.**

35 *Accident*

O Lord God Almighty, author of all knowledge, we thank you that by your everlasting power you enable your people to invent many things including instruments like vehicles and others, that make travelling easy and fast. But Lord we are sad that, many people including our *brother* here have died from accidents involving these vessels. Hear us Lord as we pray that you would instil in all drivers a sense of responsibility over the people they carry; cause them to respect the sanctity of human life and as much as possible seek to protect the lives under their care.

And when all this is done, grant us, Lord, your protection on the roads, the air and the sea, so that we may be safeguarded against sudden deaths. Through Jesus Christ our Lord. **Amen.**

There is shock and disbelief in our hearts Lord, and especially the immediate family of *N*. Why, why, why...? may be their unending question. Bring comfort, assurance and consolation to these hearts Lord and help them to cope with the trauma of the death. May they be strengthened by the sure hope that for those who die in Christ, death is only a veil, and that soon they will be reunited with their loved one who has only gone ahead of them. We pray this through Jesus Christ who conquered death and now lives and reigns for ever more. **Amen.**

36 *Death through violence*

O God our Father, see the devastation in our hearts
as we ponder the painful, helpless and desperate
struggle *N* must have gone through as he gazed death
in the face. We are tearful and bitter at what Cain can still do
to his brother Abel. Calm our hearts with the peace of Jesus who was
himself killed violently though he was innocent, and who conquered
death, even for us.

Grant us peace that passes human understanding and enable us to
release *N* to your eternal rest and peace.

Grant that the perpetrators of such evil would never find peace and
rest except through departure from sin and acceptance of the saving
power of Jesus. Grant us that security that comes through the power
of the blood of Jesus, as we live and work in a world where people
have chosen to love darkness more than the light. We thank you for
the gift of N and for all that *he* meant to us; Help us Lord to know
how to live without *him*. Through Jesus Christ who conquered death
and Satan. **Amen.**

37 *After a wasting illness*

Lord we thank you for *N*. We are sad that *he* had to suffer so much
from the illness that afflicted *his* body. We agonised as we helplessly
watched him fight for dear life. We are thankful that *he* does not have
to suffer any more because *he* is finally released from the pains and
suffering of this life and is united with you and the angels in glory.
While we prayed and wished for *his* physical recovery, we knew you
had the most perfect plan for *him*. We have no doubt now that you
have healed *him* completely, never to suffer these earthly pains or
live in constant fear of death. Death is conquered indeed. We thank
you for all who cared for *him*. Bless the efforts of the doctors who
work so hard looking for new knowledge to cure diseases and
prolong lives. Grant this knowledge Lord and bless your people with
the gift of long life. (Help us to be responsible stewards of our lives
and to guard against dangerous behaviour that can harshly cut short
our years on earth.) Through Jesus Christ our Lord. **Amen.**

38　*Old Age*

Those that wait upon the Lord have their strength renewed; they rise up with wings as eagles. They walk and do not grow weary, they run and do not grow faint.

Father we thank you for granting to *N* the gift of years. We thank you for taking *him* safely through dangers, toils and snares of this fleeting life. Your grace brought *him* safe thus far, and grace has finally led *him* home. Grant by the same grace, that our lives will be safely secured and guarded against the rolling billows of our life's tumultuous pilgrimage, and when our days on earth are over, bring us safely to the shores of our eternal home, where rested from our earthly toils, we shall live and rejoice with you eternally. Through Jesus Christ who lives and reigns forever, days without end. **Amen.**

39　*After any of these prayers, the priest may finish with the following prayer:*

Remember Lord those whose hearts are most affected by the departure of *N;* Visit them Lord, to comfort and strengthen them in this period of grief when they find it so difficult to cope with the facts. Fill them with the shining light of Jesus' resurrection, and grant them the peace that passes all understanding. Grant our prayers Father, through Jesus Christ who died for us and shares all our pain with us. **Amen.**

Burial of One Who Has Committed Suicide

NOTES

• This service is to be conducted at the graveyard.

• It may not be necessary for the ministers to robe.

ORDER OF SERVICE

1 *The minister reads some of the following sentences:*

Our Saviour Jesus Christ says: "Do not let your hearts be troubled. Trust in God; trust also in me." *(John 14:1)*

Peace I leave with you; my peace I give you. I do not give to you as the world gives. Do not let your hearts be troubled and do not be afraid. *(John 14:27)*

I have told you these things, so that in me you may have peace. In this world you will have trouble. But take heart! I have overcome the world. *(John 16:33)*

Therefore, since we have a great high priest who has gone through the heavens, Jesus the Son of God, let us hold firmly to the faith we profess. For we do not have a high priest who is unable to sympathise with our weaknesses, but we have one who has been tempted in every way, just as we are – yet was without sin. *(Hebrews 4:14-16)*

We are hard pressed on every side, but not crushed; perplexed, but not in despair; persecuted, but not abandoned; struck down, but not destroyed. *(2 Corinthians 4:8-9)*

2 *Hymn*

3 *Eulogy*

4 *MINISTRY OF THE WORD*

   1st Reading: *Job 3: 1-26 or Jeremiah 20:15-18;*
                      or Lamentations 3:19-26.

   2nd Reading: *Luke 12:22-34 or 2 Corinthians 1:8-9.*

5 *Sermon*

6 *Intercessory Prayers*

A few people may be selected to offer intercessory prayers for the family of the deceased. Prayers may be interspersed with prayerful verses of known hymns or choruses after which the minister offers the following prayer:

7 Loving Father, we thank you for *N*. It is saddening, that he had to take his own life for reasons that may never be clearly understood by any of us. We can only imagine the anguish he experienced as he pondered the meaninglessness of staying alive. You alone understand the hearts and minds of people and the motives therein. We may have failed *N* when he needed us most; forgive us Lord. Relieve us from the pain and hurt we feel his action has caused us and help us to release him to eternity. Through Jesus Christ our Lord. **Amen.**

Help us to be mindful of each other's needs, touching others' lives with love and care, understanding and acceptance; that as we trudge along life's pilgrimage, burdens might be lighter and hopes brighter. Trusting Jesus' promise to give rest to all who come to him weary and with heavy hearts, we dare to approach the throne of grace for refreshment and rest from all that weighs heavily on our hearts and consciences. Grant these our prayers Lord:

All   **Through Jesus Christ who lives and reigns for ever more. Amen.**

Remember Lord those whose hearts are most affected by the departure of *N*; Visit them Lord, to comfort and strengthen them in this period of grief when they find it so difficult to cope with the facts. Fill them with the shining light of Jesus' resurrection, and grant them the peace that passes all understanding. Grant our prayers Father, through Jesus Christ who died for us and shares all our pain with us. **Amen.**

8 *PROCESSION TO THE GRAVE*

The minister shall say some of the following verses as he leads the way towards the grave site. Pall bearers and all the rest shall follow behind.
I am the resurrection and the life (said the Lord); he who believes in me will live, even though he dies; and whoever lives and believes in me will never die. *(John 11:25-26)*

The Lord is compassionate and gracious, slow to anger, abounding in love. He will not always accuse, nor harbour his anger for ever; He does not treat us as our sins deserve or repay us according to our iniquities. *(Psalm 103:8-10)*

Because of the Lord's great love we are not consumed, for his compassions never fail. They are new every morning; great is your faithfulness. *(Lamentations 3:22-23)*

For men are not cast off by the Lord for ever. Though he brings grief, he will show compassion, so great is his unfailing love. For he does not willingly bring affliction or grief to the children of men. *(Lamentations 3: 31-33)*

Do not be amazed at this, for a time is coming when all who are in their graves will hear his voice and come forth, those who have done good, to the resurrection of life, and those who have done evil, to the resurrection of judgement. *(John 5:28)*

9   *AT THE GRAVESIDE*
The coffin is lowered into the grave. The minister says:

Bless this place O Lord, where we now put *N*'s body to rest. And because it is only you Loving Father, who truly understand us inwardly, let your will be done on the spirit of *N,* as we commit his body to the soil: *(he casts earth on the body)* earth to earth, dust to dust, ashes to ashes.

The grave is filled.

10   *BENEDICTION*

Now to him that is able to keep you from falling and to present you faultless before the presence of his glory with exceeding joy, to the only wise God our Saviour, be glory and majesty, dominion and power, both now and for ever. **Amen.** *(Jude 24-25)*

11   *Or The Grace (which may be used by a lay leader, and introduced as follows:*

Now may our Lord Jesus Christ himself, and God our
Father, who loved us and gave eternal comfort and good
hope through grace, comfort our hearts and establish
them in every good work and word.
And may the grace of our Lord Jesus Christ,
the love of God, and the fellowship of the Holy Spirit,
be with us and remain with us, now and for evermore. Amen.
(2 Thessalonians 2:16 -17)

Alternative Burial Service

NOTES:

- This service may be used for those with a Christian heritage but who die before they are baptised.

- It may also be used for people of other faiths who at the time of death were interested in joining the Christian faith.

- It may also be used in situations where the dead person's religious identity, or walk with the Lord cannot be easily ascertained.

- This service is to be conducted at the graveside.

ORDER OF SERVICE

1 *Hymn*

2 *The minister reads a few appropriate sentences from the following or other selections:*

For the Lord is good and his love endures for ever; his faithfulness continues through all generations. *(Psalm 100:5)*

He will respond to the prayer of the destitute; he will not despise their plea. *(Psalm 102:17)*

The Lord is compassionate and gracious, slow to anger, abounding in love. He will not always accuse, nor will he harbour his anger for ever; he does not treat us as our sins deserve or repay us according to our iniquities. *(Psalm 103:8,10)*

Not every one who says to me, 'Lord, Lord', will enter the kingdom of heaven, but only he who does the will of my Father who is in heaven. *(Matthew 7:21)*

I have other sheep that are not of this sheep pen. I must bring them also. They too will listen to my voice, and there shall be one flock, and one shepherd. *(John 10:16)*

Let the children come to me, and do not hinder them; for the kingdom of God belongs to such as these. *(Mark 10:14)*

See that you do not look down on one of these little ones. For I tell you that their angels in heaven always see the face of my Father in heaven. *(Matthew 18:10)*

3   *Hymn*

4   *Eulogy/Tributes*

5   *MINISTRY OF THE WORD*

One or two readings may be taken from the following selections: Ecclesiastes 3:1-11; 12:1-7; Psalm 90;130; John 10:11-16; Romans 8:35-39.

6   *Sermon*

7   *PRAYERS*

Prayers may be taken from the preceding services as may be deemed appropriate. Other prayers may be offered extemporarily.

8   *PROCESSION TO THE GRAVE*

The minister may read some of the appropriate sentences from the preceding burial services, or repeat the sentences at the start of this service.

9   *COMMITTAL*

The body is lowered into the grave, after which the minister conducts the committal thus:

We commit the body of our *brother N,* to the ground; earth to earth, ashes to ashes, dust to dust.

Then this prayer

Into your hands, O God, we commend our *brother N,* As into the hands of a faithful creator and most loving Saviour. In your infinite goodness, wisdom and power, work in him the purpose of your perfect will, Through Jesus Christ our Lord. **Amen.**

10   *The grave is filled while songs and choruses are sang.*

11   *BENEDICTION OR GRACE*

(As in the preceding service.)

Reconciliation of a Penitent

NOTES

- This liturgy is to be used in the case of a Christian who has broken fellowship with the local church through acts of sinfulness.

- The church elders are to share with the minister their opinion about the penitent and if readmission is agreed on, the following short service is used.

- The service should be conducted in the context of Holy Communion just before the *PRAYERS OF PENITENCE*.

- When it is more than one penitent the wording is to be adapted accordingly.

ORDER OF SERVICE

The penitent comes to the front and faces the congregation.

1   *Minister*   We have with us *NN* who wishes to be reconciled and readmitted to the fellowship of the church. We have examined him/her and we think he/she is truly repentant. Is it your wish that we readmit him/her?

      People   **Yes it is.**

2   *The Minister may give the penitent a chance to give his/her testimony and then lead him/her to reconciliation.*

3   *The penitent turns to the minister who asks him:*

      Minister   Is it your wish to be readmitted to the fellowship of the church?

      Penitent   **It is my wish.**

      Minister   What is your pledge?

      Penitent   **I pledge to forsake the deeds that had kept me from the fellowship of the church; I will seek to follow the Lord more closely and to honour his commands, to read the word of God and to pray constantly, that I may fully be guarded against the approaches of Satan.**

4   *The penitent kneels and prays as follows.*

Have mercy on me O Lord,
according to your unfailing love;
According to your great compassion,
blot out my transgression.
Wash away my iniquity
and cleanse me from my sin.
For I know my transgressions.
Wash away all my iniquity
and cleanse me from my sin.
Cleanse me from my sinfulness
and forgive me.
Cleanse me with hyssop and I will be clean,
Wash me, and I will be whiter than snow.
(Psam 51)

And/or

Almighty and ever-loving Father,
I approach your throne of grace in search of
mercy and forgiveness.
Forgive me of all my sinful deeds and restore
my fellowship with you and the church.
Cleanse me with the blood of Jesus
and I will be whiter than snow.
Grant me the joy of forgiveness and the strength
of the Holy Spirit to walk daily in Christ's footsteps.
Amen.

The penitent stands.

5   *Minister*   Blessed is he whose transgressions are forgiven,
                     whose sins are covered.
                     Blessed is he whose sin the Lord does not count against
                     him and in whose spirit there is no deceit.
                     Glory to the Father, Son and the Holy Spirit.

   All   **As it was in the beginning, is now and will be forever.**
                     Amen.

   Minister   May Almighty God in his mercy accept your repent-
                     ance. May he strengthen you in all goodness.

He takes the penitent's right hand and says:

On behalf of this congregation, I offer you the right hand of fellowship.

6   *Hymn, during which members of the congregation may greet the penitent.*

7   *The service of Holy Communion continues from paragraph 21*
     *(*Hear the words of challenge...).

Readmitting Christians to the Anglican Church

NOTES

- This service is to be conducted in the context of the service of Holy Communion, just before prayers of penitence.

- It is meant to cater for those Christians who had broken fellowship with the Anglican Church for some time and gone to join other Christian churches. The Christian wishing to be readmitted should take the initiative to see the Pastor about this matter.

- It is also for Christians who may have relaxed their Christian walk and stopped going to church. There are many such people whom we encounter, for instance during pastoral visits.

- The service is to be conducted by a Parish Priest.

- Prior to the service the Parish Priest and his assistants ought to have had pastoral sessions with the person.

- There should be sure proof of having belonged to the Anglican Church.

- A certificate of re-admission should be given, in cases of people who had joined other churches.

ORDER OF SERVICE

1 *HYMN. During the singing of this hymn, the persons to be readmitted draw to the front and stand facing the priest.*

2 *Priest* Blessed be God, creator and father of all.
   People **Blessed be Jesus, who reconciles us with the Father.**

   Priest Blessed be the Holy Spirit who renews and strengthens us.
   People **Blessed be Father, Son and the Holy Spirit, one God to be praised forever.**

3 *Priest* Brothers and sisters, standing before us are these beloved Christians who had broken fellowship with the Church and now wish to be readmitted.

4 *The priest reads out their names and other relevant details and may then ask the penitents to talk for themselves briefly.*

Priest: We have heard for ourselves your own testimonies,
and your desire to be admitted back to the
fellowship of the Anglican Church.
Are you convinced that you should be admitted
back to the Anglican Church?

Penitent   **Yes, I am.**

5   *The Priest turns to the congregation.*

Priest   People of God, is it your wish that these beloved
Christians be admitted back to your fellowship?

Answer   **Yes, it is.**

6   *The priest reads the following scripture*
Ephesians 4: 11-16

It was he who gave some to be apostles, some to be prophets,
some to be evangelists, and some to be pastors and teachers, to
prepare God's people for works of service, so that the Body of
Christ may be built up until we all reach unity in the faith and in
the knowledge of the Son of God, and become mature, attaining
to the full measure of the fullness of Christ. Then we will no
longer be infants, tossed back and forth by the waves, and
blown here and there by every wind of teaching and by the
craftiness of men in their deceitful scheming. Instead, speaking
the truth in love, we will in all things grow up into him who is
the Head, that is Christ. From him the whole body, joined and
held together by every supporting ligament, grows and builds
itself up in love, as each part does its work.

7   *Those to be admitted kneel facing the Priest. The congregation is led*
in a meditative song, chorus, or a psalm. Then the Priest uses
the following prayer.

We thank you Lord for these your servants whom you have given
the will to seek readmission into the fellowship of this church.
Put and sustain in them a seriousness of purpose, that they may
know and defend the truth of the Gospel, and withstand the many
winds of doctrine that threaten to sway us to and fro. May you
kindle in them the fire of the spirit, that they may move forth to
live actively for you and to exercise the gifts of ministry that you
have given them for the edification of the whole body, and for the
glory of your name. Grant that these people will be accepted fully
by this congregation and that every member shall feel him/herself

a part of the other, so that we may all be sources of
encouragement to one another in the ways of God. This we pray
and ask in Jesus Name. **Amen.**

8 *PRAYER FOR CHURCH UNITY*

Almighty God our heavenly Father, who loved the church and
gave yourself for her through your Son Jesus Christ. May it
please you to sanctify and uphold this church by your word.
Where we are weak, strengthen us; where we are defenceless,
be our defence; when we are corrupt, we beseech you to purge
and cleanse us; when we are in error as we often are, correct
and guide us. Heal our breaches, O God and save us from
needless divisions and preserve us from rivalries and bigotry.
Teach us how to live in unity and peace, bearing with one
another where we differ, and bring us into a closer, deeper
fellowship with you. Through Jesus Christ our mediator and
Lord. **Amen.**

> *People stand*

9   *Priest*   On behalf of the Bishop, and on behalf of this
                 congregation, I welcome you back to the fellowship
                 of this congregation, and of the Anglican Church.
                 In the Name of the Father, Son, and the Holy Spirit.
                 Amen

10   *The priest gives each penitent a handshake and tells him:*

         Welcome back to the fellowship of the Anglican Church.

         The penitents face the congregation.

11   *Priest*   *The peace of the Lord be always with you.*
         People   **And also with you.**

         Priest   *Let us offer one another a sign of peace.*

12   *People greet the penitents and one another, amidst joyous
         spontaneous singing.*

13   *For those who are adults and communicants, the service of
         Holy Communion continues from* PRAYERS OF PENITENCE.

Commissioning of Evangelists

NOTES

- This service is to be conducted for the evangelists who have been newly employed.

- Before commissioning, they are to undergo an acceptable course of training either through theological education by extension or other, but mainly focusing on the ministry of an evangelist.

- The service may be held once every two years at a central place and is to be conducted by the bishop or his vicar general.

- This service may be conducted in the context of another service such as a diocesan missionary service.

ORDER OF SERVICE

1   *Hymn*

2   *Bishop reads the following opening scripture.*

How, then, can they call on the one they have not believed in? And how can they believe in the one of whom they have not heard? And how can they hear without someone preaching to them? And how can they preach unless they are sent? As it is written, "How beautiful are the feet of those who bring good news!" *(Romans 10:14-17)*

3   *PRESENTATION*
A hymn is sang during which the evangelists, garbed in evangelists uniform stand in a row facing the Bishop. The patron and the director of training present the evangelists to the Bishop in these words, and indicates the parish each comes from.

Presenters   **Bishop in the service of God, we present to you the following people, that you may commission them as evangelists.**

Bishop   Take care that the people you have brought to me are truly called and more so, well prepared for the task of evangelism in this diocese.

Presenters: **We have enquired about them and have examined them; to the best of our assessment, they are fit for commissioning as evangelists.**

4   *EXHORTATION*
     A hymn is sang. The Bishop stands and exhorts the evangelists thus:

As an evangelist you are called to proclaim the Good News
of Jesus Christ; inviting those who are responsive
to turn to Christ and be saved.
 You are to testify to the truth about Jesus Christ as the Way,
the Truth and the Life.
Through the Spirit's enabling, you are to inspire
and motivate people to turn to Jesus.
You are to assist in preparing for baptism and confirmation
those who have turned to Christ, by teaching them
the fundamental truths of the Gospel and the doctrine
of the Anglican church.
   You are called to serve in your congregation,
parish, deanery and other larger circles as may be suggested by
evangelistic opportunities or by the bishop.
You are to work under the parish priest and regularly inform *him*
about the welfare of the flock.
   As an evangelist you must have a personal commitment to Christ
and be a model of a good Christian to the community.
 You are to be involved in the preaching rota of the local church
and the parish.
   You must also seek to update yourself
on the current social affairs affecting the people.
   You are to seek fellowship with other evangelists for purposes
of sharing and mutual encouragement, and further
attend meetings and forums as may be called by the Bishop
or his appointees.

5   *EXAMINATION*

Bishop   In view of the foregoing, do you believe you are truly
              called to do the work of evangelism?
Response   **I believe I am.**

Bishop   Will you seek to put the cause of Christ above all else?
Response: **Yes I will through God's help.**

Bishop   Will you endeavour to bring others to Christ by word
              and example?
Response: **Yes I will, through God's help.**

Bishop	Will you seek to study the Bible and pray often in the course of your work?
Response:	**Yes I will, through God's help.**
Bishop	Will you seek to stand by the truth of the Gospel and guard against all heresies?
Response:	**Yes I will, through God's help.**
Bishop	Will you obey the Bishop in all things just and lawful, likewise the Parish Priest and all who have authority over you?
Response:	**Yes I will, through God's help.**
Bishop	Will you accept the discipline of the church when and where your conduct might necessitate this?
Response:	**I will humbly accept it.**

6   COMMISSIONING

A hymn is sang during which the evangelists come forth and kneel or stand before the Bishop in a row. This prayer is said:

Almighty God, who appoints, anoints and sends
your servants for different ministries for the
    edification of the Church,
we thank you for these your servants who in response
to your call for evangelism
    now kneel here to be commissioned for the work of
evangelism in this diocese.
Look upon them with favour and fill them with
    your grace and power, that, unafraid and with singleness
of mind like the missioners of old, they may preach
and teach the Gospel with power and be faithful
    to the demands of the great commission,
in which your Son commanded the disciples to preach
the Gospel at home and abroad, and assured them that he
    would be with them till the close of the age.
Bless and protect them and their families against all harm;
supply them with all their needs.
    Bless their going out and their coming in,
from this day and for evermore. **Amen.**

7   *Bishop shakes hands with each one of them, saying:*
N, I commission you for the work of evangelism in this diocese.
All   **Amen.**

9   *A certificate is presented.*

10 *The evangelist is then presented with a Bible:*

Receive this Bible as a symbol of your ministry.
All   **Amen.**

11 *The patron hands the evangelist his/her scarf and other related symbols (e.g. a badge).*

12 *After all have been commissioned, they stand in a row and show up the Bible and the certificate. The Bishop, holding his staff says:*

I commission you to serve as evangelists in the Diocese of .....
Preach and teach the Good News of our Lord Jesus Christ in season and out of season. In the name of the Father, Son, and the Holy Spirit. **Amen.**

13 *Hymn*

Service of Commissioning ends there. The rest of the service continues from Prayer for the Church (in the context of Holy Communion, or with offertory (in the context of Morning Worship).

Admitting Lay Readers

NOTES

- This service may be used in the context of Holy Communion, Morning or Evening Worship, or in any other Episcopal function.

- Candidates for licensing must have undergone training that befits evangelists, such as Theological Education by Extension or other relevant resourceful training.

- There should be declaration forms which each candidate will be required to declare and sign before the service.

ORDER OF SERVICE

1 *Hymn*

2 *PRESENTATION*

Candidates for licensing line up before the Bishop, in accordance with the parishes they come from.
The presenters, preferably the director of Theological Education by Extension or/and one senior lay reader stand beside the candidates and say:

Presenters   **Bishop in the service of God, I/we present to you these persons that you may admit them as lay readers.**

Names of the candidates (and their home churches) are read out, and the latter acknowledge their presence with a wave of the hand.
The Bishop faces the congregation and says:

Brothers and sisters in Christ, these persons have been chosen, trained, and brought before God, and us, to be admitted lay readers. However, if any of you here gathered has a just cause why any of them should not be admitted, you are to come forward and say it, or else forever hold your peace. *(Pause)*

If there is no objection, the Bishop presents the candidates to the people:

Bishop   Is it your wish that we admit these people as lay readers?

People   **It is our wish.**

| *Bishop* | Will you support them in their ministry? |
| *People* | **We will support them.** |

3 *EXHORTATION*

The Bishop makes the following exhortation:

As a Lay Reader you are called to serve the church by supporting the
Parish Priest in reading the word and conducting the service; leading
in worship and expounding the scriptures so that people may well be
nurtured in the truth. You are to work under the Parish Priest, assisting him in pastoral duties such as visiting the parishioners, the sick,
the lost, praying with them and encouraging them; burying the dead;
and offering such other help and services as may be required by the
Parish Priest from time to time.

| *Bishop* | Are you willing and ready to perform these duties faithfully and without being goaded? |
| *Response* | **Yes I am.** |

4 *EXAMINATION*

Bishop examines the candidates as follows:

| *Bishop* | Will you follow the doctrine and practices of the Anglican Church of Kenya and endeavour to teach the same? |
| *Response:* | **I will, through God's help.** |

| *Bishop* | Will you, by your life and ministry set a good example to the unbelievers and those around you? |
| *Response:* | **I will, through God's help.** |

| *Bishop* | Will you endeavour to promote unity, peace and reconciliation in your ministry? |
| *Response:* | **I will, through God's help.** |

| *Bishop* | Will you also endeavour to fulfil the great commission by preaching the gospel of Jesus Christ with fervour in season and out of season. |
| *Response:* | **That is my earnest desire.** |

| *Bishop* | Will you, in all things just and lawful, obey your bishop, the parish priest and all who have authority over you? |
| *Response* | **I will, through God's help.** |

5   *ADMISSION*

Each candidate kneels before the Bishop who shakes their hands as he presents each with the licence saying:

N, I admit you to serve the Church as a Lay Reader in the name of God the Father, Son and the Holy Spirit. **Amen.**

Bishop presents the candidate with the New Testament saying:

Preach the Gospel of our Lord Jesus Christ in season and out of season. **Amen.**

The candidate is then presented with a blue scarf. After all have been licensed, they stand in a line and the bishop prays thus:

Almighty and ever living God, who sent your only Son Jesus Christ to die on the cross for us and thus reconcile us to our maker, we thank you for calling *these people* to be partakers in the great commission in which your Son Jesus commanded that we preach the gospel at home and abroad, till everyone on earth has heard it. We thank you for the confidence their respective congregations have in them, to serve the church not expecting any monetary remuneration, except for the sheer joy of serving the Church of Christ.

He stretches his right arm towards them and continues:

May God our Father, look with favour upon you.
May he equip you with the power of the Holy Spirit
that you may be fully prepared for the services ahead,
to the end that your work shall glorify God and
edify his Church. May the Lord bless your going out and your coming in, from this day and forever more. **Amen.**

6   *After this the congregation greets the new Lay Readers with ululations, songs, and other gestures of praise. The rest of the service may continue as Holy Communion beginning with Prayer for the Church.*

Visitation of the Sick

NOTES
* This service may be conducted at home, or in a hospital ward as the case might be.

* It is to be conducted by a minister or his appointed delegate.

* It may be conducted on request by the sick or his family, but it can also be the minister's sole prerogative as part of his pastoral ministry to the flock.

* Laying on of hands may be accompanied by anointing with oil.

* Anointing is a sacramental expression of healing; it may also be administered to the dying.

ORDER OF SERVICE

1   *At the entrance to the room (ward) where the sick person is, the minister says in an audible voice:*

The peace of the Lord be in this *house (or ward)* and with those who *dwell (are admitted)* herein.

2   *A hymn may be sang*

Our hope is in the Lord;
Who heals our diseases.

3   *The minister enters and proceeds to where the sick person is. He reads a few of these (or other appropriate) scripture:*

Cast all your anxieties upon the Lord for he cares for you. (*1 Peter 5:7*)

Fear not, for I have redeemed you; I have summoned you by name; you are mine. When you pass through the waters, I will be with you; and when you pass through the rivers, they will not sweep over you. When you walk through the fire, you will not be burned; the flames will not set you ablaze. For I am the Lord, your God..., your Saviour. *(Isaiah 43:1b-3a)*

God is our refuge and strength, an ever present help in trouble. Therefore we will not fear, though the earth give way and the mountains fall into the heart of the sea, though its waters roar and foam, and the mountains quake with their surging. (*Psalm 46:1-3*)

Rejoice in the Lord always. I will say it again: Rejoice! Let your gentleness be evident to all. The Lord is near. Do not be anxious about anything, but in everything, by prayer and petition, with thanksgiving, present your requests to God. And the peace of God which transcends all understanding will guard your hearts and your minds in Christ Jesus. *(Philippians 4:4-7)*

Surely he took up our infirmities and carried our sorrows, yet we considered him stricken by God, smitten by him, and afflicted. But he was pierced for our transgressions; he was crushed for our iniquities; the punishment that brought us peace was upon him, and by his wounds we are healed. *(Isaiah 53:4-5)*

Do you not know? Have you not heard? The Lord is the everlasting God, the creator of the ends of the universe. He will not grow tired or weary, and his understanding no one can fathom. He gives strength to the weary and increases the power of the weak. Even youths grow tired and weary, and young men stumble and fall; but those who hope in the Lord will renew their strength; they will soar on wings like eagles; they will run and not grow weary, they will walk and not be faint. *(Isaiah 40:28-31)*

Come to me, all you who are weary and burdened and I will give you rest. Take my yoke upon you and learn from me, for I am gentle and humble in heart, and you will find rest for your souls. For my yoke is easy and my burden is light. *(Matthew 11:28-30)*

Is anyone of you sick, he should call the elders of the church to pray over him and anoint him with oil in the name of the Lord. And the prayer offered in faith will make him well; the Lord will raise him up. If he has sinned, he will be forgiven. *(James 5:4)*

5   SCRIPTURE FOR A DYING PERSON

The person facing death may be assisted to say this scripture if he/she can.
Whom have I in heaven but you, and there is nothing I desire on earth besides you, my flesh and my heart may fail, but God is the strength of my heart and my portion for ever. (*Psalm 73:25-26*)
And I—in righteousness I shall see your face; when I awake I shall be satisfied with seeing your likeness. (*Psalm 17:15*)

6   PASTORAL TIME

The Minister may make a brief pastoral talk and give himself/herself time to listen. In circumstances like these the sick person and his family more than anything else require a message of encouragement and hope. Therefore the minister should sensitively and empathically handle this pastoral session in a way that it shall meet the people's real needs.

The minister approaches the sick person and may lay hands on him or her, or use any other gesture that portrays friendship and pastoral concern.

7   *One or more of these prayers (or other appropriate ones) may be said by the minister, standing.*

We approach your throne of grace O merciful Lord trusting in your enduring love and goodness towards us. Lord we know that nothing befalls us outside your knowledge, and in the midst of worry and anxiety you remain ever close to us for the continual supply of strength and grace as we wonder why this has happened. Comfort now, this our *brother/sister,* and grant that *she/he* shall get well and be able to look back with thankfulness at what you have done, and look into the future with hope and confidence. Through Jesus Christ our Lord. **Amen.**

In case of a road accident

Grant Lord that those who drive on our roads shall learn to respect human life and thus seek to drive safely, minding not so much about material gain but the well being of the people. Grant also that those that are responsible for the good maintenance of our roads shall ensure the same without compromise, that the vehicle owners shall seek to maintain their vehicles in good condition. May bribery cease on our roads, so that traffic law breakers may forthwith be accosted and dealt with accordingly. May all other essential aspects of road safety be looked into; and when all is done, Lord, grant us we pray, your safety and protection, that our lives may not be cut short, or our bodies maimed by road accidents. Hear us good Lord, for the sake of Jesus Christ our Lord. **Amen.**

8   *For a child*

Jesus lover of children, who implored us not to despise any of the little ones for their angels in heaven are always in your presence, look with tenderness upon your child *N.* May your healing presence be with *her* now as it was with the daughter of Jairus and the boy from the village of Nain. Lord Jesus, heal this child and grant *her* wholeness in accordance with your divine power. Grant our request Lord as it may please you so to do. Through Jesus Christ our Lord. **Amen.**

9 *At the verge of death*

Look upon your servant *N* and grant *him* the peace that transcends all understanding as *he* passes through what might appear to be like the valley of the shadow of death. Amidst pain and suffering, keep him ever joyful and abiding in you who alone are the source of life and health, strength and comfort, and who after our fleeting earthly days are over, will take us home where we belong, and where we shall reign with you days without end, freed at last from all worry, pain, sorrow and disease. Our comfort is in the knowledge that we are never ever alone. Sustain your servant *N* with this assurance and let it be enough for *him*.
Through Jesus Christ who understands and carries all our pain.
Amen.

And now we can say with *N,* "I have fought the good fight, I have finished the race, I have kept the faith. Now there is in store for me the crown of righteousness, which the Lord the righteous judge will award to me on that day—and not only to me, but also to all who have longed for his appearing".

And so, *brother/sister* as you transit from this life into the next, may the band of angels meet you and lead you to heaven, where the Lord with open hands is waiting to give you the crown of glory. At the right side of the Father, there will be no more sorrow, no more pain; and as for death, it is for ever conquered. Thank you Lord for conquering death on the cross for us. **Amen and Amen.**

10 *After one has taken the last breath*

Eternal God, you are the author and finisher of our lives. You created *N* and brought him into this life; now at your perfect time you have come to gather what is yours. We therefore release into your everlasting hands the spirit of *N*. Grant him we pray, the place you have eternally apportioned him. May he, cleansed and forgiven, be found worthy of sharing in the eternal bliss together with the angels and faithful ancestors who have gone before. Through Jesus Christ our mediator. **Amen.**

11 *After the passing away of a child*

Lord Jesus Christ, you became a baby in Bethlehem;
We commend to your loving care this child,
Lead *him/her* gently to those heavenly places where those who sleep
in you have continual peace and joy,
And fold *him/her* in the hands of your unfailing love;
As you live and reign with the Father and the Holy Spirit,
One God, world without end. **Amen.**

12 *For people keeping vigil*

God of the dark night,
You were with Jesus praying at Gethsemane
You were with him all the way to the cross
And through to the resurrection,
Help us to recognize you now as we watch with *N*
And wait for what must happen;
Help us through any bitterness and despair,
Help us accept our distress,
Help us to remember that you care for us
And that in your will is our peace. **Amen.**

13 *Before an operation*

Loving Father, look upon *N* and give *him/her* the relaxation he so much
needs as *he* now goes to be operated. Remove from *him* all fear and
anxiety and help *him* to trust you. Help the surgeon and the theatre staff
who will be carrying out this operation that they may do it with maxi-
mum care and skill, and finally grant them success, to the glory of your
name and the good health of *N*. In Jesus name we pray. **Amen.**

14 *For a person with a distressed mind*

O God Almighty, look upon your servant in *his* state of distress.
Enable *him* to cast on you all *his* cares and grant *him* peace and
calmness. May *he* know your loving presence with *him* now and
always. In Jesus name we pray. **Amen.**

15 *For one suffering from a guilty conscience*

Lord you understand our deepest thoughts, and justly judge us according to the motives of our heart. You deliver, heal and forgive those who turn to you in repentance and reward them with peace and joy. Look upon your servant *N*, and relieve *him* from the guilt that weighs *him* down. May *he* be filled with your Holy Spirit to strengthen, comfort and counsel *him*. *In* Jesus name we pray. **Amen.**

16 *Anointing and laying on of hands*

> *The minister and his assistants lay hands on each person as they kneel (if they are able to).*
> *The minister prays:*

In the name of Jesus Christ who was wounded for our sake, and who died and rose again, be healed of all infirmities in your body, mind and spirit. **Amen.**

17 *He may then anoint the forehead with oil. If the oil is not consecrated, it may be consecrated with these words:*

Consecrate this oil Lord which your servant is about to use for the anointing of your people. In the name of the Father, Son, and the Holy Spirit. **Amen.**

18 *He puts his forefinger into the oil and then makes a mark of the cross on the person's forehead and says:*

I anoint you with this holy oil.
Receive Christ's forgiveness and healing.
The power of the Saviour who suffered for you,
flow through your mind and body,
lifting you to peace and inward strength. **Amen.**

19 *Where the service does not proceed to Holy Communion, this final prayer may be said by the minister:*

We anoint you in the name of the anointed one
by whose wounds you are healed,
by whose stripes you are cured.
Receive your healing miracle in Jesus name. **Amen.**

20 *A short chorus may be sang (if desired) after which a brief service of Holy Communion follows, beginning from paragraph 28 (Our Lord's Prayer) to 36 (The Peace).*

Service of Healing

- This service is to be conducted in church as a service on its own. It may also be conducted in the context of regular Morning or Evening Worship, or Holy Communion.

- It is assumed that this type of service caters not only for those sick in body but also those suffering from mental distress, depression, sin and guilt, and those living under harsh circumstances arising from social or other ills.

- When it is in the context of Holy Communion, the service may precede the sermon.

- Seats should be provided at the front for those sick people who may want to sit. Where need be the sick should be accompanied by relatives, friends, or ushers for support, both physical and moral.

- Laying on of hands may also be accompanied by anointing with oil.

- The service is to be conducted with softness of voice and with pauses where necessary.

- The service also provides for a time of repentance and forgiveness.

ORDER OF SERVICE

1   *Hymn*

2   *The minister may read scripture sentences from the preceding service.*

3   *Minister*   Brothers and sisters, we have come together to worship God whose hands are always stretched out in blessing and healing. This, he has shown us through his Son, Jesus Christ. We come to thank him for calling us to share in this work of healing. We come to seek his grace and wisdom for a bruised and broken world. We come to give ourselves to him, that we may be instruments of his love and power to all who need his healing touch today.

People sit or kneel for confession

> **Eternal Father, God of our ancestors, before your
> power all things tremble, but through your Son we
> approach your throne. We have done wrong and
> neglected to do right; our sins weigh heavily on our
> hearts; Lord have mercy, count them not against us.
> Grant us the joy of forgiveness and lighten our
> hearts with the glory of Christ, who died and rose
> again for us. Amen.**

Minister   The God and Father of our Lord Jesus Christ rejoices at
repentance and declares his acceptance. The dead are
alive, the lost are found. His goodness and mercy shall
follow you all the days of your life, and you will live in
the house of the Lord for ever. **Amen.**

5   *1st and 2nd readings (from these or other appropriate texts)*

Isaiah 52:13-53:5
See, my servant will act wisely; He will be raised and lifted up and
highly exalted. Just as there were many who were appalled at him,
his appearance was so disfigured beyond that of any man and his
form marred beyond human likeness, so will he sprinkle many
nations, and kings will shut their mouths because of him. For what
they were not told, they will see, and what they have not heard, they
will understand. Who has believed our message and to whom has the
arm of the Lord been revealed? He grew up before him like a tender
shoot, and like a root out of dry ground, he had no beauty or majesty
to attract us to him, nothing in his appearance that we should desire
him. He was despised and rejected by men, a man of sorrows, and
familiar with suffering. Like one from whom men hide their faces, he
was despised, and we esteemed him not. Surely he took up our
infirmities and carried our sorrows, yet we considered him stricken
by God, smitten by him, and afflicted. But he was pierced for our
transgressions, he was crushed for our iniquities; the punishment that
brought us peace was upon him, and by his wounds we are healed.

6   *A prayerful chorus or hymn may be sang.*

Acts 3:1-8a, 11-16.

One day Peter and John were going up to the temple at the time of prayer-at three in the afternoon. Now a man crippled from birth was being carried to the temple gate called Beautiful, where he was put every day to beg from those going into the temple courts. When he saw Peter and John about to enter, he asked them for money. Peter looked straight at him, as did John.

Then Peter said, "Look at us!" So the man gave them his attention, expecting to get something from them. Then Peter said, "Silver or gold I do not have, but what I have I give you. In the name of Jesus Christ of Nazareth, walk." Taking him by the right hand, he helped him up, and instantly the man's feet and ankles became strong. He jumped to his feet and began to walk.

While the beggar held on to Peter and John, all the people were astonished and came running to them in the place called Solomon's Colonnade. When Peter saw this, he said to them: "Men of Israel, why does this surprise you? Why do you stare at us as if by our own power or godliness we had made this man walk?

"The God of Abraham, Isaac and Jacob, the God of our fathers, has glorified his servant Jesus. You handed him over to be killed and you disowned him before Pilate, though he had decided to let him go. You disowned the Holy and Righteous One and asked that a murderer be released to you. You killed the author of life, but God raised him from the dead. We are witnesses of this. By faith in the name of Jesus, this man whom you see and know was made strong. It is Jesus' name and the faith that comes through him that has given this complete healing to him, as you can all see."

7 *Hymn (in acclamation of the healing and saving power of Jesus) e.g. "Would You Be Free From your Burden..."*

People sit or kneel

8 *All* **Lord Jesus Christ, we are weak but you are strong; we are poor but you are rich; we are sinful but you forgive; we are sick but you give health. Come to us through your Holy Spirit, so that we may receive all that you plan for our healing and wholeness, and may all glory and honour come back to you. Amen.**

9 *Minister* Praise be to the Lord our King;
Praise be to the Lord of Lords.

He forgives sins;
He heals our ailments.

He died to give us life;
He rose to give us hope.

Christ is with us now;
He is here indeed.

The Spirit is here;
with healing in his wings.

Minister   Let us pray for health and healing.

We give thanks that God longs for healing and wholeness for all people. Let us bless the Lord.
Blessed be the name of the Lord.

For the healing ministry of Jesus Christ, touching men
and women at the place of their deepest need.
We bless the name of the Lord.

For the work of the Holy Spirit, who empowers us for
this ministry today.
We bless the name of the Lord.

For the Gospel of Christ, which embraces the whole
person: body, mind, and spirit.
We bless the name of the Lord.

Minister   We bring before you Lord, those we know who need
your healing touch, the sick, the lonely, the bereaved,
those enslaved by drugs, the displaced, the confused,
the hungry, those who have wandered away from home.
Reach out and touch them now O Lord.

Bless all in the medical profession who work to bring
health to others. Sustain those who care for the sick in
their homes. Give special grace to those who minister to
the dying.
Bless and empower.

Guide those who suffer from AIDS in the way they
should live. Lead us to show them your love.
We pray for hope and courage.

Bring healing in every family where there is stress and
conflict.

We pray for healing and reconciliation.

Minister   Bring about a healing of relationships in this church. Bring reconciliation, bring harmony, bring peace, bring unity. Just as the Father is one with the Son and the Holy Spirit, may your people, though many, enjoy that unity of purpose which the Holy Spirit alone enables and facilitates. Grant us the privilege of meeting with you today and enjoying your presence in this service as we wait with expectancy for the great things you are going to do for your people. We pray this in the name of our Lord and healer, Jesus Christ. **Amen.**

10 *Notices*

11 *Sermon*

12 *Offertory*

13 *A short relevant chorus may be sang during which people seeking to be prayed for with anointing and laying on of hands come forth and stand, sit or kneel depending on the provisions. Names of people afflicted by various conditions may be mentioned where desired.*

14 *All*   **Come Holy Spirit, we wait for you. Our lives are needy, our hearts are open. Bring to us the healing touch of Jesus. Move among us in your power and grant us healing and wholeness. In Jesus name we pray. Amen.**

Silence may be kept and then the minister continues:

15 *Minister*   We bring to you Lord, people with diseases that doctors have described as terminal;

We bring to you Lord, people whose diseases have not yet been diagnosed;

We bring to you Lord people who have been diagnosed as HIV positive;

We bring to you Lord people who have been maimed through road accidents;

We bring to you Lord, people who have been deprived of love and friendship and are in a state of deep loneliness;

We bring to you Lord those who are suffering from
numerous other conditions and who need your
healing;

We bring before you those who are sick and require
healing, but would rather their names are not
mentioned.

For all these people Lord:

All   **Bring healing, bring wholeness.**

16   *The minister may (or in addition) use this alternative general prayer.*

God the Father,
God the Son,
God the Holy Spirit,
Sanctify this hour as we stand before your holy presence, lifting our
hearts and waiting in faith and hope for the opening of your healing
springs. Open them now Lord as we stand in awe of your sovereign
majesty, and heal these your people of all that weighs them down,
physically, emotionally, and psychologically.

Release those whom Satan has held captive, comfort the disturbed
and the distressed in spirit; heal those who may be nursing deep hurts
arising from separation, divorce, failed or strained relationships;
those deeply devastated by the loss of loved ones; heal and forgive
those that may be suffering from restlessness and guilt due to un-
repented sins.

O sovereign Lord, look upon all who are involved in the rigorous
work of medical research. Grant them perseverance and renewed
energy in their crucial service to humanity; Bless and keep all who are
involved in the care of the sick and the dying both at home and in the
hospices and hospitals; fill them with love, patience and courage.

In simple faith we come to you, to draw from your healing strength.
We ask this trusting in the name of him who lives and reigns for
ever, Jesus Christ our Lord and Saviour. **Amen.**

17   *ANOINTING AND LAYING ON OF HANDS*

*The minister and his assistants lay hands on each person as they kneel at the
chancel, or other convenient positions.*

The minister prays:

In the name of Jesus Christ who was wounded for our sake, and by
whose stripes we are healed, be healed of all infirmities in your body,
mind and spirit. **Amen.**

18 *He may then anoint the forehead with oil. If the oil is not consecrated, it may be consecrated with these words:*

Consecrate this oil, Lord, which your servant is about to use for the anointing of your people. In the name of the Father, Son, and the Holy Spirit. **Amen.**

19 *He puts his thumb into the oil and then makes a mark of the cross on the person's forehead and says:*

I anoint you with this holy oil.
Receive Christ's forgiveness and healing.
The power of the Saviour who suffered for you,
flow through your mind and body,
lifting you to peace and inward strength. **Amen.**

OR

I anoint you in the name of the Anointed One;
Receive healing, receive forgiveness, receive peace,
receive fullness of life, even eternal life.
Through the merits of our Lord Jesus
Christ the great healer and Saviour. **Amen.**

20 *Hymn, after which the service of Holy Communion may follow, beginning from Sharing of Peace.*
Where the service does not proceed to Holy Communion, this final prayer may be said by the minister, and then end with the Blessing and recessional hymn. Provision could me made for people to share testimonies of healing.

21 *Minister* Almighty God, the Father of our Lord, Saviour and Healer, Jesus Christ, we thank you for your presence with us in this service; We thank you for your healing touch on distressed hearts and minds, for the healing of our physical conditions, and for the greater gift of peace and tranquility in our minds and spirits. We thank you for carrying our cares, anxieties and all that weighs us down. Thank you for the forgiveness of sins, and for deliverance from satanic invasions. We thank you that in you we are set free and free indeed, and we can therefore praise your holy name singing:
Alleluia, Alleluia, Alleluia, Alleluia,....

Thanksgiving
After a Life Threatening Experience

NOTES

- This service is to be used for those who wish to celebrate God's greatness following deliverance from a life threatening experience.

- The service is to be conducted in church by the minister or his appointed delegate, in the context of Morning or Evening Worship, or as may be desired.

- In the context of the Morning or Evening Worship, this service may come before the notices.

ORDER OF SERVICE

1 *Hymn, after which the person involved gives the testimony of deliverance, after which there follows a time of praise and worship to God for his marvellous deeds.*

2 *One or more of the following scriptural excerpts are said antiphonally. Intermittently, prayerful choruses may be slotted in.*

SCRIPTURAL SENTENCES

3 I will extol the Lord at all times;
His praise will always be on my lips.

Glorify the Lord with me:
Let us exalt his name together.

I sought the Lord and he answered me;
He delivered me from all my fears.

Those who look to him are radiant;
Their faces are never covered with shame.

The angel of the Lord encamps around those who fear him,
And he delivers them from all their problems.

The Lord is close to the broken hearted,
And saves those who are crushed in spirit.

A righteous man may have many troubles'
But the Lord delivers him from them all;

He protects all his bones,
Not one of them will be broken. *(Psalm 34: 1-20)*

OR

4   Keep me O Lord from the hands of the wicked;
Protect me from men of violence who plan to trip my feet.

O Sovereign Lord, my strong deliverer,
Who shields my head in the day of battle.

Do not grant the wicked their desires, O Lord;
Do not let their plans succeed, or they will become proud.
(Psalms 140: 4,7,8)

OR

5   Let all who take refuge in you be glad;
Let them ever sing for joy.

Spread your protection over them,
That those who love your name may rejoice in you.

For surely, O Lord, you bless the righteous;
You surround them with your favour as with a shield.
(Psalms 5:11-12)

OR

6   I love the Lord for he heard my voice;
He heard my cry for mercy.

Because he turned his ear to me;
I will call on him as long as I live.

The cords of death entangled me;
The anguish of the grave came upon me.

I was overcome by trouble and sorrow,
then I called on the name of the Lord;
O Lord Save me.

The Lord is gracious and righteous;
Our God is full of compassion.

The Lord protects the simple hearted;
When I was in great need, he saved me.

Be at rest once more O my soul;
For the Lord has been good to you.

For you O Lord have delivered my soul from death;
My eyes from tears, my feet from stumbling.

How can I repay the Lord for all his goodness to me;
I will lift up the cup of salvation and call on the name of the Lord.
(Psalms 116: 1-9,12-13)

Glory to the Father, Son and the Holy Spirit;
As it was in the beginning, is now, and ever shall be. Amen.

7 *PRAYERS*

*The minister invites someone to pray extemporarily for the prevailing
threatening circumstances (currently or previously) and to invoke God's
intervention. After that the minister prays:*

We give you thanks O Lord for your unfailing love
And your wonderful deeds to humankind
You are our refuge and underneath are your everlasting arms.
You break down Satan's gates
And cut through iron bars to set your servants free.
When we cry to you in the midst of troubles,
you run to our help and save us from our distress.
You send forth your angels to bring healing and
to rescue us from imminent danger.
Because of your great and unfailing love,
we give you thanks and praise
as we lift our hearts to you and proclaim your
Lordship from eternity to eternity.
And now we praise you Lord most high, for delivering *N* from danger
(he may mention the nature of the danger, and then say): We thank
you that in the midst of it all we have seen your salvation, through
Jesus Christ our Lord. **Amen.**

Or

8 Almighty God, you are our refuge
and our stronghold, a timely help in trouble.
We give you praise and thanks for our deliverance from those great
dangers which threatened (or compassed) us, (and for your precious
gift of peace).
Not to us, Lord, not to us, but to your name be glory,
for your goodness alone kept and preserved us.
Continue your mercies to us, we pray, that we may always acknowledge that you are our Saviour and our mighty deliverer;
Through Jesus Christ our Lord. **Amen.**

9   *He then blesses the concerned people thus, as he lays his hands on them:*

May the Lord bless you and keep you;
The Lord keep you from all harm,
The Lord watch over your life;
The Lord watch over your coming and your going,
Both now and for ever more. **Amen.**

10   *A thank offering is given by the person, with their family and friends.*
Meanwhile people join in a joyous hymn of praise. People return to their
seats and the rest of the service continues from the Notices.

Thanksgiving After Harvest
(Harvest Sunday)

NOTES

- This service is to be used during harvest time.

- Christians are to be asked to bring the best parts of the produce for offering.

- Money is also to be considered as part of harvest.

- All the members of the church are to participate in this service including children and youth.

- The service is to be conducted in the context of Morning Worship and may begin just after call to worship.

ORDER OF SERVICE

1   *An appropriate song is sang during which representatives of various age groups process into the church exhibiting various harvests.*

2   *At the Holy Table, the minister places his right hand on each of the items as a sign of acknowledgement and blessing. People return to their seats and remain standing.*
    Animals may not be brought into the church but may be tethered just outside.

3   *The minister, facing the people says:*

We are gathered here to celebrate this season's harvest, to give thanks to God the giver of all good things, and give for his work the best parts of our harvest, even as we ask for his continued blessings on us and all the good work we do.

Minister	The Lord of the harvest be always with you;
People	**And also with you.**

Minister	How priceless is your unfailing love! O God;
People	**Both high and low among humanity find refuge in the shadow of your wings.**

Minister	They feast in the abundance of your house;
People	**You give them drink from your river of delights.**

Minister	For with you is the fountain of life;
People	**In your light we see light.** *(Psalm 36:7-8)*

4   *People sit. Two to three of the following lessons, or other appropriate ones may be read.*

Leviticus 23:9-14; Deuteronomy 26:1-11 Genesis 28:20-22;
Malachi 3:8-10; Romans 13:6-7; 2 Corinthians 8: 11-12;
Luke 6:28; Matthew 25:34-36; Mark 12:41-44.

5   *Hymn, after which people remain standing for the following litany.*

6   *A LITANY OF HARVEST*

Leader   Glory and honour be to the Lord most high;
              Who made heaven and earth and all there is.

              He made man and woman in his own image;
              And set them in the garden of Eden

              Like Adam and Eve we too are managers;
              And stewards of the earth's produce.

              He who gathers crops in summer is wise;
              But he who sleeps during harvest is disgraceful.
              (Proverbs 10:5)

              Where there are no oxen the manger is empty;
              But from the strength of an ox comes an abundant
              harvest.

              A sluggard does not plough in season;
              So at harvest time he looks and sees nothing.
              (Proverbs 20:24)

Leader   As we celebrate and offer thanks for a good harvest, let
              us recall where God has graciously brought us from:

              I gave you empty stomachs in every city;
              And lack of bread in every town.

              I sent rain on one town;
              But withheld it from another.

              One field had rain;
              Another had none and dried up.

              People staggered from town to town for water;
              But did not get enough to drink. *(Amos 3:6-8)*

And so we cried to the Lord our God:
Restore our fortunes O Lord like streams in the desert.

Those who sow in tears;
Will reap with songs of joy.

He who goes out weeping, carrying seeds to sow;
Will return with songs of joy, carrying sheaves with him. *(Psalm 126:5-6)*

The Lord will indeed give what is good;
And our land will yield its harvest. *(Psalm 85:12)*

What do you have that you did not receive?
And if I received, should I boast as though I did not? *(1 Corinthians 4:7)*

It is more blessed to give than to receive;
For God loves a cheerful giver.

Remember the Lord our God;
For it is he who gives us the ability to produce wealth. *(Deuteronomy 8:18).*

7 *Hymn*

8 *Notices*

9 *Hymn*

10 *Sermon*

11 *OFFERTORY*
   The minister may give some relevant scriptural exhortation as a call to offertory.

   The minister may read this scripture:

Give and it will be given to you. A good measure, pressed down, shaken together and running over, will be poured into your lap. For with the measure you use, it will be measured to you. *(Luke 6:38)*

Or/and

Honour the Lord with your wealth, with the first fruits of all your crops; then your barns will be filled to overflowing, and your vats will brim over with new wine. *(Proverbs 3:9-10)*

12. *People are to process with joyful singing as they give to God. When all has been given, the people remain standing for prayers.*

Minister	All things come from you Lord;
People	**And of your own have we given you.**

Then this or another prayer

O Lord God our creator and keeper,
giver of sunshine and rain;
All that we are and all that we have is yours,
In gratitude we offer to you and for your work,
the produce of our farms, businesses and employment.
Accept and bless it for the furtherance of your work here and beyond.
Bless your people in their daily work. Establish their work and
multiply it to meet all their various needs. All for the glory and
honour of your holy name. **Amen.**

13 *People sit*

14 OTHER PRAYERS

*The Minister may use the prayers in other parts of the this book as may be desirable and appropriate. (See **Prayers and Intercessions for Different Times and Purposes**).*

15 PRAYER FOR PROTECTION

16 BLESSING
This or other form of blessing may be used

He who supplies seed to the sower and bread for food will also
supply and increase your store of seed and will enlarge the harvest of
your righteousness, and make you rich in every way so that you can
be generous on every occasion *(see 2 Corinthians 9:10-11)*. You will
still be eating last year's harvest when you will have to make room
for the new ... *(Leviticus 26:10)*.
... And the blessing of God Almighty, Father, Son, and the Holy
Spirit, be with you and remain with you now and for ever, **Amen.**

17 *Recessional Hymn*

Thanksgiving After Childbirth

NOTES

- This service is to be conducted in the church. Thanksgiving after childbirth does not in any way stand for baptism.

- The service may be done on request by families other than professing Christians because it is most importantly a service of thanksgiving for the safe arrival of the baby into the world, (and the safety of the mother).

- The service may be conducted in the context of Morning or Evening Worship, Holy Communion service, or separately, but not followed by Baptism.

- As a thanksgiving gesture to the Lord, the parents, backed up by relatives and friends, bring a thank offering.

- The service is to be conducted by the priest but in his absence he may ask his assistants to conduct it.

- The service should preferably be conducted within one month of the baby's arrival.

- The baby should be baptised within the first three months of its arrival.

- In case of more than one child the pronouns should be adjusted accordingly to cater for the plurality.

- In the case of adoption of a child, the service may start from item No. 7 - Prayer for Adoption.

ORDER OF SERVICE

1   *Hymn. The parents and friends come forward with the baby and stand before the Holy Table facing the Priest.*

2   *Minister*   The Lord be with you.
    And also with you.

We have come here before God, to join the family of *N* and *N* in offering thanks to God for blessing them with the gift of a child, and for granting *N* protection and safety during the delivery.

Let us pray:

Almighty God, we thank you for the gift of life,
    and for the joy and challenges of parenthood.

Thank you for the gift of this child *N*,
whom you have graciously given your servants *N* and *N*
who humbly come before you in gratitude.
Accept our worship and praise as we join them in
thanksgiving for your wondrous deeds.
Through Jesus Christ our Lord. **Amen.**

3   *The minister leads the people in the following antiphonal recitation.*

Because the Lord our God is so good:
We shall praise him with Psalms.

Give thanks to the Lord for he is good;
His love endures for ever.

Let all who fear the Lord say:
His love endures for ever.
(Psalm 118: 1-4)

Unless the Lord builds a house,
Its builders labour in vain.

Unless the Lord watches over a city,
The watchmen stand guard in vain.

In vain you rise up early and stay up late, toiling for
food to eat,
To those he loves, he grants them sleep.

Sons are a heritage from the Lord,
Children are a reward from the Lord.

Like arrows in the hands of a warrior,
Are children born in one's youth.

Blessed is the man whose quiver is full of them,
**They will not be put to shame when they
contend with their enemies in the gate.**
(Psalm 127)

Minister   Glory to the Father, Son and the Holy Spirit.
All   **As it was in the beginning, is now and ever shall be,
Amen.**

4   *Hymn*

5   *The minister holds the baby in his arms and says the following prayer and/or,
the ensuing litany.*

A woman giving birth to a child has pain because her time has come; but when her baby is born she forgets the anguish because of her joy that a child is born into the world. *(John 16:21)*

O God our heavenly Father, we thank you and praise your holy name for blessing your servants *N* and *N* with the gift of this child, *N*. We thank you for delivering *N* from the pangs of labour through which she brought forth this beautiful child.
Bless this child Lord and guard *him* against all dangers as *he* grows up. Grant that *he* shall grow to become a responsible and useful member of society. Guard *him* against wrong company and grant *him* good and useful friends as *he* grows. Through Jesus Christ our Lord. **Amen.**

Grant that the parents of this child shall bring *him* up in the way of Christ so that *he* shall grow up in wisdom, in stature and in favour with God and people, to the glory of him who said, "Let the children come to me, for the Kingdom of God is for such as these". We pray this in the name of the same Jesus Christ our Lord and Saviour. **Amen.**

6   *Prayer for an adopted baby*

O God our Father,
to whom we are related through adoption,
yet enjoying the full benefits of being called your children,
bless now this child *N,* who through adoption
henceforth becomes truly the daughter/son of *N* and *N*.
Adoptive love is redemptive and sacrificial,
leaving no regrets in its way.
Father, may your blessings be richly bestowed upon this family.
Provide for their every need for the wholistic nurturing of this child.
May *N* find total favour in the hearts of *his* adopting parents,
and may he grow to become truly loving and loveable;
and as Jesus did, may *N* grow in wisdom and in stature,
and in favour with God and the community. **Amen.**

7   *Then this litany*

Lord we thank you for this child;
For his safe arrival.

Lord protect *him* against diseases;
Lord protect him.

Lord protect *him* from childhood accidents;
Lord protect him.

May *he* be nurtured and nourished well;
May *he* enjoy a good appetite.

May *he* grow in wisdom and stature;
And in favour with God and people.

May *he* grow to become a staunch witness of Christ.
In both Church and society.

May the path of *his* life be swept of all dangers.
That *he* may enjoy the wealth of many happy years.

8   *He gives the child back to the parents. There follows ululations and joyful singing and dance.*

9   *A special thank offering is taken. People go back to their seats.*

10 *In the context of Holy Communion, Morning or Evening Worship, the service is to continue from the Ministry of the Word. If the service stands on its own, a Lesson is read, then a short exposition, the Lord's Prayer, and Benediction or Grace.*

A Thanksgiving Service

NOTES

- Christians are encouraged to regularly find cause to offer open thanksgiving to God in church, in acknowledgement of his greatness in their lives.

- The Service may be conducted in the context of the usual Morning Worship or Evening Worship, and may be inserted before Notices.

- It is to be conducted by the Parish minister or his assistant; but a lay minister may also conduct it through delegation by the minister.

- The Dedication aspect in this service is also to be understood to mean re-dedication, a renewed commitment to continue serving God and seeking to live according to his will and for his glory.

- The Service can also be used on a special thanksgiving day which the church or parish may wish to set apart for giving thanks to God and for re-dedication of the Christians for greater service to God.

ORDER OF SERVICE

1 *A Hymn. During the singing of this hymn, the people giving thanks move forward and stand facing the sanctuary.*

2 *The people concerned are given a chance to state briefly the reason for thanksgiving. The congregation may respond with a hand clap or other forms of acceptable applause.*

3 *The minister leads the congregation in reciting the following psalm, or other relevant scripture. See suggestions below the psalm.*

PSALM 147
Praise the Lord.
 How good it is to sing praises to our God,
how pleasant and fitting to praise him!
The Lord builds up Jerusalem;
 he gathers the exiles of Israel.
He heals the brokenhearted and binds up their wounds.

He determines the number of the stars
 and calls them each by name.
Great is our Lord and mighty in power;
 his understanding has no limit.
The Lord sustains the humble

but casts the wicked to the ground.

Sing to the Lord with thanksgiving;
    make music to our God on the harp.
He covers the sky with clouds;
    He supplies the earth with rain
and makes grass grow on the hills.
    He provides food for the cattle
and for the young ravens when they call.

His pleasure is not in the strength of the horse,
    nor his delight in the legs of a man;
the Lord delights in those who fear him,
    who put their hope in his unfailing love.

Extol the Lord, O Jerusalem;
    praise your God, O Zion,
for he strengthens the bars of your gates
    and blesses your people within you.
He grants peace to your borders
    and satisfies you with the finest of wheat.
He sends his command to the earth;
    his word runs swiftly.
He spreads the snow like wool
    and scatters the frost like ashes.
He hurls down his hail like pebbles.
    Who can withstand his icy blast?
He sends his words and melts them;
    he stirs up his breezes, and the waters flow.

He has revealed his word to Jacob,
    his laws and decrees to Israel.
He has done this for no other nation;
    they do not know his laws.
Praise the Lord.
Glory be to the Father, Son, and the Holy Spirit;
As it was in the beginning,
is now and ever shall be. Amen.

*Other useful texts: Psalm 65; 103; 107; 116; 117;
Deuteronomy 8; 26:1-11; 32:7-15,45-47; Joshua 24:1-14;
1 Chronicles 29:9-15, 17-18; Habbakuk 3: 17-19;
Luke 12:22-23; 17:11-19; Romans 4:3, 13-22;*

Romans 8:24-28, 35-39; Galatians 6:6-10; Colossians 3:1-17.

4   *People offer their gifts. Others in the congregation may join in this expression.*

5   OPTIONAL
     PRAYER OF DEDICATION TO GOD
     The minister offers this prayer through which the people may be dedicated to God and for his service. People kneel on the chancel.

Minister   Bless these your servants O Lord, who have publicly come to offer thanks and praise to you in acknowledgement of your goodness towards them. And as they now dedicate themselves to your service, we ask that you would anoint them with the anointing of the Holy Spirit so that the services they render to you and in your name, to the Church and all in need, would bring glory to your holy name. Bless their going and their coming, from this day and for ever more. **Amen.**

6   *The minister assisted by his assistants lays his hands on each person's head and the minister says:*

Be dedicated to the Lord. In all your doings, with all your talents, and with your very lifestyle, may you always seek to glorify the Lord. In the name of the Father, Son, and the Holy Spirit. Amen.

7   *An appropriate hymn is given, during which the people go back to their seats and the rest of the service continues.*

A Litany for the
Preservation of Environment

NOTES

- This litany is to be used on its own.

- It is to be used as a way of celebrating God's gift of the created order and reminding people of their obligation to be responsible stewards of the same.

- The Service may be used inside the church or near a threatened environmental site.

- It is to be presided by an ordained minister assisted by others.

- It serves best when several people are involved in leading different sections.

ORDER OF SERVICE

1   *An appropriate song is sang in praise of God for his creation. People sit. The minister standing facing the people says:*

Minister   As we ponder the awesome wonder of God's creation let us with the psalmist and the prophets, thank him and hear his warning of judgement on those who destroy it, and rejoice in the hope of its future.

The earth is the Lord's and everything in it.
He has founded it upon the seas and established it upon the waters. *(Psalm 24:1-2)*

The trees of the Lord are watered abundantly, the cedars of Lebanon which he planted.
In them the birds build their nests; the stork has her home in the pine trees. *(Psalm 104:16-17)*

Who shall ascend the hill of the Lord
And stand in his holy place?
**He who has clean hands and a pure heart
and does not swear deceitfully.** *(Psalm 24:3-4)*

2   *JUDGEMENT ON THOSE WHO DESTROY THE ENVIRONMENT*

Minister   Let us hear the warning words of Isaiah.
Woe to those who call evil good and good evil,
who put darkness for light and light for darkness.
Who put bitter for sweet and sweet for bitter!

Woe to those who are wise in their own eyes
And shrewd in their own sight! *(Isaiah 5:20-21)*

On a bare hill raise a signal, cry aloud to them;
Wave the hand for them to enter the gates of the nobles. *(Isaiah 13:2)*

3 SCRIPTURE PORTIONS

Reader The Lord enters into judgement
with the elders and princes of his people:
"It is you who have devoured the vineyard,
the spoil of the poor is in your houses.
What do you mean by crushing my people,
by grinding the face of the poor?"
Says the Lord God of Hosts. *(Isaiah 3:14-15)*

Reader Woe to those who join house to house,
who add field to field,
until there is no more room,
and you are made to dwell alone
in the midst of the land.
The Lord of hosts has sworn in my hearing;
"Surely many houses shall be desolate,
large and beautiful houses, without inhabitants".
(Isaiah 5:8-9)

Reader Woe to those who decree iniquitous decrees,
and the writers who keep writing oppression,
to turn aside the needy from justice
and to rob the poor of my people of their right,
that widows may be their spoil,
People **and that they make the fatherless their prey.**
(Isaiah 10:1-2)

Reader Whom have you mocked and reviled?
Against whom have you raised your voice
And haughtily lifted your eyes?
People **Against the holy one of Israel!**

Reader By your servants you have mocked the Lord
And you have said, "With many chariots
I have gone up the heights of the mountains
to the far heights of Lebanon;

I felled its tallest cedars, its choicest pine trees;
I came to its remotest height,
its densest forest. *(Isaiah 37:23-24)*

4   *Minister*   Thus says the Lord!
"Because you have raged against me
And your arrogance has come to my ears
I will put my hook into your nose
and my bit into your mouth,
And I will turn you back on the way
by which you came.

      People   **The way by which you came.** *(Isaiah 37:28-29)*

HOPE FOR THE FUTURE

5   *Minister*   But the words of Job give us hope for the future.
For there is hope for a tree,
if it be cut down, that it will sprout again,
and that its shoots will not cease.
Though its roots grow old in the earth,
and its stump die in the ground,

      People   **Yet at the scent of water it will bud**
and put forth branches like a young plant.
(Job 15:7-9)

      Minister   Let the fields exult and everything in them,
the trees of the wood sing for joy
for the Lord comes to judge the earth.

      People   **He will judge the world with his truth and justice.**
(Psalm 96:12-13)

6   *Reader*   The Lord has broken the staff of the wicked,
the sceptre of rulers,
that smote the peoples in wrath
with unceasing blows.
The pine trees and cedars of Lebanon
exult over you and say,

      People   **"Now that you have been laid low, no woodsman**
comes to cut us down". *(Isaiah 14:8)*

7   *CELEBRATION OF CREATION*

*Either this litany, or, Psalm 148 which may be used antiphonally by the
minister and the congregation.*

Minister	For you shall go out in joy, and be led forth in peace; the mountains and the hills before you shall break forth into singing,
People	**And all the trees of the field shall clap their hands.** *(Isaiah 55:12)*
Minister	Cypress trees will grow where there are briers; myrtle trees will come up in place of thorns. This will be a sign that will last for ever;
People	**The Lord has done it!** *(Isaiah 55:13)*
Minister	We thank you Lord for the forests of this land.
People	**We thank you Lord.**
Minister	We are sad that the hills have been shaved of trees:
People	**We are very sad.**
Minister	We are sad the trees have been wantonly felled and not replanted.
People	**We are very sad.**
Minister	But we are hopeful that the trees will sprout.
People	**They will sprout and joyfully clap their hands, Alleluia.**

People clap their hands

8 EPILOGUE *(may be said antiphonally)*

O Lord of all creation, who viewed
all you had created and concluded
it was all very beautiful,
grant that your people, whom you created in your image
shall seek to safeguard and not destroy your beautiful creation.

May the shaved hills be reforested;
and turn flourishingly green again.

May the forests grow denser and greener;
and the encroachment of the deserts be averted.

May the rivers stay in their courses;
and be safeguarded against pollution.

May the fields yield a hundred fold;
and people be well fed.

May the herds and flocks ever find green pasture and cooling streams;
May our seas, oceans and lakes teem with aquatic life.

May all wildlife be protected;
May it be safeguarded against poaching and fire catastrophes.

May water gush forth in the deserts and springs in the wastelands.
May creation harmony be furthered and humanity be truly good stewards as was decreed in the garden of Eden.

Glory to the Father, Son, and the Holy Spirit,
As it was in the beginning, is now and ever shall be. Amen.

9   *Hymn*

10   *Notices*

11   *Sermon*

14   *Offertory*

15   *Final Prayers and Blessing*

Restoration of Things Profaned

NOTES

- This service is to be used for the restoration of holy places of worship and/or things therein after any kind of defilement of the same has taken place through people's wrongful use, unholy invasion, wicked behaviour.

- The service is to be conducted by the bishop but he may also delegate to a priest to do it.

- If the local priest, and/or any of the elders had a part to play in the profane act, they are not to take part in the cleansing ceremony; the service of Reconciliation of a Penitent is appropriate for use in restoring them back to the fellowship of the Church.

- Water for cleansing should be put in a bowl and consecrated.

- Following the act of profanity, especially if it touches on the worship life of the people, this service of restoration is to precede any other service that is to be conducted in the premises.

ORDER OF SERVICE

1 *Hymn*

2 *Bishop*   Brothers and sisters in the Lord, today we gather here to restore what the devil had destroyed and what the evil one profaned. Remember the Lord restores the treasures of the righteous. He guards his foot against stumbling. For this reason we have gathered here to restore this place of worship, and all the holy vessels that have been profaned.

3 *He reads a few of the scripture sentences below.*

If we say we have no sins we deceive ourselves and the truth is not in us. If we confess our sins in repentance and trust, God is faithful and just and will forgive us our sins and purify us from all unrighteousness. *(1 John 1:8,9)*

My soul has a desire and longing to enter into the courts of the Lord; My heart and my flesh rejoice in the living God. *(Psalm 84:2)*
Wash and be clean: put away evil deeds from your sight. Cease to do evil and learn to do good. *(Isaiah 1:16b)*

Come, let us go to the mountain of the Lord, that he may teach us his ways, and that we may walk in his paths. *(Isaiah 2:3)*

This is the person to whom I'll look to; he that is humble and contrite in spirit, and trembles at my word. *(Isaiah 66:2)*

I will get up and go to my Father, and I will say to him: "Father, I have sinned against heaven and before you. I am no longer worthy to be called your son." *(Luke 15:18,19a)*

4   *CONFESSION*

All   **Eternal Father, God of our ancestors,**
             before your power all things tremble,
             but through your Son, we approach your throne.
             We have done wrong and neglected to do right;
             Our sins weigh heavily on our hearts;
             Lord have mercy, count them not against us.
             Grant us the joy of forgiveness and lighten our hearts
             with the glory of Christ, who died and rose again for
             us. Amen.

5   *ABSOLUTION*

Bishop   The God and Father of our Lord Jesus Christ rejoices at
             repentance and declares his acceptance. The dead are
             alive, the lost are found.
             His goodness and mercy shall follow you all the days of
             your life, and you will live in the house of the Lord for
             ever. **Amen.**

6   *CONSECRATION OF WATER*

The water should be consecrated thus:

Bless this water Lord, which we are about to use as a sign for the cleansing and restoration of this house of worship and other holy items therein, to their original holy use. We consecrate this water in the name of the Father, Son, and the Holy Spirit. **Amen.**

7   *PROCESSION ROUND THE CHURCH AND SPRINKLING OF THE WATER ON THE OUTER WALLS*

Appropriate hymn(s) may be sang as the cleansing goes on.
Bishop then leads people into the church. As the procession enters the church a hymn is sang.

The following psalm is read antiphonally and solemnly as the people stand.

Psalm 106 (v 3,6,39, Psalm 27:9,10)

Happy are those who obey the Lord's commands;
who always do what is right.

We have sinned as our ancestors did;
We have been wicked and evil.

They made themselves impure by their actions;
And were unfaithful to God.

So God was angry with his people;
He was disgusted with them.

Yet the Lord heard them when they cried out;
and he took notice of their distress.

Do not hide yourself from me;
Do not be angry with me.

You have been my help;
Don't leave me, don't abandon me, O God my Saviour.

Glory to the Father, Son and the Holy Spirit;
As it was in the beginning, is now and ever shall be. Amen.

8   *A prayerful chorus*

9   *Bishop then goes to each item that has been profaned, sprinkles it with the
holy water and says:*

I declare this *(name the item)* restored to the use for which it was
consecrated.
People   **Thanks be to God.**

10   *When all the items have been re-consecrated, the bishop announces:*

Bishop   I declare the whole of this building and all the profaned
items herein, restored to the original use for which they
were dedicated and consecrated.
People   **Alleluia, thanks be to God.**

11   *People stand. Bishop conducts the following:*

Bishop   Give thanks to the Lord for he is good;
People   **His love endures for ever.**

Bishop	Let everybody say:
People	**His love endures for ever.**
Bishop	Let those who fear the Lord say:
People	**His love endures for ever.** *(see Psalm 118:1-4)*
Bishop	The Lord is my strength and my song;
People	**He has become my salvation.**
Bishop	Shouts of joy and victory;
People	**Resound in the tents of the righteous.** *(ululation & drums) (v 14-15)*
Bishop	Blessed is he who comes in the name of the Lord;
People	**From the House of the Lord we bless you.**
Bishop	The Lord is God;
People	**And he has made his light shine upon us.**
Bishop	With boughs in hand, join in the festal procession;
People	**Up to the horns of the altar.** *(v 26-27)*
Bishop	The Lord's right hand is lifted high;
People	**The Lord's right hand has done mighty things!** *(v 16)*
Bishop	Open for me the gates of righteousness;
People	**I will enter and give thanks to the Lord.**
Bishop	This is the gate of the Lord;
People	**Through which the righteous may enter.** *(v 19-20)*
Bishop	The stone the builders rejected;
People	**Has become the capstone.**
Bishop	The Lord has done this;
People	**And it is marvellous in our eyes.**
Bishop	This is the day the Lord has made;
People	**Let us rejoice and be glad in it.** *(v 22-24)*
Bishop	Alleluia!
People	**Amen and Amen.**
12 *Bishop*	Let us pray. *(Silence is observed.)*

Almighty God, by the radiance of your Son's appearing,
You have purified a world corrupted by sin:
We humbly pray that you would continue to be our
Strong defence against the attacks of our enemies;
Grant that [*this* _____, and] whatsoever in this *church*
has been stained or defiled through the craft of Satan or by human
malice, may be purified and cleansed by your abiding grace; that this
place, purged from all pollution, may be restored and sanctified, to
the glory of your name;
Through Jesus Christ our Lord, who lives and reigns with you and
the Holy Spirit, one God, now and for ever. **Amen.**

(Service of Restoration ends here.)

13   *Recessional hymn*

Freeing a Building From Holy to Ordinary Use

NOTES

- Before the onset of the service, all consecrated items that the congregation wishes to retain for continued use, are to be removed from the building.

- The service is to be conducted by the Bishop or his appointee.

- Once freed, the building, may be demolished or used for other ordinary (but not profane) purposes.

- The service is to be conducted only for those buildings that had once been consecrated as places of worship. It is non applicable for instance where people have been worshipping in a classroom awaiting the completion of their church.

ORDER OF SERVICE

1   *People are seated inside the church, or else they remain standing if pews have been removed.*

2   *The Bishop and others with him enter the Church and proceed to the sanctuary.*

    Bishop   The Lord be with you.
    People   **And also with you.**

3   *People stand as the Bishop reads the Sentence of Freeing. He may use these or other words:*

Brothers and Sisters in Christ, many of you may have intimate connections with this place because you have worshipped here for many years, and the fact that it has been the centre of worship for people from around. Those of us who are older know the history of this Church/building; how it was consecrated for worship purposes on *(he states date, month, and year)*. Since that time, many memorable events have taken place here such as baptisms, confirmations, weddings; not to mention the normal Sunday services that take place here Sunday after Sunday.

To all who cherish such fond memories and who may experience a deep sense of loss following the eventual freeing, I pray for peace and consolation, and trust that the experience of having to worship in a different and more magnificent building will reduce the sense of loss.

4   *After this, the following:*

Bishop	The Lord be with you.
People	**And also with you.**

Bishop	Let us pray.
	Lord we thank you for all the time this building has been used as the place of worship for your people in this locality.
People	**We thank you Lord.**

Bishop	For all that it has meant to them.
People	**We thank you Lord.**

Bishop	For all the acceptable services that were rendered here.
People	**We thank you Lord.**

Bishop	For all the edifying sermons that were delivered here.
People	**We thank you Lord.**

Bishop	For all who have been baptised and confirmed here.
People	**We thank you Lord.**

Bishop	For all whose marriages were conducted here.
People	**We thank you Lord.**

Bishop	For all the times we received spiritual nourishment through the Holy Communion.
People	**We thank you Lord.**

Bishop	Glory to the Father, Son and the Holy Spirit.
People	**As it was in the beginning, is now and ever shall be. Amen.**

5   *Then follows the declaration of freeing, which may be drafted in the following, or other manner (See Appendix):*

6   *The Bishop offers this prayer:*

Guide us Lord with your mercies and divine protection as we live and work for you. Reveal your face whenever we seek you. Guide our faltering steps as we struggle to walk in your footsteps in the sandy and miry ground of our existence. Keep our faith steadfastly focused on you, to the end that our joy in serving the church on earth will be crowned in our being partakers of the wedding of the Lamb, when Jesus will receive his bride, the Church, holy and pure. Through Jesus Christ who lives and reigns with the Father, for ever and ever. **Amen.**

Go out into the world in peace; be brave,
keep hold of what is good, never pay back wrong for wrong,
encourage the faint hearted, support the weak and the
distressed, give due love to everyone.

And the blessing of God Almighty,
Father, Son and the Holy Spirit, be with you and remain with you
now and for ever more. **Amen.**

Bishop   Go in peace to love and serve the Lord
People   **In the name of Christ, Amen.**

7   *An appropriate hymn may be sang as the people leave the church.*

APPENDIX

Sentence of Freeing of a Church Building
For Ordinary Use

(On behalf of the Diocesan Bishop) I declare that this building shall no
longer be a recognized place of worship. I declare that the building is free
from use as a place of worship and sacramental practices of the Anglican
Church of Kenya. I declare this building freed for (demolition, or) other
use. In the name of the Father, Son, and the Holy Spirit. **Amen.**

Dated this day of _____(date) _____(month), in the year of
our Lord _____ (Year)

Signed: _____

Bishop of: _____

Diocese: _____

The Litany

God the Father, creator of the universe and all that is there.
Have mercy on us.

God the Son, the Saviour of the world.
Have mercy on us.

God the Holy Spirit the comforter of humanity.
Have mercy on us.

Holy, blessed and glorious Trinity.
Have mercy on us.

From all satanic plottings against your Church.
O Lord deliver us.

From malice and hatred, from all forms of corruption and worldliness.
O Lord deliver us.

From all fear of persecution and the dread of death.
O Lord deliver us.

From disordered and sinful affections and from the deceits of the world, the flesh and the devil.
O Lord deliver us.

From drought and floods, from earthquakes and other disasters, from wicked people who plan evil against us, from gangsters, robbers, murderers, hijackers and kidnappers, from carjackers and reckless drivers, from slanderers and rumour mongers.
O Lord deliver us.

Protect and direct your holy Church to the source of truth; govern and encourage her to speak the truth in love, both in season and out of season.
Hear us O Lord.

Endow your servants with your Holy Spirit and let them serve you faithfully and courageously without fear or favour; enlighten them with knowledge and understanding, that by their teaching and their lives, they may proclaim your Word.
Hear us O Lord.

For their homes and families, that they may be adorned with all Christian virtues.
Hear us O Lord.

Give your people grace to hear and receive your word, and bring forth the fruit and the gifts of the Spirit.
Hear us O Lord.

Hear us as we remember the bishops and all ministers of the Gospel who have died in the peace of Christ and have been promoted to glory *(pause in silence)... .*
Grant us with them a share in your eternal kingdom.

For all in the communion of your Church, who have died in Christ; that we may walk in their footsteps and be fully united with them in your everlasting kingdom.
Hear us O Lord.

For the nations of the world that they may peacefully co-exist, and that a spirit of respect and forbearance may grow among nations and peoples.
We beseech you O Lord.

For the poor, the persecuted and the suffering; for prisoners and the detained, refugees and all in danger; that they may be relieved and protected.
We beseech you O Lord.

For the terminally ill and all who are living with dreadful scourges, that they may be comforted in their suffering. May they place all their hope in you and hence find peace that passes all understanding.
We beseech you O Lord.

For doctors and scientists in the medical research who spend many hours in various laboratories of the world in search of cures for diseases.
Grant them patience, endurance and success.

For the little children and babies: born and unborn, that their tender lives may be protected and their rights guarded.
We beseech you O Lord.

Guide and govern your holy Church, fill it with love and truth, and grant it that unity which is your will, binding it together with your Spirit.
We beseech you O Lord.

Give courage to our bishops, clergy, and all church leaders, that they may courageously proclaim the Good News of the Kingdom, and fearlessly challenge injustices in the nation.
We beseech you O Lord.

Give sufficient grace to our Archbishop in his rigorous task of leading the Church in this country, and in his many other callings. Grant him strength, courage and wisdom for every day's tasks.
We beseech you O Lord.

Direct and guide all church based organizations that work for peace, justice and reconciliation, and for the wholistic development of God's people; that they may achieve their mission goals, for the glory and honour of your holy name.
We beseech you O Lord.

Bring into the way of truth, all who have erred and are deceived and those who have been tossed to and fro by every wind of doctrine.
We beseech you O Lord.

Strengthen those who stand, comfort and help the fainthearted, raise up the fallen and finally beat down Satan under your feet.
We beseech you O Lord.

Guide our President and other leaders of this country into ways of justice, peace and unity. Grant that there will be peace within our borders, that all the people in this region may live in harmony and enjoy good neighbourliness.
Hear us O Lord.

For political tolerance among people of different political persuasions, for greater respect for one another's opinions and convictions, for greater thirst after truth and justice for all, that political thuggeries and assassinations may come to an end, that people may enjoy fullness of life as God intended for them.
Hear us O Lord.

Guide and bless those who administer the law; that honesty and truth may be upheld, and that they may proclaim justice without fear or favour except the fear of God.
Hear us O Lord.

Help and comfort the lonely, the bereaved, the oppressed and the voiceless.
Help and comfort them.

Protect our Archbishop, Bishops and Ministers from threats and intimidations of all kinds.
Lord protect them.

Heal the sick in body and mind, provide for the widows and the orphans, the homeless, the hungry and the destitute.
Lord have mercy.

Watch over the aged in their faltering steps, diminishing eyesight and failing strength. Grant that they shall soar up with wings as eagles, run and not be weary, walk and not faint, as they continue putting their hope in you.
Hear us O Lord.

Remember, we beseech you, school leavers and graduates from institutions of learning, that they may get employment and stop idling, for an idle mind is the devil's workshop.
Hear us O Lord.

Pour your blessing on all human labour, that your people may enjoy good output, be well fed and live in economic comfort.
Hear us O Lord.

Preserve and guard the integrity of creation against exploitation; that forests, lakes, game reserves and other natural and environmental resources may be safeguarded against misuse or abuse.
Hear us O Lord.

Grant us favourable climate and sufficient rain, that our herds may be fed, the fields be fruitful and the harvest plentiful.
Hear us O Lord.

For all of us here gathered in your name and for your service; for the forgiveness of our sins, and for the grace of the Holy Spirit to amend our lives.
Hear us O Lord.

Watch over us when we sleep, and protect us against those of evil intent who lurk around homes at night, attacking people and harvesting where they never planted.
Hear us O Lord.

Almighty God, grant that we might receive what we have earnestly asked in faith, that in all the services we render to you and in your name, we may find true fulfilment, and that your people may be well nourished in their souls, to the glory and honour of your holy name. **Amen.**

Collects for Sundays, Principal Holy Days and Festivals

NOTES

- Normally, on any occasion, only one Collect is used.

- The Collect for each Sunday is used on the following weekdays except where other provision is made.

- At Evening Worship on Saturdays other than the Easter Eve, Christmas Eve or Principal Feasts or Festivals, the Collect appointed for the ensuing Sunday shall be used. When Evening Worship on the day before a Festival makes use of the lessons relating to that Festival, the Collect of that Festival shall be used.

- The framework in which the Collects have been written has been borrowed from the Common Worship of the Church of England. We acknowledge this with gratitude. The difference is that our Collects do not necessarily have a Trinitarian ending. Rather, they tend to take our normal (varied) Kenyan style of saying and ending prayers.

- We have tried as much as possible to write our own authentic Collects but excluding the Post Communions except for limited instances, and also for Festivals. We have retained the Festival Collects as they are in Common Worship, but have left out those that are specifically relevant to the people in England.

- The Collects are largely (if not) purely based on the Gospel readings taken from the Second Service in the Lectionary.

Collects for Seasons

ADVENT

The First Sunday of Advent *Purple*
Matthew 24:15-28; Matthew 21:1-13; John 3:1-17.

Collect
Almighty God,
give us grace to cast away the works of darkness
and to put on the armour of light,
now in the time of this mortal life,
in which your Son Jesus Christ came to us in great humility;
that on the last day,
when he shall come again in his glorious majesty
to judge the living and the dead,
we may rise to the life immortal;
through him who is alive and reigns with you,
in the unity of the Holy Spirit,
one God, now and for ever.

This Collect may be used as the Post Communion on any day from the Second Sunday of Advent until Christmas Eve instead of the Post Communion provided.

Post Communion
O Lord our God,
make us watchful and keep us faithful
as we await the coming of your Son our Lord;
that, when he shall appear,
he may not find us sleeping in sin
but active in his service
and joyful in his praise;
through Jesus Christ our Lord.

The Second Sunday of Advent *Purple*
Matthew 11:2-11; Luke 1:1-25; John 1:19-28.

Collect
O God our Father, we thank you for your servant
John, who like a burning lamp and faithful to his
calling, announced the advent of our Lord and people
rejoiced for a while in his light, for he was just a witness
to the greater light of your Son Jesus Christ, the light of the World.
May we too through the enabling of your Son Jesus,
be like lights in a dark world, to lead the people into the
knowledge of Jesus our Lord and the light of the world.

The Third Sunday of Advent *Purple*
Matthew 14:1-12; Luke 1:57-66 (or 67-80); John 5:31-40.

Collect
Lord Jesus, we know we are privileged to share
in the sufferings of those like your servant John for whom
bold honesty led to his death. Lead us to boldly stand
for the truth and declare the same with courage and wisdom
that comes from you. Stand with your servants in times of
crises and hardships that they may not compromise their stand,
but continue shining like heavenly lights
in a world that is so full of darkness and sin.

The Fourth Sunday of Advent *Purple*
This provision is not used on weekdays after 23 December.
Luke 1:39-55; Matthew 1:18-25; Luke 1:39-45.

Collect
Lord Jesus, our Saviour and redeemer,
we glorify you for your wonderful purpose
of salvation, for you came not to condemn the world,
but that the world through you might be saved.
and as Mary treasured all the messages of the divine errands,
so do our hearts burn within us as we await the imminence
of your return as King and judge. Help us to be ready. **Amen.**

24 December **Christmas Eve** *Purple*
Luke 1:67-79.

Collect
Almighty God,
you make us glad with the yearly remembrance
of the birth of your Son Jesus Christ:
grant that, as we joyfully receive him as our redeemer,
so we may with sure confidence behold him
when he shall come to be our judge.

Post Communion
Eternal God, for whom we wait,
you have fed us with the bread of eternal life:
keep us ever watchful,
that we may be ready to stand before the Son of man,
Jesus Christ our Lord.

CHRISTMAS

25 December **Christmas Night** *Gold or White*
Principal Feast
Luke 2:1-14(15-20); John 1:1-14.

Collect
Eternal God,
who made this most holy night
to shine with the brightness of your one true light:
bring us, who have known the revelation of that light
on earth, to see the radiance of your heavenly glory;
through Jesus Christ your Son our Lord, who is alive and
reigns with you, in the unity of the Holy Spirit,
one God, now and for ever.

Post Communion
O God our Father,
in this night you have made known to us again
the coming of our Lord Jesus Christ: confirm our faith
and fix our eyes on him until the day dawns and Christ
the Morning Star rises in our hearts.
To him be glory both now and for ever.

25 December **Christmas Day** *Gold or White*
Principal Feast
Luke 2:1-7(8-20); John 1:1-14; Luke 2:1-14 (15-20).

Collect
Glory to God on the highest heaven,
And on earth peace among those he favours!
For the unspeakable gift of his Son Jesus our Saviour.
Everlasting Father, we give you honour, praise and adoration,
throughout eternity.

Post Communion
Almighty Father we thank you that
the Word of Life became flesh
and lived among us, and we have seen his glory,
the glory of a Father's only Son,
full of grace and truth. Amen.

The First Sunday of Christmas *White*
This provision is not used on weekdays after 5 January.
Luke 2:41-52 (yr 1&2); Luke 2:15-21.

Collect
Lord Jesus, as a young boy you fully expressed
yourself as you listened to the teachers of Jerusalem
and asked them questions to the astonishment of your
parents and all around you.
Be with our children as they learn, that in their listening
and asking of questions, they may grow up in wisdom and in
stature and in favour with God and society.

Or

O God the rock of our salvation
we thank you for wonderfully purposing that
your Son should become one of us, yet without sin,
a sympathetic high priest on our behalf.
Grant us like Mary to treasure and to ponder in our
hearts all the wonders of your Son, our redeemer,
Jesus Christ.

The Second Sunday of Christmas *White*
This provision is not used on weekdays after 5 January.
Matthew 2:13-23 (yr 1,2 &3).

Collect
Most loving Father,
we thank you for the obedience
of your servant Joseph who, in response to your call,
got up at night and took Jesus and his mother to Egypt,
that the prophecy might be fulfilled: "Out of Egypt I have
called my son".
Lead us in similar obedience to the glory of Jesus our Lord.

EPIPHANY

6 January **The Epiphany** *Gold or White*
Principal Feast
John 2:1-11

Collect
Almighty redeemer,
grant that in obedience to the words of Mary
we may do what your Son bids us do,
and share with the world the joy of the new wine
of our obedience to him.

The Baptism of Christ *Gold or White*
The First Sunday of Epiphany
Luke 3:15-22; Matthew 3:13-17; Mark 1:4-11.

Collect
Eternal Father,
grant us today as you did then,
that we would see the Spirit descending on Jesus
and hear afresh your declaration and instruction,
"This is my beloved Son with whom am well pleased";
and give us O Lord, ears that would listen,
and hearts that would obey him.

The Second Sunday of Epiphany *White*
John 1:43-51; Matthew 8:5-13; John 1:29-42.

Collect
Precious Jesus,
through the riches of your Grace and in
response to faith, you transformed
the people's desperate situations, restoring all
to health and wholeness.
Speak your word now O Lord, and we shall be healed.

The Third Sunday of Epiphany *White*
Luke 4:14-21; Matthew 4: 12-23; Mark 1:21-28.

Collect
Almighty and most gracious Father,
as your Son Jesus called the first disciples
and changed them from fish catchers to soul winners,
we ask that like them we too may respond with
zeal and passion in obedience to his call.

The Fourth Sunday of Epiphany *White*
Mark 1:21-28; Matthew 13:10-17; John 4:19-29a.

Collect
Dear Jesus,
you taught with authority and gave spiritual insight
to those who followed you, lifting them from the
darkness of ignorance to the glorious light of the gospel truths.
Grant us we pray the insight to understand what you say to us in the
parables.

2 February **The Presentation of Christ in the Temple** *Gold or White*
Candlemass
Principal Feast
Luke 2:22-40

Collect
Almighty God
Your Son Jesus the Saviour of the world and first born
of all creation was in his infancy consecrated before you.
Grant that we too following in his footsteps might be
wholly consecrated to you and glorify you in all that we do,
awaiting to be gloriously presented by Jesus before your throne,
when he comes again.

ORDINARY TIME

The Fifth Sunday before Lent *Green*
Mark 1: 29-3; Luke 5:1-11; Matthew 5:13-20.
This provision is always used from the day after the Presentation
of Christ in the Temple until the first of the Sundays before Lent.

Collect
O Lord our God,
In as much as we are dedicated to your service,
it is only you who can give the results or else we
labour in vain.
Show us and lead us into those mission fields,
where the harvest is ripe but the reapers are few.
Glorify yourself in our work for your kingdom's sake. **Amen.**

The Fourth Sunday before Lent *Green*
Mark 1:40-45; Luke 6:17-26; Matthew 5:21-37.

Collect
Father in the name of Jesus,
we are not able without the continuous supply of your
abundant grace, to lead lives that glorify you.
We are overwhelmed by your power, might and Love.
Do not hide your face from us when we seek you,
for health and the healing of relationships,
for forgiveness of sins and for guidance
in our service to you and for your kingdom. **Amen.**

The Third Sunday before Lent *Green*
Mark 2:1-12; Luke 6:27-38; Matthew 6:1-8.

Collect
Almighty God,
Your Son, our Saviour Jesus
manifested your power in a manner that
was never witnessed before, and further taught
us how to love our enemies.
Grant us the ability and courage to do likewise,
and the power and wisdom to challenge
all in our society who promote
values that stand in opposition to your will.
Through Jesus Christ who chose
to die that the world may be won for God.

The Second Sunday before Lent *Green*
Luke 12:16-31; Luke 8:22-35; Matthew 6:25-34.

Collect
Almighty God,
We are often tossed up and down by the
storms of this life, and at such times
we get afraid and anxious. May we be awake to
the fact that your divine hand is in control.
Therefore, trusting in your power that is at work within us,
we release all our cares and anxieties to you and ask for
inner refreshment and peace that passes all
understanding, to reign in our hearts always. **Amen.**

The Sunday next before Lent *Green*
Matthew 17:9-23 (or 1-23); Mark 9:2-8 (or 9-13); John 12:27-36a.
This provision is not used on or after Ash Wednesday.

Collect
Almighty Father,
your Son accepted to suffer the death of a criminal
that we may be set free.
Help us to understand the mystery of his death,
through which we have come to life,
and grant that we shall be counted worthy to share
in the glory of Him who sits at your right hand on high,
Jesus Christ our Lord.

LENT

Ash Wednesday *Purple or Lent Array*
Principal Holy Day
Luke 15:11-32

Collect
Almighty and everlasting God,
you hate nothing that you have made
and forgive the sins of all those who are penitent:
create and make in us new and contrite hearts
that we, worthily lamenting our sins
and acknowledging our wretchedness,
may receive from you, the God of all mercy,
perfect remission and forgiveness;
through Jesus Christ your Son our Lord,
who is alive and reigns with you,
in the unity of the Holy Spirit,
one God, now and for ever.

This Collect below may be used as the Post Communion
on any day from the First Sunday of Lent until the Saturday
after the Fourth Sunday of Lent instead of the Post Communion provided.

Post Communion
Almighty God,
you have given your only Son to be for us
both a sacrifice for sin
and also an example of godly life:
give us grace
that we may always most thankfully receive
these his inestimable gifts,
and also daily endeavour
to follow the blessed steps of his most holy life;
through Jesus Christ our Lord. **Amen.**

The First Sunday of Lent *Purple or Lent Array*
Luke 15:1-10; Luke 13: 31-35; Luke 18:9-14.

Collect
Loving Father,
our Lord Jesus was full of sorrow as he wept
over Jerusalem for her failure to repent.
Teach us the humility to look at ourselves by
the light of the cross, and be moved to repent of
all our wrongdoing, for you delight in restored fellowship
through him who plunged the depths that we might be
raised to the highest glory.

The Second Sunday of Lent *Purple or Lent Array*
Luke 14:27-33; John 8:51-59; Luke 14:27-33.

Collect
Almighty God,
Our Lord Jesus promises eternal life to
all who follow him;
Help us to know that there is a cost in being his disciples,
but that greater is the reward of being alive with you
for ever more.

The Third Sunday of Lent *Purple or Lent Array*
John 2:13-22; Matthew 10:16-22; John 1:35-51.

Collect
Almighty God,
Father of our Lord Jesus Christ,
you know our thoughts even before we speak them out;
 for there is no secret we can hide from you.
Grant us wisdom to know your will for us, courage to
stand for what is true, and patience to endure to the end.
Through your Son Jesus Christ our Lord. **Amen.**

The Fourth Sunday of Lent *Purple or Lent Array*
John 3:14-21; John 12:1-8; John 11:17-44.
Mothering Sunday may be celebrated in preference to the provision for
the Fourth Sunday of Lent.

Collect
Merciful Father,
we thank you for sending your Son,
our Lord Jesus to die that we may live.
Grant that we shall wake up from our slumber,
denounce all the works of darkness and embrace
Him who is our light and our life, to the end
that when our lives here are over, we shall eternally
reign with him, days without end. **Amen.**

Mothering Sunday *Purple or Lent Array*
Luke 2:33-35 or John 19:29-27.
Mothering Sunday may be celebrated in preference to
the provision for the Fourth Sunday of Lent.

Collect
God of compassion,
whose Son Jesus Christ, the child of Mary,
shared the life of a home in Nazareth, and on
the cross drew the whole human family to himself:
strengthen us in our daily living that in joy and in
sorrow we may know the power of your presence,
to bind together and to heal; through Jesus Christ your
Son our Lord, who is alive and reigns with you,
in the unity of the Holy Spirit,
one God, now and for ever. **Amen.**

Post Communion
Loving God,
as a mother feeds her children at the breast
you feed us in this sacrament with the food and drink of eternal life:
help us who have tasted your goodness
to grow in grace within the household of faith;
through Jesus Christ our Lord.

The Fifth Sunday of Lent *Purple or Lent Array*
Passiontide begins
Matthew 20:17-24; Luke 22:1-13; Luke 22:1-13.

Collect
Almighty God, holy and eternal,
grant us to know the virtue of humility
and sincerity in our walk with you,
that we may shun the futile lures of this life
and put first the eternal gains of being true
followers of Christ.
Through Jesus Christ our Lord. **Amen.**

Palm Sunday *Red*
Matthew 26:14-27; 66 or 27:11-54;
Mark 14:1-15, 47 or 15:1-39 [40-47]; Luke 22:14-23, 56 or 23:1-49.

Collect
Hosanna to the Son of David!
Hosanna to the King of Kings!
Who for our sake and our salvation
Was content to be betrayed by sinners,
willingly offering himself as the living bread.
Grant that we shall follow you truly,
sincerely and selflessly as you taught us. **Amen.**

Maundy Thursday *White*
Principal Holy Day
John 13:31b-35

At Morning and Evening Prayer the Collect of
Palm Sunday is used.
At Holy Communion this Collect is used.

Collect
Eternal Father
Your Son our Lord Jesus was presented to be tried
yet no fault was found in him, but they condemned him still.
He who knew no sin became sin for us
that he might pay a ransom to secure our redemption.
Grant that as we share in his passion, we may be made like him.
In his holy name we pray. **Amen.**

Good Friday *Hangings removed Red for the liturgy*
Principal Holy Day
John 19:38-42 or Colossians 1:18-23.

Collect
Almighty Father,
Your Son our Lord Jesus cried from the Cross,
"It is finished"! Grant that by his death we shall be reconciled
to you and live our lives in honour of him who is the head of the
Church and the first-born among the dead. **Amen.**

Easter Eve *Hangings removed*
John 2:18-22.

Collect
Everlasting Father,
Grant that we who are baptized into the death
of your Son our Saviour Jesus Christ
may continually put to death our evil desires
and be buried with him;
and that through the grave and gate of death
we may pass to our joyful resurrection;
through the merits of he who died and rose again for us,
Jesus Christ our Lord. **Amen.**

EASTER

Easter Day *Gold or White*
Principal Feast
John 20:1-18 or Matthew 28:1-10; John 20:1-18 or Mark 16:1-18;
John 20:1-18 or Luke 24:1-12.

Collect
Christ is risen!
He is risen indeed, Alleluyia!
He broke the chains of death and Hades
and gloriously resurrected
and now lives and reigns forever.
Through his death and resurrection we have
the assurance of eternal life
Help us Lord to die daily to sin,
that we may evermore live with you in the joy of
his risen life. In your name we pray. **Amen.**

The Second Sunday of Easter *White*
Mark 15:46-16:8; Luke 24:1-12; Luke 24:13-35.

Collect
The angel asked the women:
"Why do you look for the Living among the dead?"
Jesus Christ conquered death and sin and is alive for ever more.
Lord Jesus, grant us your divine presence, and the joy of knowing that no
amount of persecution can bend our hope of eternity with you.
In your precious name we pray and believe. **Amen.**

The Third Sunday of Easter *White*
John 2:13-22; Luke 16:19-31; John 11:[17-26]27-44.

Collect
Almighty Father,
Holy and revered, grant that our lives shall manifest faith,
holiness, reverence for God and humility to put the needs of
others before our own, and thus lay for ourselves treasure in heaven,
indestructible and eternal. Through Jesus Christ our Lord. **Amen.**

The Fourth Sunday of Easter *White*
Luke 19:37-48; John 6:30-40; Luke 24:36-49.

Collect
Almighty God,
Thank you for giving us Jesus the bread of life.
Send us the power of the Holy Spirit that we may
ever boldly testify to the truth of the Gospel in season
and out of season, and by our example lead
many to the saving knowledge of our Saviour Jesus Christ
our Lord. **Amen.**

The Fifth Sunday of Easter *White*
Luke 2:25-32[33-38]; Mark 16:9-16; Mark 15:46-16:8.

Collect
Almighty God,
We thank you for your Son Jesus
the Saviour who was prophesied about
from days of old, and whose birth
brought the dawn of salvation for all who
would believe in him.
Grant that we shall be his
faithful ambassadors on earth, and in his power
proclaim the Gospel in all its manifestations.
Through him who conquered death and now lives
with you in the unity of the Holy Spirit, one God,
now and for ever. **Amen.**

Ascension Day *Gold or White*
Principal Feast
Luke 24:44-53.

Collect
Almighty God,
We thank you for Jesus your Son, our Lord,
for his ascension to glory, having accomplished
your purpose on earth.
Grant we pray, that through the power of the Holy Spirit,
we shall ever seek to glorify him in all our doings,
awaiting the greater glory of his second coming when we too
shall be taken where he is and live with him eternally.
Through his wonderful name we pray and believe. **Amen.**

Sunday after Ascension *White*
(The Sixth Sunday of Easter)
John 21:1-14; Luke 22:24-30; Matthew 28:1-10, 16-20.
This provision is not used on or after Ascension Day.

Collect
Almighty Father,
in our efforts to fulfil the great commission of our Lord,
help us to remember that it is Jesus who equips and directs
our mission focus, for on our own we are helpless and foolish.
Grant us the grace to depend on you in all our difficulties,
and to exercise humility in times of success, that all glory,
honour and praise may belong to Jesus our Master and King,
now and for ever. **Amen.**

The Seventh Sunday of Easter *White*
Sunday after Ascension Day
Mark 16:14-20; Luke 4:14-21; Luke 24:44-53.

Collect
Lord Jesus, you bid your disciples to
"go into all the world and preach the good news to all creation..."
Grant that we too shall be committed to this commission. Send us
Lord wherever you chose, whenever you will, and we shall gladly go
in your name and by the power of the Holy Spirit. **Amen.**

Day of Pentecost *Red*
Whit Sunday
Principal Feast
This provision is not used on the weekdays after the Day of Pentecost.
Acts 2:1-21; John 20:19-23; John 14:18-17[25-27].

Collect
Almighty and ever living God,
we thank you for the gift of the Holy Spirit
who sets our hearts on fire.
Grant that we shall understand afresh what the presence
of the Holy Spirit means for us today as we seek to effectively
fulfil the Lord's great commission in our day, to the glory of
Jesus Christ our Lord and King. **Amen.**

Or

O God our Father,
We pray that you may release the power of
the Holy Spirit upon all who believe,
that we may become powerful witnesses of Jesus Christ our Lord
who died and rose again and now reigns with you and the Holy Spirit,
for ever and ever. **Amen.**

ORDINARY TIME

Trinity Sunday *Gold or White*
Principal Feast
Mark 1:1-13

Collect
Holy Trinity,
God the Father, God the Son, and God the Holy Spirit,
we worship you, adore you and put all our faith in you.
Help us ever to abide by this faith, and zealously defend it for
it is eternally abiding. Through the merits of our Saviour Jesus Christ who
reigns with you and the Holy Spirit, days without end. **Amen.**

The Thursday after Trinity Sunday may be observed as

**The Day of Thanksgiving for the
Institution of Holy Communion** *White*
(Corpus Christi)
John 6:51-58

Collect
Lord Jesus Christ,
we thank you that in this wonderful sacrament
you have given us the memorial of your passion:
grant us so to reverence the sacred mysteries
of your body and blood that we may know within ourselves
and show forth in our lives the fruits of your redemption;
for you are alive and reign with the Father in the unity of the Holy Spirit,
one God, now and for ever. **Amen.**

Post Communion
All praise to you, our God and Father,
for you have fed us with the bread of heaven and
quenched our thirst from the true vine: hear our prayer that,
being grafted into Christ, we may grow together in unity
and feast with him in his kingdom; through Jesus Christ our Lord. **Amen.**

The Second Sunday of Pentecost *Green*
Mark 2:1-12; Luke 6:27-38; Matthew 6:1-8.

Collect
O God our Father whose Son our Saviour
Jesus healed and restored many to perfect health,
We pray that you would extend your mercies today
to all the sick in our midst, touching them with your divine
hand and healing them from all that afflicts and weighs them down.
Through Jesus Christ the great physician. **Amen.**

The Third Sunday of Pentecost *Green*
Matthew 10:40-42; Mark 5:21-43; Luke 9:51-62.

Collect
Gracious Father, you were so generous that you
 gave us your Son Jesus, that his power and mercy may
 reach the ends of the world, bringing wholeness to nations and people.
Grant that we may welcome and receive your anointed ones
and in your name attend the hungry and the thirsty.
And as we seek in faith your healing touch upon our lives,
 may we hear you say to us "Your faith has made you whole".
Through that great physician Jesus Christ. **Amen.**

The Fourth Sunday of Pentecost *Green*
Matthew 11:16-19, 25-30; Mark 6:1-13; Luke 10:1-11, 16-20

Collect
I thank you, Father, Lord of heaven and earth,
because you have hidden these things
from the wise and the intelligent
and have revealed them to infants;

Yes Father for such was your gracious design.
Grant that we, like babes, would embrace the imperatives of the kingdom
and so conduct our lives in a manner that solely brings glory to your
name. **Amen.**

The Fifth Sunday of Pentecost *Green*
Matthew 13:1-9, 18-23; Mark 6:14-29; Luke 10:25-37.

Collect
Merciful Father,
grant that all who love you may hear the good news of Jesus Christ
and take them to heart. Let your words to us be as the falling
of the seeds on good soil, that we may bring forth an abundant harvest.
For your name's sake. **Amen.**

The Sixth Sunday of Pentecost *Green*
Matthew 13:24-30, 36-43; Mark 6:30-34,53-56; Luke 10:38-42.

Collect
Father, through your enduring patience with us,
you have designed that wheat and tares
should grow together until the great day of harvest
Help us to shun hypocrisy in our Christian walk,
that our lives may truly and boldly exemplify our faith in Jesus Christ
our Lord and Saviour. **Amen.**

The Seventh Sunday of Pentecost *Green*
Matthew 13:31-33,44-52; John 6:1-21; Luke 11:1-13.

Collect
Almighty Father,
we thank you for Jesus our Lord and Bread of Life,
who desires of his children to be nourished physically but more so,
spiritually by accepting him as Lord and Saviour in their lives.
Grant us so to receive Jesus,
be cleansed of all our sins and eternally be fed,
never to hunger again. **Amen.**

Eighth Sunday of Pentecost *Green*
Matthew 14:13-21; John 6:24-35; Luke 12:13-21.

Collect
Our God and Father, we praise you for our Saviour Jesus.
He saw the needs of all who followed him and had
compassion on them, graciously providing for their needs.
We pray that you will show compassion on all who seek you today,
and abundantly supply their needs according to your riches in glory.
Amen.

Ninth Sunday of Pentecost *Green*
Matthew 14:22-33; John 6:35, 41-51; Luke 12:32-40.

Collect
Loving Father,
You know the dispositions of our hearts
and you read our thoughts as one would an open book.
You know when we are afraid and shaken by the events
in our transient life.
Lead us into greater knowledge of you and cause us to be
practical in our Christian walk, ready at all times for the second coming
of Jesus our Lord and King. **Amen.**

Or

Lord you reach out in love
and mercy to those who cry out to you for help.
Reach out O Lord to rescue us in our day when
we call upon your name. May your mercy engulf
us and your love enfold us for the honour
and glory of your name. **Amen.**

The Tenth Sunday of Pentecost *Green*
John 6:51-58; Luke 12:49-56; Matthew 20:1-16.

Collect
Eternal Father,
We are feeble minded and often fail to fully grasp
the mysteries of salvation.
How we pray that you would deepen our understanding

and strengthen our resolve to serve you zealously
and faithfully for your kingdom's sake.
Through Jesus our Lord. **Amen.**

The Eleventh Sunday of Pentecost *Green*
Matthew 16:13-20; John 6:56-69; Luke 13:10-17.

Collect
Almighty God,
through your Son our Saviour Jesus,
you heal our diseases and infirmities.
Help us like Peter to know Jesus as he truly is,
and that by eating and drinking of him we may
 get the assurance of life eternal.

The Twelfth Sunday of Pentecost *Green*
Mark 7:1-8, 14,15,21-23; Matthew 4:23-5:20; John 3:22-36.

Collect
Eternal Father,
we thank you for Jesus our redeemer,
for his compassion on all the sick and the suffering,
for his willingness to be mistaken for a criminal and for accepting to die
in our place. Grant us joy and humility in our service to him who must
increase while we decrease. To him be glory, honour and praise, now and
for ever more. **Amen.**

Bible Sunday *Green*
*Bible Sunday is to be observed on the second Sunday of September or as
is celebrated by the Bible Society of Kenya.*
Luke 4:14-30; Matthew 22:34-40; Luke 4:14-30.

Collect
Blessed Lord,
who caused all holy Scriptures to be written for our learning:
help us so to hear them,
to read, mark, learn and inwardly digest them
that, through patience, and the comfort of your holy word,
we may embrace and for ever hold fast
the hope of everlasting life,
which you have given us in our Saviour Jesus Christ,

who is alive and reigns with you,
in the unity of the Holy Spirit,
one God, now and for ever.

Post Communion
God of all grace,
your Son Jesus Christ fed the hungry
with the bread of his life
and the word of his kingdom:
renew your people with your heavenly grace,
and in all our weakness
sustain us by your true and living bread;
who is alive and reigns, now and for ever.

The Thirteenth Sunday of Pentecost *Green*
Mark 7:24-37; Matthew 6:1-18; Luke 14:25-33.

Collect
Our gracious Heavenly Father,
You challenge us to count the cost of discipleship,
and thus make firm our commitment to you.
Help us to be different from the Pharisees and become selflessly
charitable and merciful,
That, laying aside the things that hold us, we may faithfully follow you
the rest of our lives. In Jesus name we pray. **Amen.**

The Fourteenth Sunday of Pentecost *Green*
Mark 8: 27-38; Matthew 7:1-14; John 6:51-69.

Collect
O righteous Father,
You require of us to shun all worldly concerns
and to depend on you for our every need.
We ask you through your Son our Saviour Jesus to cleanse us
from all unrighteousness and hypocrisy, that we may love and
value one another, through Jesus Christ who died for us. **Amen.**

The Fifteenth Sunday of Pentecost *Green*
Mark 9:30-37; Matthew 8:23-34; John 7:14-36.

Collect
Father, You are the Alpha and Omega,
supreme over all that you created.
We acknowledge your presence in all the
difficult situations we encounter from time to time.
Help us, we pray that in all our achievements we would learn the humility
of Jesus who gave up heavenly privileges for our sake.
And that in all our difficulties, recognize your Lordship.
Through Jesus Christ our Lord. **Amen.**

The Sixteenth Sunday of Pentecost *Green*
Mark 9:38-50; Matthew 9:1-8; John 8:31-38, 48-59.

Collect
O God of our ancestors,
God of Abraham, Isaac and Jacob.
Your Son our Saviour is the way the truth and the life.
May he abide in us and enable us to walk in his way,
live by his truth, serve in his power, and share in his life.
Through the merits of the same Jesus Christ our Lord we pray. **Amen.**

The Seventeenth Sunday of Pentecost *Green*
Mark 10:2-16; Matthew 10:1-22; John 9.

Collect
O God our King and lover of children,
You demand of all who would inherit your kingdom,
 to be like children in character. Open our eyes and deepen our faith
and loyalty to you, that shunning the deceptions of worldly riches we may
carry our cross and faithfully follow you without ever looking back.
 In Jesus name to pray. **Amen.**

The Eighteenth Sunday of Pentecost *Green*
Mark 10:17-31; Matthew 11:20-30; John 15:12-27.

Collect
Almighty Father,
We often hurt your love through our disobedience,
and by failing to love others as we ought to.
But we thank you for your enduring love and care towards us.
Help us Lord to keep our focus fixed on Jesus,
that we may zealously love and serve him with all that we are
and all that we have, to the glory and honour of his name. **Amen.**

The Nineteenth Sunday of Pentecost *Green*
Mark 10:35-45; Matthew 12:1-21; John 16:1-11.

Collect
Loving Father,
We thank you for teaching us through your Son Jesus,
that the way to greatness is through servanthood. We thank you
that Jesus taught us this by his own example. Help us like Jesus,
to serve others selflessly no matter the cost,
to the glory of his holy name. **Amen.**

The Twentieth Sunday of Pentecost *Green*
Mark 12:28-34; Luke 18:9-14; Matthew 22:34-46.

Collect
Father, in the name of Jesus,
We thank you for teaching us that the greatest commandment is
to love you and to love our neighbours.
Though we often fall short of this requirement, our confidence
and trust is in Jesus Christ our Lord who alone is able to form us to
be what we ought to be. So help us Lord, for the glory and honour of your
name.

The Twenty First Sunday of Pentecost *Green*
Matthew 8:23-34; John 7:14-36; Mark 9: 30-37.

Collect
O Lord our God,
who alone are able to know the end from the beginning,

and to whom the mysteries of life and death are an open secret;
open our feeble minds that we may truly know the depths
of your salvific purpose for humanity and for each one of us
individually, and thus purposefully work our salvation
with fear and trembling, as we seek to model our lives in your
likeness, knowing well that the way of salvation is the way of the cross.
Give us courage to walk that way, as Jesus did. **Amen.**

The Twenty Second Sunday of Pentecost *Green*
Mark 9:38-50; Luke 16:19-31; Matthew 21: 23-32.

Collect
Eternal Father,
grant, we beseech you,
that the ministers of the Gospel will truly be ambassadors of
Truth and righteousness in the world, that people who hear the
message of the Gospel will be drawn to you in faith and practice,
and further embrace the power thereof, even to perform miracles
in your name. **Amen.**

*If there are twenty-three Sundays after Trinity, the provision for the Third
Sunday before Lent is used on the Twenty-second Sunday after Pentecost.*

1 November **All Saints' Day** *Gold or White*
Principal Feast
John 11:32-44; Luke 6:20-31; Matthew 5:1-12.

Collect
Almighty God,
you have knit together your elect
in one communion and fellowship
in the mystical body of your Son Christ our Lord:
grant us grace so to follow your blessed saints
in all virtuous and godly living
that we may come to those inexpressible joys
that you have prepared for those who truly love you;
through Jesus Christ your Son our Lord,
who is alive and reigns with you,
in the unity of the Holy Spirit,
one God, now and for ever.

Post Communion
God, the source of all holiness and giver of all good things:
may we who have shared at this table
as strangers and pilgrims here on earth
be welcomed with all your saints
to the heavenly feast on the day of your kingdom;
through Jesus Christ our Lord.

The Fourth Sunday before Advent *Red or Green*
Mark 10:2-16; Matthew 10:1-22; John 9.

Collect
Almighty and eternal God,
Who equips and sends your saints for the work of ministry,
Equip us even now, that we may show forth thy power
To an unbelieving world; thy love and care to the troubled;
And bring restoration and hope to the lost; and courageously withstand
the opposition of all who fight the truth of the gospel.

The Third Sunday before Advent *Red or Green*
John 15:12-27; Matthew 11:20-30; Mark 10:17-31.

Collect
Almighty Father, in the name of Jesus
Who lived and ministered in the cities of his day,
Equip we beseech you, your servants who minister in urban settings.
Give them love and unity of purpose in their evangelistic and
Pastoral tasks, that people of all walks of life may know Jesus
And live their lives for him and for his glory. Through Jesus Christ who
healed the sick, sought the lost, raised the dead,
fed the hungry and challenged the rich to share their wealth.

The Second Sunday before Advent *Red or Green*
Luke 9:1-6; Matthew 13:24-30,36-43; Matthew 13:1-9,18-23.

Collect
Heavenly Father,
Your Son and our Saviour Jesus came to weed out
Satan's works from the world. Enable us in the power
Of the Holy Spirit to work alongside our Saviour in weeding

out the injustices and corruption in our society,
thus producing the fruit of righteousness, that Christ may
be manifested in both our talk and our walk.
To the glory of our Saviour Jesus Christ, the righteous.

The Sunday next before Advent (Christ the King) *Red or White*
John 18:33-37; Luke 23:33-43; Matthew 25:31-46.

Collect
Eternal Father,
whose Son Jesus Christ ascended to the throne of heaven
that he might rule over all things as Lord and King:
keep the Church in the unity of the Spirit
and in the bond of peace,
and bring the whole created order to worship at his feet;
who is alive and reigns with you,
in the unity of the Holy Spirit,
one God, now and for ever.
Post Communion (which may also be used as the Collect at Morning and
Evening worship during this week)
Stir up, O Lord,
the wills of your faithful people;
that they, plenteously bringing forth the fruit of good works,
may by you be plenteously rewarded;
through Jesus Christ our Lord.

FESTIVALS

The Naming and Circumcision of Jesus *White*
1 January

Collect
Almighty God,
whose blessed Son was circumcised
in obedience to the law for our sake
and given the Name that is above every name:
give us grace faithfully to bear his Name,
to worship him in the freedom of the Spirit,
and to proclaim him as the Saviour of the world;
who is alive and reigns with you,

in the unity of the Holy Spirit,
one God, now and for ever.

Post Communion
Eternal God,
whose incarnate Son was given the Name of Saviour:
grant that we who have shared
in this sacrament of our salvation
may live out our years in the power
of the Name above all other names,
Jesus Christ our Lord.

18 Jan – 25 January **The Week of Prayer for Christian Unity**

Collect
Lord God,
renew your Church and begin with me.
Heal our land, tend our wounds,
make us one and use us in your service:
for Jesus Christ's sake. **Amen.**

25 January **The Conversion of Paul** *White*

Collect
Almighty God,
who caused the light of the gospel
to shine throughout the world
through the preaching of your servant Saint Paul:
grant that we who celebrate his wonderful conversion
may follow him in bearing witness to your truth;
through Jesus Christ your Son our Lord,
who is alive and reigns with you,
in the unity of the Holy Spirit,
one God, now and for ever.

Post Communion of Apostles and Evangelists
Almighty God,
who on the day of Pentecost sent your Holy Spirit
to the apostles with the wind from heaven and in tongues of flame,
filling them with joy and boldness to preach the gospel:
by the power of the same Spirit strengthen us to witness to your truth

and to draw everyone to the fire of your love;
through Jesus Christ our Lord.

(or)

Lord God, the source of truth and love,
keep us faithful to the apostles' teaching and fellowship,
united in prayer and the breaking of bread,
and one in joy and simplicity of heart,
in Jesus Christ our Lord.

19 March **Joseph of Nazareth** *White*

Collect
God our Father,
who from the family of your servant David
raised up Joseph the carpenter to
be the guardian of your incarnate
Son and husband of the Blessed
Virgin Mary: give us grace to follow him in
faithful obedience to your commands;
through Jesus Christ your Son our Lord,
who is alive and reigns with you,
in the unity of the Holy Spirit,
one God, now and for ever.

Post Communion
Heavenly Father,
whose Son grew in wisdom and stature
in the home of Joseph the carpenter of Nazareth
and on the wood of the cross perfected
the work of the world's salvation:
help us, strengthened by this sacrament
of his passion,
to count the wisdom of the world as foolishness,
and to walk with him in simplicity and trust;
through Jesus Christ our Lord.

25 March **The Annunciation of Our Lord** *Gold or White*
Principal Feast

Collect
We beseech you, O Lord,
pour your grace into our hearts, that as we have
known the incarnation of your Son Jesus Christ
by the message of an angel, so by his cross and passion
we may be brought to the glory of his resurrection;
through Jesus Christ your Son our Lord,
who is alive and reigns with you, in the unity of the Holy Spirit,
one God, now and for ever.

Post Communion
God most high,
whose handmaid bore the Word made flesh:
we thank you that in this sacrament of our redemption
you visit us with your Holy Spirit
and overshadow us by your power;
strengthen us to walk with Mary the joyful path of obedience
and so to bring forth the fruits of holiness;
through Jesus Christ our Lord.

25 April **Mark** *Red*
Evangelist

Collect
Almighty God,
who enlightened your holy Church
through the inspired witness of your evangelist Saint Mark:
grant that we, being firmly grounded
in the truth of the gospel, may be faithful to its teaching both in word and
deed; through Jesus Christ your Son our Lord,
who is alive and reigns with you, in the unity of the Holy Spirit,
one God, now and for ever.

Post Communion
One of the Post Communions of Apostles and Evangelists is used.
See St. Paul 25th January.

1 May **Philip and James** *Red*
Apostles

Collect
Almighty Father,
whom truly to know is eternal life:
teach us to know your Son Jesus Christ
as the way, the truth, and the life;
that we may follow the steps
of your holy apostles Philip and James,
and walk steadfastly in the way that leads to your glory;
through Jesus Christ your Son our Lord,
who is alive and reigns with you,
in the unity of the Holy Spirit,
one God, now and for ever.

Post Communion
One of the Post Communions of Apostles and Evangelists is used.
See St. Paul 25th January.

14 May **Matthias** *Red*
Apostle

Collect
Almighty God,
who in the place of the traitor Judas
chose your faithful servant Matthias
to be of the number of the Twelve:
preserve your Church from false apostles
and, by the ministry of faithful pastors and teachers,
keep us steadfast in your truth;
through Jesus Christ your Son our Lord,
who is alive and reigns with you,
in the unity of the Holy Spirit,
one God, now and for ever.

Post Communion
One of the Post Communions of Apostles and Evangelists is used.
See St. Paul 25th January.

31 May **The Visit of the Blessed Virgin Mary to Elizabeth** *White*

Collect
Mighty God,
by whose grace Elizabeth rejoiced with Mary
and greeted her as the mother of the Lord:
look with favour on your lowly servants
that, with Mary, we may magnify your holy name
and rejoice to acclaim her Son our Saviour,
who is alive and reigns with you, in the unity of the Holy Spirit,
one God, now and for ever.

Post Communion
Gracious God,
who gave joy to Elizabeth and Mary
as they recognized the signs of redemption
at work within them:
help us, who have shared in the joy of this Eucharist,
to know the Lord deep within us
and his love shining out in our lives,
that the world may rejoice in your salvation;
through Jesus Christ our Lord.

11 June **Barnabas** *Red*
Apostle

Collect
Bountiful God, giver of all gifts,
who poured your Spirit upon your servant Barnabas
and gave him grace to encourage others:
help us, by his example, to be generous in
our judgements and unselfish in our service;
through Jesus Christ your Son our Lord,
who is alive and reigns with you,
in the unity of the Holy Spirit,
one God, now and for ever.

Post Communion
One of the Post Communions of Apostles and Evangelists is used.
See St. Paul 25th January.

24 June **The Birth of John the Baptist** *White*

Collect
Almighty God,
by whose providence your servant John the Baptist
was wonderfully born, and sent to prepare the way
of your Son our Saviour by the preaching of repentance:
lead us to repent according to his preaching
and, after his example, constantly to speak the truth,
boldly to rebuke vice, and patiently to suffer for the truth's sake;
through Jesus Christ your Son our Lord,
who is alive and reigns with you, in the unity of the Holy Spirit,
one God, now and for ever.

Post Communion
Merciful Lord,
whose prophet John the Baptist proclaimed your Son
as the Lamb of God who takes away the sin of the world:
grant that we who in this sacrament have known
your forgiveness and your life-giving love may ever tell
of your mercy and your peace; through Jesus Christ our Lord.

29 June **Peter and Paul** *Red*
Apostles

Collect
Almighty God,
whose blessed apostles Peter and Paul
glorified you in their death as in their life:
grant that your Church, inspired by their teaching
and example, and made one by your Spirit,
may ever stand firm upon the one foundation,
Jesus Christ your Son our Lord, who is alive and reigns
with you in the unity of the Holy Spirit,
one God, now and for ever.

Or
where Peter is celebrated alone

Almighty God,
who inspired your apostle Saint Peter

to confess Jesus as Christ and Son of the living God:
build up your Church upon this rock,
that in unity and peace it may proclaim one truth
and follow one Lord, your Son our Saviour Christ,
who is alive and reigns with you,
in the unity of the Holy Spirit,
one God, now and for ever.

Post Communion
One of the Post Communions of Apostles and Evangelists is used.
See St. Paul 25th January.

3 July **Thomas** *Red*
Apostle

Collect
Almighty and eternal God,
who, for the firmer foundation of our faith,
allowed your holy apostle Thomas
to doubt the resurrection of your Son
till word and sight convinced him:
grant to us, who have not seen, that we also may believe
and so confess Christ as our Lord and our God;
who is alive and reigns with you,
in the unity of the Holy Spirit,
one God, now and for ever.

Post Communion
One of the Post Communions of Apostles and Evangelists is used.
See St. Paul 25th January.

22 July **Mary Magdalene** *White*

Collect
Almighty God,
whose Son restored Mary Magdalene
to health of mind and body and called her to be a witness
to his resurrection: forgive our sins and heal us by your grace,
that we may serve you in the power of his risen life;
who is alive and reigns with you, in the unity of the Holy Spirit,
one God, now and for ever.

Post Communion
God of life and love,
whose risen Son called Mary Magdalene by name
and sent her to tell of his resurrection to his apostles:
in your mercy, help us, who have been united with him
in this Eucharist, to proclaim the good news
that he is alive and reigns, now and for ever.

25 July **James** *Red*
Apostle

Collect
Merciful God,
whose holy apostle Saint James,
leaving his father and all that he had,
was obedient to the calling of your Son Jesus Christ
and followed him even to death:
help us, forsaking the false attractions of the world,
to be ready at all times to answer your call without delay;
through Jesus Christ your Son our Lord,
who is alive and reigns with you, in the unity of the Holy Spirit,
one God, now and for ever.

Post Communion
One of the Post Communions of Apostles and Evangelists is used.
See St. Paul 25th January.

6 August **The Transfiguration of Our Lord** *Gold or White*
This is a principal festival and supersedes a Sunday. When it occurs on a
Sunday it is Celebrated then and not transferred.

Collect
Father in heaven,
whose Son Jesus Christ was wonderfully transfigured
before chosen witnesses upon the holy mountain,
and spoke of the exodus he would accomplish at Jerusalem:
give us strength so to hear his voice and bear our cross
that in the world to come we may see him as he is;
who is alive and reigns with you,

in the unity of the Holy Spirit,
one God, now and for ever.

Post Communion
Holy God,
we see your glory in the face of Jesus Christ:
may we who are partakers at his table
reflect his life in word and deed,
that all the world may know his power to change and save.
This we ask through Jesus Christ our Lord.

15 August **The Blessed Virgin Mary** *White*

Collect
Almighty God,
who looked upon the lowliness of the Blessed Virgin Mary
and chose her to be the mother of your only Son:
grant that we who are redeemed by his blood
may share with her in the glory of your eternal kingdom;
through Jesus Christ your Son our Lord,
who is alive and reigns with you,
in the unity of the Holy Spirit,
one God, now and for ever.

Post Communion
God most high,
whose handmaid bore the Word made flesh:
we thank you that in this sacrament of our redemption
you visit us with your Holy Spirit
and overshadow us by your power;
strengthen us to walk with Mary the joyful path of obedience
and so to bring forth the fruits of holiness;
through Jesus Christ our Lord.

24 August **Bartholomew** *Red*
Apostle

Collect
Almighty and everlasting God,
who gave to your apostle Bartholomew grace
truly to believe and to preach your word:

grant that your Church may love that word which he believed
and may faithfully preach and receive the same;
through Jesus Christ your Son our Lord,
who is alive and reigns with you, in the unity
of the Holy Spirit, one God, now and for ever.

Post Communion
One of the Post Communions of Apostles and Evangelists is used.
See St. Paul 25th January.

14 September **Holy Cross Day** *Red*

Collect
Almighty God,
who in the passion of your blessed Son
made an instrument of painful death
to be for us the means of life and peace:
grant us so to glory in the cross of Christ
that we may gladly suffer for his sake;
who is alive and reigns with you, in the unity
of the Holy Spirit, one God, now and for ever.

Post Communion
Faithful God,
whose Son bore our sins in his body on the tree
and gave us this sacrament to show forth his death until he comes:
give us grace to glory in the cross of our Lord Jesus Christ,
for he is our salvation, our life and our hope,
who reigns as Lord, now and for ever.

21 September **Matthew** *Red*
Apostle and Evangelist

Collect
O Almighty God,
whose blessed Son called Matthew the tax collector
to be an apostle and evangelist:
give us grace to forsake the selfish pursuit of gain
and the possessive love of riches
that we may follow in the way of your Son Jesus Christ,
who is alive and reigns with you,

in the unity of the Holy Spirit,
one God, now and for ever.

Post Communion
One of the Post Communions of Apostles and Evangelists is used.
See St. Paul 25th January.

29 September **Michael and All Angels** *White*

Collect
Everlasting God,
you have ordained and constituted
the ministries of angels and mortals in a wonderful order:
grant that as your holy angels always serve you in heaven,
so, at your command,
they may help and defend us on earth;
through Jesus Christ your Son our Lord,
who is alive and reigns with you,
in the unity of the Holy Spirit,
one God, now and for ever.

Post Communion
Lord of heaven,
in this Eucharist you have brought us near
to an innumerable company of angels
and to the spirits of the saints made perfect:
as in this food of our earthly pilgrimage
we have shared their fellowship,
so may we come to share their joy in heaven;
through Jesus Christ our Lord.

18 October **Luke** *Red*
Evangelist

Collect
Almighty God,
you called Luke the physician,
whose praise is in the gospel, to be an evangelist
and physician of the soul: by the grace of the
Spirit and through the wholesome medicine of the
gospel, give your Church the same love

and power to heal; through Jesus Christ your Son our Lord,
who is alive and reigns with you, in the unity of the Holy Spirit,
one God, now and for ever.

Post Communion
One of the Post Communions of Apostles and Evangelists is used.
See St. Paul 25th January.

28 October **Simon and Jude** *Red*
Apostles

Collect
Almighty God,
who built your Church upon the foundation
of the apostles and prophets,
with Jesus Christ himself as the chief cornerstone:
so join us together in unity of spirit by their doctrine,
that we may be made a holy temple acceptable to you;
through Jesus Christ your Son our Lord, who is alive and
reigns with you, in the unity of the Holy Spirit,
one God, now and for ever.

Post Communion
One of the Post Communions of Apostles and Evangelists is used.
See St. Paul 25th January.

30 November **Andrew** *Red*
Apostle

Collect
Almighty God,
who gave such grace to your apostle Saint Andrew
that he readily obeyed the call of your Son Jesus Christ
and brought his brother with him:
call us by your holy word,
and give us grace to follow you without delay
and to tell the good news of your kingdom;
through Jesus Christ your Son our Lord,
who is alive and reigns with you,
in the unity of the Holy Spirit,
one God, now and for ever.

Post Communion
One of the Post Communions of Apostles and Evangelists is used.
See St. Paul 25th January.

26 December **Stephen** *Red*
Deacon, First Martyr

Collect
Gracious Father,
who gave the first martyr Stephen
grace to pray for those who took up stones against him:
grant that in all our sufferings for the truth
we may learn to love even our enemies
and to seek forgiveness for those who desire our hurt,
looking up to heaven to him who was crucified for us,
Jesus Christ, our mediator and advocate,
who is alive and reigns with you,
in the unity of the Holy Spirit,
one God, now and for ever.

Post Communion
Merciful Lord,
we thank you for the signs of your mercy
revealed in birth and death:
save us by the coming of your Son,
and give us joy in honouring Stephen,
first martyr of the new Israel;
through Jesus Christ our Lord.

27 December **John** *White*
Apostle and Evangelist

Collect
Merciful Lord,
cast your bright beams of light upon the Church:
that, being enlightened by the teaching
of your blessed apostle and evangelist Saint John,
we may so walk in the light of your truth
that we may at last attain to the light of everlasting life;

through Jesus Christ your incarnate Son our Lord,
who is alive and reigns with you,
in the unity of the Holy Spirit,
one God, now and for ever.

Post Communion
Grant, O Lord, we pray,
that the Word made flesh
proclaimed by your apostle John
may, by the celebration of these holy mysteries,
ever abide and live within us;
through Jesus Christ our Lord.

28 December **The Holy Innocents** *Red*

Collect
Heavenly Father,
whose children suffered at the hands of Herod,
though they had done no wrong:
by the suffering of your Son
and by the innocence of our lives
frustrate all evil designs
and establish your reign of justice and peace;
through Jesus Christ your Son our Lord,
who is alive and reigns with you,
in the unity of the Holy Spirit,
one God, now and for ever.

Post Communion
Lord Jesus Christ,
in your humility you have stooped to share our human life
with the most defenceless of your children:
may we who have received these gifts of your passion
rejoice in celebrating the witness of the Holy Innocents
to the purity of your sacrifice
made once for all upon the cross;
for you are alive and reign, now and for ever.

Dedication Festival *Gold or White*

Collect
Almighty God,
to whose glory we celebrate the dedication
of this house of prayer:
we praise you for the many blessings
you have given to those who worship you here:
and we pray that all who seek you in this place may find you,
and, being filled with the Holy Spirit,
may become a living temple acceptable to you;
through Jesus Christ your Son our Lord,
who is alive and reigns with you,
in the unity of the Holy Spirit,
one God, now and for ever.

Post Communion
Father in heaven,
whose Church on earth is a sign of your heavenly peace,
an image of the new and eternal Jerusalem:
grant to us in the days of our pilgrimage
that, fed with the living bread of heaven,
and united in the body of your Son,
we may be the temple of your presence,
the place of your glory on earth,
and a sign of your peace in the world;
through Jesus Christ our Lord.

Harvest Thanksgiving *Green*
Harvest Thanksgiving may be celebrated on a Sunday in October or any
other Month of Harvest and may replace the provision for that day,
provided it does not supersede any Principal Feast or Festival.

Collect
Eternal God,
you crown the year with your goodness
and you give us the fruits of the earth in their season:
grant that we may use them to your glory,
for the relief of those in need and for our own well-being;
May the people calmly and peacefully enjoy the gains of their harvest,
free of illness or any sudden mishaps through Jesus Christ your Son our
Lord, who is alive and reigns with you,
in the unity of the Holy Spirit,
one God, now and for ever.

Post Communion
Lord of the harvest,
with joy we have offered thanksgiving for
your love in creation and have shared in the bread
and the wine of the kingdom,
by your grace plant within us a reverence for
all that you give us
and make us generous and wise stewards of the
good things we enjoy;
through Jesus Christ our Lord.

Summary of Prayers and Intercessions

1. For a New Year
2. For Harvest
3. During Election of Leaders
4. For Peace of Mind
5. For Patience
6. For Strength
7. For Zeal in Service
8. For Education and Learning
9. For the Environment
10. For the Synod
11. For the Homeless
12. For the Healing Ministry
13. For the Hungry
14. For the Unemployed
15. Dedication of Offerings
16. Prayer for Protection
17. Prayer of St Augustine
18. Prayer for Guidance
19. Prayer for Africa
20. Prayer for Christian Unity (January 8-25)
21. Prayer for Rain
22. Prayer for Mission and Evangelism
23. Prayer for Life in Towns and Cities
24. Blessing at a Funeral
25. Prayer for the Primate
26. Prayer for the Blessing of Eternal life
27. Prayer for the Blessing of Mutual Love and Faithfulness
28. A Personal Prayer at the Beginning of Each Day
29. A Morning Commitment
30. A Night Prayer
31. For Animals
32. Prayers for Those Infected with HIV/AIDS
33. Succumbing to AIDS
34. Ecological Concerns
35. Prayer for a Pregnant Person

Prayers and Intercessions
for Different Times and Purposes

1. *For a New Year*

Eternal God
your everlasting mercy
rises new in the morning of another year.
Give us grace to arise with Christ
who is our morning light.
In this new year of our life's journey,
may we walk by our faith in him,
and with a willing spirit
persevere to the end;
through the same Jesus Christ our Lord. **Amen**

2. *For Harvest*

God of faithfulness
your generous love supplies us
with the fruits of the earth in their seasons.
Give us grace to be thankful for your gifts,
to use them wisely,
and to share with others;
Through Jesus Christ our Lord. **Amen**

3. *During Election of Leaders*

Almighty God,
you are the source of wisdom and justice.
Guide us in the same,
as we elect leaders to serve among us,
lead us to elect the right people
who would serve in the Spirit of Christ who,
though he was God,
he did not consider equality with God,
something to be grasped.
But instead he lowered himself to the level of a servant leader!
Grant that those we elect shall be guided by
love, truth and justice and shall pursue the same,
for the good welfare of those they serve,
and for the glory of God.
Through Jesus Christ our Lord. **Amen**

4. *For Peace of Mind*

> Set free O Lord the souls of your servants
> from all restlessness and anxiety.
> Give us your peace and power,
> and so keep us that,
> in all perplexity and distress,
> we may abide in you,
> upheld by your strength,
> and stayed on the rock of your faithfulness;
> through Jesus Christ our Lord. **Amen.**

5. *For Patience*

> Bless us Lord,
> with the vision of your being and beauty
> that in the strength of it
> we may be neither hasty nor slothful in our work.
> And grant us the grace to be patient with others
> as you are patient with us,
> that we may gently bear with their faults
> while we strive at all times to root out our own;
> for your mercy's sake. **Amen.**

6. *For Strength*

> God of might and power,
> you support us in danger
> And carry us through temptation.
> give us grace to trust in you
> that, though by nature we are frail and weak,
> we may stand upright in any time of trial;
> through the strength of him
> who makes us more than conquerors,
> even Jesus Christ our Lord. **Amen.**

7 *For Zeal in Service*

> God of unfailing power,
> you give vigour to the weary,
> fresh hope to the exhausted.
> We look to you for new strength,
> that we may soar as on eagles' wings,

run and not feel faint,
march on and not grow weary.
Keep us aglow with your Spirit,
that with unflagging zeal
we may serve the Lord. **Amen.**

8   *For Education and Learning*

God of all knowledge and wisdom,
we pray that you would bless the work of all
institutions of learning,
that in them the right knowledge may be taught
and that truth shall be upheld and pursued.
May the knowledge acquired benefit
both the student and the community.
Through Jesus Christ our Lord. *Amen.*

9   *For the Environment*

O Lord our God and creator of all,
we thank you for the beauty of creation,
show us we pray, how to respect
the fragile balance of life.
Guide by your wisdom those who have power
to care for or to destroy the environment,
that by the decisions they make
life may be cherished
and a good and fruitful earth
be preserved for future generations;
through Jesus Christ our Lord. **Amen**

10   *For the Synod*

Lord Jesus,
we acknowledge your headship of the Church;
grant that trusting in your Lordship,
this synod shall be conducted through
the knowledge that comes from you,
may all the deliberations be conducted
with wisdom, sensitivity and a spirit of discernment,
may all difficult issues be tackled in truth and love,
all for the good governance of the church, unity of Christians,
and for the glory of your name. **Amen.**

11 *For the Homeless*

Have compassion Lord
on all who are poor and homeless,
or who live in overcrowded conditions,
give them strength and hope
and keep them close to you.
Help us to work and pray for the day when
all your children are housed and healthy,
and free to live full and happy lives;
Through Jesus Christ our Lord,
who had nowhere to lay his head. **Amen.**

12 *For the Healing Ministry*

We commit into your loving care,
all who suffer pain and ill health,
all who have for long been bedridden,
all who are up and walking but who carry
with them a persistent condition of ill-health,
all who must undergo an operation and are afraid,
surround them all with your presence;
that they may be comforted in the assurance that
they are not alone, because you bore all the pain for us,
and finally crushed the power of death under your foot.
And because you overcame, we too shall overcome,
trusting in the name of the mighty healer,
Jesus Christ our Lord. **Amen.**

13 *For the Hungry*

Lord we bring to you all the hungry
people of the world.
May the love of Christ touch all who have,
To share with the needy,
For it is in sharing that we are blessed,
As we fulfill Christ's mission when he said,
"I came that you may have life and have it in abundance."
Touch our money, even the abundance of our stores,
And move us to give, so that no child of God will suffer want,
When there is so much around.
Grant this our prayer, for your name's sake. **Amen.**

14 *For the Unemployed*

Gracious Lord,
look with favour upon all who suffer due to
unemployment, underemployment
and even unemployability;
all who possess various skills,
knowledge and zeal for work but cannot find jobs.
Strengthen their resolve to keep trying, and more
so to find alternative jobs that are sufficiently
rewarding and equally fulfilling.
Grant understanding, sympathy and greater affection
in family members
so that relationships will not be torn apart,
and mutual family life affected by matters
of material concern. Grant these our prayers,
for the sake of Jesus Christ who himself was
a carpenter in Nazareth. **Amen.**

15 *Dedication of Offerings*

We bring our gifts to you Lord
with cheerfulness and a joyful heart.
grant that with our gifts
we may also offer a ready mind and a willing spirit
to show forth in our lives the truth of the Gospel;
through Jesus Christ our Lord.
Gracious and loving God,
if we have gifts to bring,
it is of your free mercy,
for all things are yours,
and what we have comes from you.
Accept the offerings we make,
and grant that gifts which can never be worthy
may yet be hallowed by your blessing
and used in your service;
through Jesus Christ our Lord. **Amen.**

16 *Prayer for Protection*

O Lord our God,
how majestic is your name in all the earth.
Created from the dust of the ground,
inspired with your Spirit, we live:
breathless at the end, we die,
and return to the dust of death.
Grant us your blessings this night
in the sure hope of rising with Christ
and rejoicing with him in your glory;
through him who is alive and reigns with you
and the Holy Spirit, one God world without end.
Amen.

17 *Prayer of St Augustine*

Almighty God,
to turn away from you is to fall,
to turn towards you is to rise,
and to stand in you is to live for ever.
Grant us in all our duties your help,
in all our problems your guidance,
in all our dangers your protection,
and in all our sorrows your peace;
Through Jesus Christ our Lord. **Amen.**

18 *Prayer for Guidance*

Guide us, Lord, in all we do
with your grace and love,
and grant us your continual help;
in all our problems your guidance,
in all our dangers your protection,
and in all our sorrows your peace;
Through Jesus Christ our Lord. **Amen.**

19 *Prayer for Africa*

God bless Africa,
Guard her children,
Guide her leaders,
And give her peace;
For Jesus Christ's sake. **Amen.**

20 *Prayer for Christian Unity* (January 8-25)

Lord God,
Renew your Church and
Begin with me;
Heal our land, tend our
Wounds, make us one
And use us in your service;
For Jesus Christ's sake. **Amen.**

21 *Prayer for Rain*

Almighty God, Giver of life and strength,
creator of rain and sky, dust and earth,
preserver of people and plants and animals:
as our cattle leave their enclosures,
as we work on a dry and weary land
we look to you for heavenly showers,
quench our thirst, strengthen our herds,
raise our crops and refresh our land;
Through Jesus Christ, the water of life. **Amen.**

22 *Prayer for Mission and Evangelism*

O God our Father,
give us your passion for your Word and
boldness in telling our neighbour
about your grace,
may the Holy Spirit convict
the lost and draw them to the
Saviour, Jesus Christ our Lord. **Amen.**

23 *Prayer for Life in Towns and Cities*

Creator God, our heavenly Father,
your Son was a carpenter in Nazareth:
we pray for all those who labour
in our factories and shops.
Grant them wisdom and honesty, strength and skill,
to provide for themselves
and for the needs of our country.
Look with compassion on the landless poor,
the unemployed and homeless,
the orphans and the hungry,

and grant us your power to work towards justice
in transforming their lives for your glory;
through our risen Lord Jesus Christ,
who had nowhere to lay his head. **Amen**

24 *Blessing at a Funeral*

Grant to the living, Grace,
to the departed, rest,
to the Church and our government
and to all people,
peace and concord,
and to us and all his servants,
life everlasting.

And the blessing of God almighty, Father, Son and the Holy
Spirit, be with us all now and for evermore. **Amen**

25 *Prayer for the Primate*

Give sufficient grace to our Archbishop in his
rigorous task of leading the Church in this country,
and in his many other callings. Grant him strength,
courage and wisdom for every day's tasks – big and small,
sophisticated and simple; and may your Holy Spirit
richly indwell him, to the end that in all his services,
rendered to you and in your name, he shall portray the image
of a good and faithful shepherd of the flock you've put
under his care, to the glory and honour of your name.
Amen.

26 *Prayer for the Blessing of Eternal Life*

God of Abraham, God of Isaac, God of Jacob
And God of our ancestors;
Bless these servants, and sow the seed
Of eternal life in their hearts
That whatever they learn in your Holy Word
They may indeed fulfil.
Look in love upon them, Father, and bless them with
The blessing you sent to Abraham and Sarah
That obeying your will and secure in your protection,
They may abide in your love to their lives' end,
Through Jesus Christ our Lord. **Amen.**

27 *Prayer for the Blessing of Mutual Love and Faithfulness*

EITHER:

Almighty God, who by joining man and woman together taught us
from the beginning, that we should not separate what you have
joined as one, we praise you that you have consecrated
the state of matrimony to such an excellent
purpose that in it is signified the spiritual
marriage and unity between Christ and his Church.
Look mercifully on these your servants,
that this man may love his wife,
according to your word, as Christ loved his bride
the Church, and gave himself for it;
cherishing it as himself; and also that
this woman may be loving and generous,
responsive and faithful to her husband.
O Lord, bless them both and grant
them to inherit your everlasting kingdom, through
Jesus Christ our Lord. **Amen**

OR

O God, you have so consecrated the covenant
of marriage that in it is represented the spiritual
unity between Christ and his Church.
Send therefore, you blessing upon these your servants
that they may so love, honour and cherish each other
In faithfulness and patience, in wisdom and true godliness,
That their home may be a haven of blessing and peace,
Through Jesus Christ our Lord,
Who lives and reigns with you and the Holy Spirit,
One God, now and for ever. **Amen.**

OR

Almighty God, who created our first parents and sanctified and
joined them together in marriage, pour upon you the riches of his
love, sanctify and bless you, that you may please him both in
body and soul, and live together in holy love to your lives end.
Amen.

OR

God the Father enrich you with his grace
God the Holy Spirit strengthen you with his joy
The Lord bless and keep you in eternal life. **Amen.**

28 *A Personal Prayer at the Beginning of Each Day*

I thank you Lord for keeping me through the night,
and for the promise of this new day.
I pray that I would begin it with you,
and that it may be to me a day of growth in the spirit,
and of service to you and your kingdom in the world.
Help me to meet with quiet confidence
whatever trials the day holds for me;
Strengthen me against temptation and keep me always
loyal to our Lord and Saviour Jesus Christ. **Amen.**

29 *A Morning Commitment*

I commit myself to God for today.
By the help of his grace, I will endeavour to keep
His commandments, and to follow faithfully
in the way of Jesus Christ my Lord. **Amen.**

30 *A Night Prayer*

The day is over and now I turn to you Lord,
before I take my night's rest.
You have been with me all the day long
and for all your mercies, perceived and unperceived,
I give thanks.
I repent of my sins of omission and commission
through my thoughts, words and deeds;
graciously forgive me Lord, as I also forgive all
who have offended me.
Grant me now the blessing of a quiet mind
and a trustful spirit, freed from all fear of the night.
At peace with you and all people, I now take my rest,
through Jesus Christ our Lord. **Amen.**

31 *For Animals*

O God, who has made the earth and every crature that dwells therein,
help us, we pray thee, to treat with compassion the living creatures
            entrusted to our care,
that they may not suffer neglect, nor be cruelly treated.

Bless all who serve in their behalf, and help us in our care for them,
to have a deeper understanding of your love for all creation;
through Jesus Christ our Lord. **Amen.**

32 *Prayers for Those Infected with HIV/AIDS*

Lord we pray for those infected with HIV/AIDS;
That you may lift them from their despair as they constantly ponder
and dread the imminence of death.
We think of spouses and children whose lives are interrupted
and cut back by this cureless disease of our age.
We pray that they will be sustained by your mercies.
Fill them with hope and grant them the peace
that passes all understanding.
We pray for those affected by Aids,
who have to care for the sick.
Refresh them anew everyday and may
their service to the needy
Be service to you. **Amen.**

Forgive us for victimizing AIDS sufferers and for
avoiding them when they need us most.
Forgive us for our fears and horror when we
were too concerned with saving our skin.
Remind us afresh the words of our Lord that
in seeking to save our lives we lose them,
but in accepting to lose our lives for his sake
we shall save our very lives.
May Christ be a good hiding place for us and for them,
and may he give us the courage to sere our fellows
in their need. **Amen**

33 *Succumbing to AIDS*

O Lord, like your Son,
I am acquianted with sorrow and grief.
Support me all the day long of this
troublous life, until the shades lengthen, and
the evening comes, and the busy world
is hushed, the fever of life is over, and my work is
done. Then, Lord, in your mercy grant me a safe
lodging, a holy rest, and peace at the last;
through Jesus Christ our Lord. **Amen.**

34 *Ecological Concerns*

Lord you made a world that is interrelated and interconnected,
when we use toxic substance for our crops we poison the food
We are yet to harvest and put on our tables to eat.
When we seek a higher yield through science alone
we poison the earth and generations to come.
Polluted rivers and fields, polluted forests and
countless ecosystems mean a polluted earth!
Lord teach us how to live in harmony with nature
and one another for Christ's sake. **Amen.**

35 *Prayer for a Pregnant Person*
(To be used upon request)

We thank you Lord for making us procreators
together with you,
thereby bringing forth new life to this world.
We thank you for the ability to get pregnant
and the joy of parenthood.
We ask that you look upon these your maidservants
in their present state and in their different stages of pregnancy.
Bless them and the tender lives that are growing inside them.
Grant them your care and protection against all dangers
in this nine-month long process;
and finally grant us the joy of seeing and welcoming the new borns.
We ask this for the sake of Jesus Christ
who was himself born and nurtured like all of us. **Amen.**

Printed in the United States
127360LV00001BF/97-999/P